PRINCIPLES OF MANAGERIAL FINANCE

Rexcel Lagare

TAP

Toronto Academic Press

PRINCIPLES OF MANAGERIAL FINANCE

Rexcel Lagare

Toronto Academic Press
4164 Lakeshore Road
Burlington ON L7L 1A4
Canada
www.tap-books.com

Email: orders@arclereducation.com

ISBN: 978-1-77956-295-1

ABOUT THE AUTHOR

Rexcel is an MBA graduate from Arizona State University's Thunderbird School of Global Management, ranked No. 1 in the world for international trade by the QS International Trade Rankings, ahead of Cambridge, Harvard, and Stanford. Arizona State University ranked No. 1 as the "Most Innovative School" in the nation by U.S. News & World Report for eight years in succession. Rex graduated magna cum laude with a bachelor's degree in accounting from the University of San Carlos in the Philippines. Spanning over a decade of experience in finance, supply chain & operations projects with Fortune 500 clients and Business World's Top 1000 Corporations, as well as with startup and midsize companies, Rexcel Lagare is proficient in guiding clients enhance their business performance in his role as a management consultant.

Table of Contents

List of Figures

List of Table

PREFACE

The concept that all significant business decisions are heavily influenced by the effective management of money highlights the importance of finance as a key function in every organization, regardless of the sector in which they operate in. This foundational role of finance underscores its criticality, leading to an increased demand for individuals who combine expertise in finance with managerial skills.

In the field of managerial finance, the focus shifts more towards evaluating the effectiveness of various financial strategies rather than just dealing with the nuts and bolts of financial operations—like measuring financial performance or ensuring funds are correctly categorized. This approach goes beyond the basics to explore the deeper implications of financial data, aiming to understand what the numbers really mean and how they can elevate better decision-making.

Unlike a purely technical perspective that might limit itself to the quantitative aspect of finances, managerial finance seeks to unearth the potential improvements within financial practices. It looks for opportunities to make adjustments that could mitigate risks, reduce financial losses, and enhance overall profitability. Essentially, managerial finance is about leveraging financial techniques to their fullest potential to support the organization's goals.

Managerial finance blends elements from corporate finance, which deals with the financial activities that fund the operations and growth of a company, and managerial accounting, which focuses on providing internal financial information to managers for decision-making. This interdisciplinary approach is designed to not only strategize but also to track the performance of these strategies in achieving business objectives.

Effective financial management is pivotal in creating value and ensuring that the limited resources of an organization are used wisely and strategically. Focusing on the optimal allocation of these resources, managerial finance plays a crucial role in guiding companies toward achieving their goals and maintaining financial health.

The aim of the book "Principles of Managerial Finance" is to introduce readers to the basic concepts and techniques of financial management that are essential for making informed business decisions. This book is specially designed for college students studying business, management, or finance. It is also a valuable resource for anyone new to managerial finance, including small business owners or individuals looking to understand the financial aspects of managing a business.

The book covers key topics such as financial analysis, planning and forecasting, budgeting, managing working capital, and making long-term investment decisions. It explains complex financial concepts in a simple and understandable way, using real-world examples and case studies to show how these principles can be applied in practical business situations.

Through this book, readers will learn how to assess the financial health of a business, make sound investment decisions, and develop strategies to finance operations and growth. The goal is to equip future managers and business professionals with the financial tools and knowledge they need to make effective decisions that enhance the value of their organizations.

–Author

CHAPTER 1

Introduction to Managerial Finance

LEARNING OBJECTIVES

After studying this chapter, you will be able to:

- Understand the finance and business
- Focus on goal of the firm in finance
- Describe the managerial finance function
- Discuss on financial systems
- Identify the managerial accounting

INTRODUCTORY EXAMPLE

Finance: Finance is a fundamental concept that permeates every aspect of our lives, from personal money management to the operations of multinational corporations. It is the art and science of managing money, assets, and liabilities to ensure sustainable growth and profitability. For individuals and businesses alike, understanding finance is vital for making informed decisions, allocating resources effectively, and achieving financial goals.

In the context of this book, an example of finance refers to a practical illustration or scenario that helps clarify various financial concepts and principles. Examples of finance serve as valuable tools for understanding complex financial topics by providing real-world applications and scenarios. They provide clarity, applicability, and context to theoretical frameworks, enabling individuals to grasp financial concepts with greater ease. One example of finance is financial planning. Let's consider an individual who wants to retire comfortably in 30 years. Financial planning involves analyzing income, expenses, assets, and liabilities to determine how much money must be saved each year to achieve this goal. By using financial models, the individual can calculate factors such as inflation, investment returns, and life expectancy to create a comprehensive plan. This serves as an example of finance as it applies the principles of budgeting, investing, and risk management to achieve a long-term financial objective.

In the realm of business finance, an example of finance can be seen in capital budgeting. When a company evaluates various investment opportunities, such as building a new factory or acquiring another business, it must assess the potential returns and risks associated with each project. This analysis involves estimating future cash flows, discounting them to their present value, and comparing them against the cost of capital. By considering these factors, businesses can make informed decisions about which projects to pursue, ensuring efficient use of financial resources.

Billing and invoicing provide another example of finance, particularly in the realm of accounting. Let's imagine a small business that sells products or services to customers. The billing process involves generating invoices, which detail the items purchased, their prices, and any applicable taxes or discounts. A clear and accurate invoice not only ensures that the customer is properly billed but also helps the business track its sales, manage inventory, and maintain cash flow. This example of finance emphasizes the importance of accurate recording, financial transparency, and effective communication in the billing and invoicing process.

Every aspect of finance, from personal financial planning to corporate financial management, consists of numerous examples that illustrate different principles and concepts. Examples serve as practical guides, allowing individuals and businesses to navigate the intricacies of finance with confidence and understanding. Whether it's a case study analyzing the financial performance of a company, a scenario demonstrating the impact of interest rates on borrowing costs, or a real-life example of financial fraud, these illustrations help deepen our comprehension of the subject matter.

UNIT INTRODUCTION

Managerial finance integrates accounting and economics. Finance managers utilize cash flows, accounting data, and other financial information to allocate and organize the company's financial resources. Additionally, managers make financial decisions that are in the best interests of the company guided by economic principles. Put differently, the field of finance is an application of economics that relies on accounting data. Finance managers are crucial members of the business community for most companies, as they reflect what brings value to the organization.

Financial managers monitor the company's progress, assess the financial implications, identify trends, and make recommendations regarding the best use of the organization's resources to ensure the long-term viability of the enterprise. Additionally, financial managers seek out top external financial institutions and propose the optimal blend of financial assets for the organization's shareholders.

In the current business landscape, having the resources and instruments necessary to compete is essential; a business must have an end-to-end vision that transcends all boundaries in order to be successful and ensure its long-term survival. To ensure that the company's assets are utilized appropriately, decision-making based on various scenarios is necessary.

1.1. FINANCE AND BUSINESS

→Learning Objectives

- To describe career opportunities in finance
- To know legal forms of business organization
- Why study managerial finance?

Finance encompasses the study of capital assets, money, and of related topics. Whereas economics studies how goods and services are produced, distributed, and consumed. Financial economics serves as the bridge between the two disciplines. The field of finance can be broadly categorized into three main areas: personal finance, corporate finance, and public finance. Financial activities take place within financial systems at various levels. Within a financial system, assets such as currencies, loans, bonds, shares, stocks, options, futures, and other similar contracts are purchased, sold, or traded as financial instruments. Furthermore, assets can be invested, banked and insured to enhance value and mitigate loss. Risk can only be mitigated and not eliminated as risk is inherent in all financial actions.

Because of its broad scope, finance encompasses a wide range of subfields. Value maximization and volatility reduction are the goals of asset, money, risk, and investment management. A given action's viability, stability, and profitability are evaluated through financial analysis. Experiential finance examines how financial theories can occasionally be put to the test through the scientific method. In contrast, business refers to a wider range of activities that are involved in the creation, marketing, and trade of goods and services. Value creation for customers, stakeholders, and society at large entails strategic decision-making, resource allocation, market analysis, and operations management. The integration of finance and business serves as the cornerstone for organizations to establish their competitive edge, adjust to evolving market conditions, and maneuver through intricate economic landscapes. Organizations can effectively manage risks, seize opportunities, and create sustainable value in today's dynamic and interconnected global marketplace by integrating financial principles and business strategies.

1.1.1. Career Opportunities in Finance

Careers in finance typically fall into one of two broad categories:

1. Financial Services; and
2. Managerial Finance.

Both types of workers rely on a common analytical "tool kit," but the problems to which they apply it differ significantly depending on their career path.

1. **Financial Services:** The field of finance that deals with creating and supplying financial products and advice to people, companies, and governments is known as financial services. The fields of banking, investments, real estate, insurance, and personal financial planning all offer a wide range of fascinating career opportunities.
2. **Managerial Finance:** The responsibilities of the financial manager employed by a company are the focus of managerial finance. All kinds of businesses, big and small, profit-seeking, and non-profit, have their financial affairs managed by financial managers. They carry out an array of diverse responsibilities, including creating a financial plan or budget, giving credit to clients, assessing proposed major expenses, and raising capital to support the business's operations.

Keyword

Financial Service is not the financial good itself—say a mortgage loan to buy a house or a car insurance policy—but something that is best described as the process of acquiring the financial good.

The significance and intricacy of the financial manager's responsibilities have grown in recent years due to several factors. These elements include growing competition, technological advancement, the recent global financial crisis and the regulatory responses that followed.

Because of these changes, there is a greater need for financial professionals who can handle cash flows in various currencies and guard against the risks associated with doing business internationally. These modifications add to the complexity of the finance function but also open doors to more fulfilling careers. Numerous professional certification programs are becoming more and more popular as a result of the financial manager's increasingly complex job responsibilities. Corporate strategies that help the company expand and strengthen its competitive position are actively developed and implemented by financial managers nowadays. Because of this, a lot of corporate presidents and chief executive officers (CEOs) got to the top of their companies by first doing exceptionally well in the finance department.

Remember

Sole proprietors report their income and expenses on their personal tax returns and pay income and self-employment taxes on their profits.

1.1.2. Legal Forms of Business Organization

Selecting a legal structure for a business is one of the most crucial decisions to make. This choice has significant financial ramifications because a company's legal structure affects the risks that its owners must take, how it can raise capital, and how its earnings are taxed. The sole proprietorship, partnership, and corporation are the three most popular legal forms of business organization. Though sole proprietorships are the most common type of business structure, corporations are nearly always used by the biggest companies. Nevertheless, there are benefits and drawbacks to every kind of organization.

1. **Sole Proprietorships:** A business owned by one person and run for that person's personal gain is known as a sole proprietorship.

Usually, the proprietorship is run by the owner, or proprietor, and a small staff. The owner raises capital through loans or personal savings and is in charge of all business decisions. Therefore, independent-minded entrepreneurs find this type of organization appealing. One of the main disadvantages of being a sole proprietor is that you have unlimited liability for the debts of the business. This means that if the business can't pay its creditors, the entrepreneur could be held personally liable.

Keyword

Preferred stock is a component of share capital that may have any combination of features not possessed by common stock, including properties of both an equity and a debt instrument, and is generally considered a hybrid instrument.

2. **Partnerships:** When two or more owners collaborate to make money, that arrangement is known as a partnership. In the real estate, insurance, and finance sectors, partnerships are typical. Partnerships in public accounting and law frequently have a large number of partners.
3. **Corporations:** A corporation is a legally recognized entity. A corporation can make and be a party to contracts, bring legal action, and purchase property in its own name, just like an individual. . A corporation's equity, or ownership, is represented by its stockholders, who may hold common stock or, less frequently, preferred stock. Limited liability protects stockholders of a corporation from personal liability for the debts of the company, unlike owners of sole proprietorships or partnerships. Their losses are capped at what they paid for the company's stock when they bought shares. Investors anticipate receiving a return in the form of dividends, which are recurring payments of cash, or gains from rising share prices. Because a company's profits are typically where the funds needed to pay dividends come from.

Periodically, the owners, or stockholders, cast votes to choose the directors and to make other decisions, like changing the corporate charter. Generally speaking, the board of directors is in charge of approving major expenditures, directing corporate affairs, establishing general policy, and approving strategic goals and plans. Above all, the board sets the pay scales for the highest ranking executives and determines when to promote or fire senior managers. Key corporate executives and other "outside" or "independent" directors, such as executives from other companies, significant shareholders, and local or national leaders, make up the board.

1.1.3. Why Study Managerial Finance?

Anybody hoping to succeed in a variety of positions within companies and sectors must study managerial finance. Gaining an understanding of managerial finance gives people the information and abilities they need to make wise choices about risk management, financing, and investments — all important facets of running a business. People who study managerial finance are better equipped to assess investment opportunities, allocate resources effectively, and maximize financial performance because they have a deeper understanding of financial principles, valuation techniques, and financial analysis. Furthermore, managerial finance serves as a basis for strategic decision-making, enabling people to successfully navigate intricate financial environments, predict market trends, and propel organizational success. In today's fast-paced and cutthroat business world, those with managerial finance expertise can pursue a variety of career paths in accounting, finance, consulting, and entrepreneurship. This will help organizations grow and survive.

Did you get it?

1. What do you mean by managerial finance?

1.2. GOAL OF THE FIRM

→Learning Objectives

- To discuss maximize shareholder wealth
- To define maximize profit

The firm's objective, also known as the overarching goal of business operations, includes creating value and assuring long-term sustainability and shareholder wealth. According to this fundamental principle, any business entity's main goal should be to maximize returns for its shareholders through effective resource allocation, risk management, and the pursuit of strategic initiatives that will eventually increase profitability and shareholder value. The idea of maximizing shareholder wealth acknowledges the significance of taking opportunity costs, risk, and time value of money into account when making decisions, even though profit maximization was traditionally thought to be the main objective. By concentrating on maximizing shareholder wealth, businesses give top priority to projects that increase positive net present value (NPV), improve the organization's overall financial performance, and connect shareholders' interests with the company's strategic goals. Furthermore, this goal emphasizes the necessity of sustainable and ethical business practices by highlighting the significance of social responsibility, corporate governance, and ethical behavior in business operations.

1.2.1. Maximize Shareholder Wealth

According to finance theory, managers' main objective should be to maximize the wealth of the company's stockholders, who are its owners. The share price of the company is the easiest and most reliable indicator of stockholder wealth. There is a widespread misperception that companies that prioritize their shareholders' needs come at the expense of other stakeholders, like suppliers, employees, or customers. This way of thinking ignores the fact that managers typically have to appease these other interest groups before they can enrich shareholders. Stockholders receive dividends from the company's profits in the end. A company that experiences dissatisfied customers, disgruntled employees, or reluctance from suppliers to ship raw materials is unlikely to enrich shareholders because it will probably be less profitable in the long run than a company that effectively manages its relationships with these stakeholder groups.

Thus, we contend that the company's and managers' primary objective ought to be to maximize the wealth of the owners for whom the business is run, which is generally the same as maximizing the stock price. This objective translates into a simple guideline for managers to follow when making decisions: only act in a way that is anticipated to boost shareholder wealth. That objective may seem straightforward, but it's not always easy to accomplish. Managers must evaluate the potential return (cash inflows net of cash outflows) and risk associated with a given course of action in order to decide whether it will increase or decrease shareholders' wealth. In fact, we can argue that return (cash flows) and risk are the two main factors that managers need to take into account when making business decisions.

1.2.2. Maximize Profit

The short or long term process by which a business can ascertain the price, input, and output levels that will result in the maximum potential total profit (or just profit, for short) is known as profit maximization. The firm is considered to be a "rational agent" in neoclassical economics, the current mainstream approach to microeconomics. This agent seeks to maximize its total profit, which is the difference between its total revenue and its total cost, regardless of whether it operates in a perfectly competitive market or not.

It is frequently impractical to measure total cost and total revenue because businesses lack the trustworthy data needed to calculate costs across the board. Rather, they adopt a more pragmatic approach by analyzing how minor adjustments to production affect costs and revenues. The extra money made from selling a product that a company produces in excess is known as the marginal revenue (MR), and the additional expenses incurred in producing that extra unit are known as the marginal costs (MC).

Keyword

Marginal revenue is the revenue generated for each additional unit sold relative to marginal cost (MC). This is useful for businesses to balance their production output with their costs to maximize profit.

When the level of output is such that the marginal revenue is equal to the marginal cost (MR=MC), then the firm's total profit is said to be maximized. If the marginal revenue is greater than the marginal cost (MR>MC), then its total profit is not maximized, because the firm can produce additional units to earn additional profit. In other words, in this case, it is in the "rational" interest of the firm to increase its output level until its total profit is maximized. On the other hand, if the marginal revenue is less than the marginal cost (MR<MC), then too its total profit is not maximized, because producing one unit less will reduce total cost more than total revenue gained, thus giving the firm more total profit. In this case, a "rational" firm has an incentive to reduce its output level until its total profit is maximized.

1.2.2.1. Total Revenue: Total Cost Perspective

Recognizing that profit is equal to total revenue (TR) minus total cost (TC) is the first step towards determining the output quantity that maximizes profit. The output that maximizes profits is the one where this difference is greatest. The scenario where the company is a perfect competitor in the goods market and cannot determine its own selling price is represented by the linear total revenue curve in the accompanying diagram. The profit-maximizing output level is represented as the one at which total revenue is the height of C and total cost is the height of B; the maximal profit is measured as the length of the segment $\overline{CB}$.

The total profit curve reaches its maximum at this output level as well. The price to sell the product at can be read off the demand curve at the firm's optimal quantity of output if, contrary to what is implied in the graph, the firm is not a perfect competitor in the output market. The amount of output at which marginal revenue and marginal cost are equal is the optimal quantity (Figure 1.1).

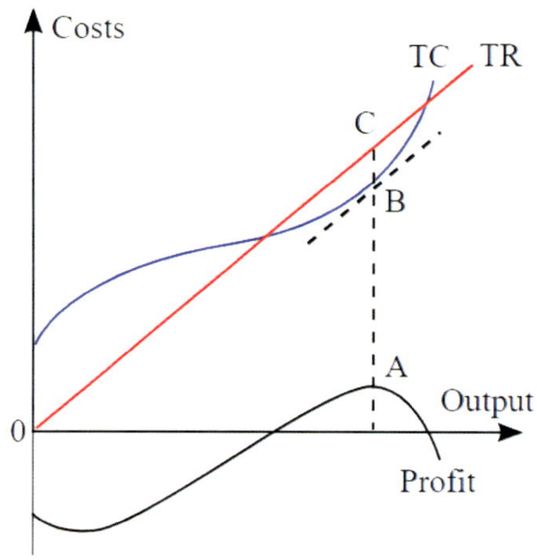

Figure 1.1. *Profit maximization using the total revenue and total cost curves of a perfect competitor.*

1.2.2.2. Marginal Revenue: Marginal Cost Perspective

An equivalent perspective relies on the relationship that, for each unit sold, marginal profit ($M\pi$) equals marginal revenue (MR) minus marginal cost (MC). At some output level, if marginal revenue exceeds marginal cost, marginal profit is positive and more should be produced; conversely, if marginal revenue falls short of marginal cost, marginal profit is negative and less should be produced. The quantity that maximizes profit is found at the output level where marginal profit is zero, or when marginal revenue and marginal cost are equal. Total profit must reach a maximum where marginal profit is zero—where marginal cost equals marginal revenue—and where lower or higher output levels result in lower profit levels. This is because total profit increases when marginal profit is positive and decreases when marginal profit is negative.

1.2.2.3. Case in Which Maximizing Revenue is Equivalent

There are situations when a firm's cost and demand characteristics allow for marginal profits to be higher than zero at all production levels, up to a predetermined maximum. In this case marginal profit plunges to zero immediately after that maximum is reached;

hence the $M\pi = 0$ rule implies that output should be produced at the maximum level, which also happens to be the level that maximizes revenue.

Setting marginal revenue to zero, which happens at the maximum level of output, allows one to determine the quantity and price that will maximize profits. When the total revenue curve hits its peak, marginal revenue is equal to zero. An airline scheduled flight would be one example. Even if every seat is taken, there is no marginal cost associated with adding one more passenger to the flight. If every seat was occupied, the airline would make the most money.

Did you get it?

1. **What strategies can be employed to maximize profit from a total revenue and total cost perspective?**
2. **What factors influence total revenue and total cost, and how can they be optimized to enhance profitability?**
3. **How do changes in production levels and pricing strategies impact total revenue and total cost, and ultimately, profit maximization?**

1.3. MANAGERIAL FINANCE FUNCTION

→Learning Objectives

- To understand organization of the finance function
- To deal relationship to economics
- To discuss relationship to accounting
- To describe primary activities of the financial manager

The managerial finance function within organizations encompasses a spectrum of responsibilities aimed at optimizing financial resources and achieving strategic objectives. This function involves overseeing financial planning, budgeting, and forecasting to align financial goals with broader organizational goals. Additionally, managerial finance entails making informed decisions regarding investment opportunities, capital structure, and risk management to maximize shareholder wealth and ensure long-term sustainability. Managers responsible for the finance function analyze financial data, assess performance metrics, and develop strategies to enhance profitability, mitigate risks, and capitalize on opportunities in the marketplace. They also play a crucial role in financial reporting, compliance, and governance, ensuring transparency, accuracy, and adherence to regulatory standards.

People in all areas of responsibility within the firm must interact with finance personnel and procedures to get their jobs done. For financial personnel to make useful forecasts and decisions, they must be willing and able to talk to individuals in other areas of the firm. For example, when considering a new product, the financial manager needs to obtain sales forecasts, pricing guidelines, and advertising and promotion budget estimates from marketing personnel. The managerial finance function can be broadly described by considering its role within the organization, its relationship to economics and accounting, and the primary activities of the financial manager.

1.3.1. Organization of the Finance Function

The size of the company affects the scope and magnitude of the managerial finance function. In small businesses, the accounting department typically handles the finance function. As a company expands, the finance department usually becomes its own department and is directly accountable to the CEO or president through the chief financial officer (CFO). The controller and treasurer answer to the CFO. Usually in charge of the company's cash, the treasurer (also known as the chief financial manager) invests excess money when it becomes available and obtains outside funding when required. In addition, the treasurer is in charge of the company's pension plans and takes care of important risks involving changes in interest rates, commodity prices, and foreign exchange values. Accounting tasks like corporate accounting, tax management, financial accounting, and cost accounting are usually handled by the controller, who also serves as the chief accountant. The controller has a more internal focus, while the treasurer tends to be more externally focused.

A company that values foreign sales or purchases may hire one or more finance specialists whose responsibility it is to track and control the company's exposure to currency fluctuation losses. Using a range of financial instruments, a skilled financial manager can "hedge," or protect against, such a loss, at a reasonable cost. The treasurer of the company usually receives reports from these foreign exchange managers.

1.3.2. Relationship to Economics

Economics and finance are closely related fields. Financial managers need to be aware of the implications of shifting economic conditions and policy shifts, as well as the overall economic framework. They must also be able to apply economic theories as a means of determining the most effective ways to run businesses. Supply and demand analysis, profit-maximizing tactics, and price theory are a few examples. Marginal cost-benefit analysis, the idea that financial decisions and actions should only be taken when the added benefits exceed the added costs, is the main economic principle used in managerial finance. Nearly all financial decisions ultimately come down to an assessment of their marginal benefits and marginal costs.

Remember

Recognizes revenues and expenses only with respect to actual inflows and outflows of cash.

1.3.3. Relationship to Accounting

The accounting and finance departments of the company typically work together and are closely related. Accountants typically handle the finance function in small businesses, while financial analysts typically assist in gathering accounting data in larger businesses. Nonetheless, there are two distinctions between accounting and finance: one has to do with decision-making, and the other with the focus on cash flows.

1. **Emphasis on Cash Flows:** The principal duties of an accountant include creating and disseminating data to evaluate the firm's performance, assessing its financial standing, complying with regulatory requirements, filing

reports, and filing and paying taxes. The accountant creates financial statements by applying generally accepted accounting principles, which identify revenue at the time of sale (regardless of whether payment has been received) and expenses at the time of incurrence. This method is known as the accrual basis.

In contrast, the financial manager prioritizes cash flows, or the coming in and going out of cash. He or she plans the cash flows required to meet the company's obligations and buy the assets required to meet the company's objectives in order to keep the business solvent. Using this cash basis, the financial manager only records income and expenses in relation to actual cash inflows and outflows. Regardless of whether a business makes money or loses money, it needs to have enough cash on hand to pay its bills on time.

2. **Decision Making:** Making decisions is the subject of the second significant distinction between accounting and finance. The gathering and presentation of financial data takes up the majority of an accountant's time. Financial managers assess the associated returns and risks, review the accounting statements, and create additional data before making decisions. It does not, of course, imply that financial managers and accountants never make decisions or obtain information; rather, it just indicates that the two fields' main objectives are very different.

Keyword

Market volatility is an investment term that describes when a market or security experiences periods of unpredictable, and sometimes sharp, price movements.

1.3.4. Primary Activities of the Financial Manager

The primary activities of the financial manager revolve around strategic financial planning, resource allocation, and risk management to optimize the organization's financial performance and support its overarching goals. Financial managers are tasked with analyzing financial data, assessing market trends, and forecasting future financial needs to develop comprehensive financial strategies aligned with the organization's objectives. They play a pivotal role in capital budgeting decisions, evaluating investment opportunities, and determining the allocation of financial resources across various projects and initiatives to maximize returns and minimize risks. Additionally, financial managers are responsible for managing the organization's capital structure, including debt and equity financing, to ensure optimal funding sources and cost-effective capital utilization. Risk management is another critical aspect of their role, involving the identification, assessment, and mitigation of financial risks such as market volatility, credit risk, and liquidity constraints. By employing financial analysis tools, implementing risk management strategies, and adhering to regulatory compliance standards, financial managers contribute to the organization's stability, profitability, and long-term sustainability in dynamic and competitive market environments.

Did you get it?

1. **What are the primary functions and responsibilities of a managerial finance department within an organization?**
2. **How does the managerial finance function contribute to strategic decision-making and resource allocation within the organization?**

1.4. FINANCIAL SYSTEMS

→Learning Objectives

- To discuss the objectives of financial system
- To explain the components of financial system

A financial system is one that permits money transfers between lenders, investors, and debtors, among other participants in the financial market. Financial systems function both domestically and internationally. Financial institutions are made up of intricately linked markets, services, and organizations designed to facilitate regular and effective connections between lenders and investors. Anywhere there is a financial medium exchange (the exchange of money for other financial instruments) and a reallocation of funds to areas in need (banks, businesses, and financial markets) in order to take advantage of the potential of ideal money and use it to get benefits out of it, financial systems can be understood. We refer to this entire system as a financial system. In financial systems, credit, money, and finance are used as exchange mediums. As an alternative to bartering, they act as a medium of known value for which goods and services can be traded. Financial markets, financial instruments, banks (public or private), and financial services can all be found in a modern financial system. Financial systems facilitate the allocation, investment, and transfer of funds among economic sectors, while also allowing individuals and companies to assume joint risks.

1.4.1. Objectives of Financial System

A financial system's main goals are to create capital, make investments easier, and generate profits. The significance or importance of the financial system in an economy is also one of these goals. The major and primary objectives of a financial system are as follows:

- **To Mobilize the Savings:** The financial system begins its operations by the mobilizing of savings from the small saving community. It collects the funds by offering different schemes which attract the investors' i.e., savers to fund their savings in different institutions, services, securities etc.
- **To Distribute the Savings for the Industrial Investment:** The money from the saving community is being mobilized with the intention of investing it in various industries. Thus, it satisfies the industrial sector's funding requirement. Thus, it promotes the expansion of the industrial sector.
- **To Stimulate Capital Formation:** The approval of funding for the industries does not mean that the goal of supporting them is achieved. Additionally, it forces them to set aside money from their earnings for industrial investments and additional capital requirements.

- **To Accelerate the Pace of Economic Growth:** The financial institutions' overarching goal is to assist a country's economic development. Allocating savings funds towards industrial capital requirements and encouraging capital formation can expedite the economic growth process.

1.4.2. Components of Financial System

The financial system comprises of four major components. These components are:

1. Financial Institutions
2. Financial Markets
3. Financial Instruments
4. Financial Services

1.4.2.1. Financial Institutions

Financial organizations serve as a go-between for investors and debtors. They offer members and clients financial services. Because they serve as middlemen between savers and borrowers, they are also known as financial intermediaries. The financial markets are used to either directly or indirectly mobilize investor savings. They provide services to businesses looking to manage their financial assets and raise capital from the markets (deposits, securities, loan, etc.).

1.4.2.1.1. Feature of Financial Institutions

The following salient features of financial institutions:

- It is an institution as well as intermediary.
- It channelizes savings fund into investment fund.
- It creates financial assets such as deposits, loans, securities etc.
- It includes banking and non-banking institutions.
- It includes both organized and unorganized institutions.
- Established with a clear operating function.
- Regulated by the government and regulating authority.
- It accepts deposits.
- It provides commercial loans, real estate loans and mortgage loans.

Remember

Financial institutions help keep capitalist economies running by matching people who need funds with those who can lend or invest it. They offer a wide range of business operations within the financial services sector including banks, credit unions, insurance companies, and brokerage firms.

- Financial institutions keep money flowing through the economy among consumers, businesses, and government.

1.4.2.1.2. Classification of Financial Institutions

The financial institutions are divided into four categories: state-level institutions, investment institutions, term lending institutions, and refinance institutions. They should be divided into banking and non-banking establishments as well.

1. **Banking Institutions:** Financial institutions of this kind take deposits from the general public and lend the money to clients who are in need. Their primary goal is to make money, and their secondary goal is to protect the members' interests. The banking organizations make sure that the money that customers deposit is used for worthwhile purposes.
   i. **Commercial Banks:** These are also called as business banks. The following are the types of commercial banks.
      - Public sector.
      - Private sector.
      - Regional Rural Banks (RRB`s)
      - Foreign banks.

   ii. **Cooperative Banks:** These were put in place to protect its members' interests. They function as cooperative organizations, take deposits, and lend money to the necessary members.
2. **Non-banking Institutions:** These are the financial organizations that offer banking services but don't fit the bank classification under the law. Financial resources are also raised from the public, either directly or indirectly, by non-banking financial institutions. They lend the money that has been raised. Financial institutions that are not banks are divided into two categories: organized and unorganized.

The following are examples of non-banking institutions:

- Provident and pension fund.
- Small Saving organization.
- Life Insurance Corporation (LIC).
- General Insurance Corporation (GIC).
- Mutual funds.
- Investment Trust, etc.

Non-banking financial institutions can also be categorized as investment companies housing companies, leasing companies, hire purchase companies, specialized financial institutions (EXIM Bank), Investment Institutions, State level institutions etc.

1.4.2.1.3. Importance of Financial Institutions

The main organizations that supply funding for economic activity are financial institutions. A nation can reap numerous benefits from having strong and stable financial institutions. The importance of FI is as follows:

- **Provide Funds:** Funds for industrial and investment activities are provided by financial institutions.
- **Infrastructural Facilities:** financial institutions also offer basic infrastructural facilities needed for the development and promotion of lucrative ventures. Infrastructural facilities involve development of

industrial estates tech parks, road, and water etc.

- **Promotional Activities:** Financial institutions engage in promotional activities to raise capital, lower the risk associated with selling financial securities, and arrange working and long-term capital for their businesses.
- **Development of Backward Areas:** apart from the financial activities, financial institutions also take some social responsibilities of developing the backward areas at free of cost by offering credit facilities, free education, employment creation etc.
- **Planned Development:** Financial institutions start all planned developments with the goal of boosting the state's economy. The government plan and social welfare are synchronized with all planned developments.
- **Accelerating Industrialization:** since the financial institutions are established to earn the profit and safeguard interest of its members, they accelerate the industrialization to contribute industrial growth. They support industries by granting finance, project development and consultancy.
- **Employment Generation:** Using the money for investments, the construction of infrastructure, and the expansion of industry creates jobs for the state's educated and skilled workforce.

1.4.2.1.4. Functions of Financial Institutions

There are two categories for the roles that financial institutions play: primary and secondary.

1. **Primary Functions:** These are the basic functions of financial institutions which come in the respective group of institutions like banks, co-operative societies, insurance industries etc., the primary functions are as follows:
   - The majority of financial institutions, including cooperative societies and commercial banks, accept deposits. Take in deposits from the general public. They provide a variety of programs to encourage public deposits from their patrons. Financial institutions provide returns in the form of interest for accepted deposits based on the deposit tenure.
   - **Providing Commercial Loans:** Loans, advances, cash credits, bill discounting, and other commercial lending operations are supported by the deposits that are accepted. These bring in a healthy profit for the banks.
   - **Providing Real Estate Loans:** the financial institutions also provide loans and advances for real estate industries to purchase sit, build premises, construction of industrial and residential parks.
   - **Providing Mortgage Loans:** the financial institutions also provide loans to the needy group on mortgage of properties and collateral securities. For example, gold loan, property loan etc., where gold and properties are mortgaged to avail the loan.

- **Issuing Share Certificates:** financial institutions also undertake the job of issuing share certificates of any established corporate to its share-holders. It also constitutes accepting shares investment money from the investors and issuing them certificates on behalf of the companies.

2. **Secondary Functions:** These are the extra duties that financial institutions carry out in addition to the aforementioned core duties. Secondary functions are as follow:
   - **Act as an Intermediary:** Financial institutions serve as a go-between for the industrialists and the savings community. They lend the same money to the needy group at a higher interest rate after receiving the public deposit at a lower rate. The profit for their intermediary work is represented by the difference in interest.
   - **Facilitate the Flow of Money:** They also make it easier for money to move and channelize it toward investment activities. The interconnected stepping stones that enable money to move smoothly from small savers to massive corporate endeavors are financial institutions.

1.4.2.2. Financial Markets

Any location or framework that enables buyers and sellers to exchange financial instruments, such as derivatives, bonds, stocks, and different foreign currencies, is referred to as a financial market. The exchange of capital between investors and those in need of capital is facilitated by financial markets. Financial markets enable participants to transfer risk (usually through derivatives) and advance commerce in addition to facilitating capital raising.

1.4.2.2.1. Functions of Financial Markets

The important functions performed by Financial Markets are as follows:

- **Facilitation of Price Discovery:** Anything's price is determined by two things: the market's supply and demand. Therefore, the price of various financial securities is determined in part by the supply and demand of assets and financial securities.
- **Mobilization of Savings and Channelizing the Savings into the most Productive Uses:** The financial markets facilitate the transfer of savers' savings to the most profitable and suitable investment opportunities by serving as a conduit between investors and savers.
- **Providing Liquidity to Financial Assets:** Because financial securities are easily bought and sold in this market, financial markets give investors and savers a platform to convert their securities into cash.
- **Reduction of the Cost of Transaction:** Prior to making an investment in financial securities, companies and investors must gather information about them, which can take a lot of time. By giving them access to complete information about financial securities, such as their price,

availability, and cost, the financial markets assist these investors and businesses.

1.4.2.2.2. Classification of Financial Market

The Financial Market is divided into two broad categories:

- **Capital Market: A** capital market is a marketer that includes all organizations, institutions, and instruments that offer medium- and long-term funding. Short-term financing instruments and institutions are not included in a capital market. A capital market may include common instruments like bonds, shares, mutual funds, debentures, and public deposits. An ideal capital market is one in which traders can access finance at a reasonable cost, where investors receive adequate information, where capital is allocated productively, where market operations are fair, free, competitive, and transparent.
- **Money Market:** Money markets are where short-term funds that are intended for usage for up to a year are sold. The money market typically provides the funding or financing for working capital. In addition to the short-term lending and borrowing of cash, the money market also sees the buying and selling of securities with a one-year term or securities that are redeemed (paid back) within that same year. Some of the common instruments of the money market are Call Money, Commercial Bills, T. Bills, Commercial Paper, Certificates of Deposits, etc.

1.4.2.3. Financial Instruments

Financial assets, securities, and financial instruments are the commodities that are exchanged or dealt in a financial market. The financial markets offer a wide range of securities due to the different needs of lenders and borrowers. Financial assets are claims to principal repayment at a later time and/or payments of periodic or final amounts, such as dividends or interest. Some of the examples of these financial instruments are equity shares, preference shares debentures, bonds, etc.

1.4.2.3.1. Characteristics of Financial Instruments

The important characteristics of financial instruments are as follows:

- **Liquidity:** Financial instruments provide liquidity. These can be easily and quickly converted into cash.
- **Marketing:** Financial instruments facilitate easy trading on the market. They have a ready market.
- **Collateral Value:** Financial instruments can be pledged for getting loans.
- **Transferability:** Financial instruments can be transferred from one person to another.
- **Maturity Period:** The maturity period of financial instruments may be short term, medium term or long term.
- **Transaction Cost:** Financial instruments involve buying and selling cost. The buying and selling costs are called transaction costs.
- **Risk:** Financial instruments carry risk. Equity based instruments are

riskier in comparison to debt-based instruments because the payment of dividend is uncertain. A company may not declare dividend in a particular year.

- **Future Trading:** Financial instruments facilitate future trading so as to cover risks arising out of price fluctuations, interest rate fluctuations etc.

1.4.2.3.2. Classification of Financial Instruments

There are two categories for financial instruments: term financial instruments and type financial instruments.

1. **Term Financial Instruments:** These are the tradable financial assets and exchanged on term basis. These are again classified into short term, medium term and long term securities.
    - **Short Term Securities:** This sub category comprises securities with maturity of one year or less.
    - **Medium Term Securities:** Basis for classifying securities under this sub category depends on practices applied in financial markets of the given Country. Normally, this sub-category includes securities with maturity from 1 to 5 years.
    - **Long Term Securities:** This sub-category comprises securities with maturity longer than those of short and medium term securities.
2. **Type Based Securities:** Under this classification financial securities are classified into primary, secondary, and innovative securities.
    - **Primary Instruments/ Securities:** Primary securities are characterized as financial instruments whose value is set by the market and not by comparison with other instruments. These are released by organizations that are not financial. Debentures, preference shares, and equity shares are some examples of the main instruments.
    - **Secondary Instruments/ Securities:** An instrument that financial institutions issue directly to an investor is known as a primary security. Investing in a mutual fund, for instance, is investing in a secondary security. Additional instances of primary securities include money market funds, certificates of deposits, mutual funds, and commercial paper.
    - **Innovative Instruments:** these are the financial innovative instruments to suit the need of co-operates and investors group. For example, Derivatives, securitized assets, foreign currency mortgages and so on.

1.4.2.4. Financial Services

Financial services are those that have a financial component and are provided to customers by financial industries. Its goal is to act as a middleman and help institutional and individual investors with their financial transactions. Stated differently, financial services refer to the goods and services provided by organizations such as banks, credit card issuers, insurers, stock brokerages, and so forth. Financial intermediation is another term for financial services. Financial intermediation is the process of organizing surplus personnel and distributing raised funds to different charitable organizations (industries, companies, business people, individuals etc) for economic development.

Financial services include asset and insurance management, personal financial planning, leasing, investment, and related institutions, as well as the creation and provision of financial instruments and advisory services to businesses and individuals in the banking and related industries. These financial services are necessary for economic growth, industry expansion, and the establishment of new businesses.

Keyword

Financial intermediation refers to the practice of linking an investor and borrower. Acting as a third party, an intermediary aims to meet the financial needs of both parties to mutual satisfaction.

1.4.2.4.1. Classification of Financial Services

Financial services are divided into two categories: fee-based services and fund-based services. The former are listed below.

1. **Fund Based Services:** Financial services that are provided on a commission basis or for a set amount of interest are referred to as fund-based or asset-based financial services.
   - **Leasing:** It refers to a written agreement between lessor and lessee where lessor allows lessee to use his property for specified period of time or rent is called lease.
   - **Factoring:** Factoring is a service that a factor (financial institution) offers to its clients (businesses). Factors buy their clients' accounts receivable and debt at a discount and provide instant cash. We refer to this facility as factoring. Another name for it is finance on accounts receivable.
   - **Bills Discounting:** Discounting a bill of exchange is the act of trading or selling bills to a financial institution before the bills' maturity period for the discount rate. The amount of the discount is determined by the risk involved and the amount of time until the bill matures.
   - **Venture Capital:** Venture capital is a type of funding that investors provide to businesses to support their launch and growth. Investors share returns and risk with entrepreneurs as co-promoters.
   - **Loan:** A loan is an agreement, either written down or verbal, between a lender and a borrower for the temporary transfer of property (cash) from the lender to the borrower, with the borrower promising to repay the lender for the cash plus agreed-upon interest.

- **Housing Finance:** A housing finance company offers financing for the purchase or building of homes, including the purchase or development of land needed for such projects.
- **Hire Purchase:** A hire purchase system is a way to sell products on credit in which the buyer can buy the goods and pay for them in installments. At the conclusion of the financial installment, the buyer will receive title to the goods.

2. **Fee Based Services:** Fees based financial services are those which are paid for a flat fee rather than commission. Those services are known as fees based services are as follows:

- **Portfolio Management:** The process of managing and allocating money among different options for a portfolio in order to lower uncertainty is called portfolio management.
- **Loan Syndication:** The process of loan syndication involves many lenders pooling their funds to lend money to a company or project while sharing the risk and rewards.
- **Corporate Counselling:** Corporate counseling refers to a set of activities performed to ensure the efficient running of a corporate enterprise and to improve the performance.
- **Foreign Collaboration:** A corporate alliance consisting of both resident and non-resident entities working together to accomplish a predetermined task is known as foreign collaboration.

Did you get it?

1. Identify the characteristics of financial instruments
2. Discuss the financial services

1.5. MANAGERIAL ACCOUNTING

→Learning Objectives

- Discuss on objectives of managerial accounting.
- Write the features of managerial accounting
- Describe how to techniques used in managerial accounting

The field of accounting known as managerial accounting, sometimes called cost accounting or management accounting, is focused on identifying, measuring, analyzing, and interpreting accounting data so that managers can use it to guide operational decisions. Unlike financial accounting, which is primarily concentrated on the coordination and reporting of the company's financial transactions to outsiders (e.g., investors, lenders), managerial accounting is focused on internal reporting to aid decision-making. Managerial accountants are responsible for interpreting data into actionable insights that the company's management can use to make decisions by analyzing a variety of events and operational metrics.

1.5.1. Objectives of Managerial Accounting

The objectives of managerial accounting encompass several key goals aimed at providing relevant information, facilitating decision-making, and enhancing organizational performance. Some primary objectives include:

- **Decision Support:** Managerial accounting seeks to provide decision-makers within an organization with timely and relevant information to support strategic, tactical, and operational decision-making processes. This includes information on costs, revenues, profitability, and performance metrics that enable managers to evaluate alternatives, allocate resources effectively, and pursue opportunities that align with organizational objectives.
- **Planning and Forecasting:** Managerial accounting assists managers in developing comprehensive plans and forecasts for future operations and financial performance. By analyzing historical data, market trends, and operational metrics, managers can forecast future revenues, expenses, and resource requirements to guide strategic planning, budgeting, and goal-setting processes.
- **Performance Evaluation:** Managerial accounting enables managers to evaluate the performance of individuals, departments, and business units within the organization. This involves comparing actual results against budgeted targets,

analyzing variances, and identifying areas of strength and weakness to drive continuous improvement and accountability throughout the organization.

- **Cost Management:** Managerial accounting focuses on managing costs and improving cost-efficiency across various functions and processes within the organization. By identifying cost drivers, analyzing cost behavior, and implementing cost-control measures, managers can minimize wasteful spending, optimize resource utilization, and enhance overall profitability.
- **Strategic Alignment:** Managerial accounting aligns financial and operational activities with the organization's strategic objectives and goals. By providing insights into the financial implications of strategic decisions, managers can ensure that organizational resources are allocated in a manner that maximizes shareholder value, promotes long-term sustainability, and maintains competitiveness in the marketplace.
- **Risk Management:** Managerial accounting helps managers identify, assess, and manage financial risks inherent in business operations. By conducting sensitivity analysis, scenario planning, and risk assessment, managers can anticipate potential risks, develop contingency plans, and mitigate adverse financial outcomes to safeguard organizational assets and reputation.
- **Resource Allocation:** Managerial accounting assists managers in allocating scarce resources, such as capital, labor, and materials, to the most productive and profitable uses within the organization. By analyzing cost-benefit trade-offs, investment opportunities, and return on investment metrics, managers can prioritize investments, projects, and initiatives that generate the highest returns and create sustainable competitive advantages.

1.5.2. Features of Managerial Accounting

Managerial accounting encompasses several distinctive features that distinguish it from other branches of accounting and make it particularly relevant for managerial decision-making and internal management purposes within organizations. Some key features of managerial accounting include:

- **Internal Focus**: Managerial accounting primarily serves the internal needs of management and decision-makers within an organization. Unlike financial accounting, which focuses on providing financial information to external stakeholders, managerial accounting is geared towards supporting internal management functions, such as planning, control, and decision-making.
- **Future Orientation**: Managerial accounting emphasizes forward-looking information and analysis to assist managers in planning and decision-making for the future. It involves forecasting, budgeting, and projecting future financial outcomes based on historical data, market trends, and management's strategic objectives.
- **Decision-Relevance**: Managerial accounting information is tailored to meet the specific needs of

managers and assist them in making informed decisions. It provides relevant and timely information on costs, revenues, profitability, and performance metrics to support strategic planning, resource allocation, and performance evaluation.

- **Flexibility**: Managerial accounting systems are designed to be flexible and adaptable to the unique needs and requirements of different managerial levels and functions within an organization. They can be customized to provide detailed or summarized information, as well as different types of reports and analyzes, to meet the diverse informational needs of managers.
- **Internal Control**: Managerial accounting systems often incorporate mechanisms for internal control and performance evaluation to ensure accountability, transparency, and efficiency in organizational operations. They may include variance analysis, performance metrics, and budgetary controls to monitor and evaluate actual performance against planned targets.
- **Cost-Volume-Profit Analysis**: Managerial accounting utilizes cost-volume-profit (CVP) analysis to examine the relationships between costs, sales volume, and profitability. This analysis helps managers make strategic decisions regarding pricing, product mix, and sales strategies to maximize profitability and break-even points.
- **Decision Models and Techniques**: Managerial accounting employs various decision models and techniques, such as relevant costing, differential analysis, and capital budgeting methods, to support managerial decision-making across different functional areas, including production, marketing, and investment.

Did you know?

Grenzplankostenrechnung (GPK) is a German costing methodology, developed in the late 1940s and 1960s, designed to provide a consistent and accurate application of how managerial costs are calculated and assigned to a product or service. The term Grenzplankostenrechnung, often referred to as GPK, has best been translated as either marginal planned cost accounting or flexible analytic cost planning and accounting.

1.5.3. Techniques used in Managerial Accounting

Managerial accounting relies on a variety of different techniques, including the following:

1. **Margin Analysis:** It is the analysis of an activity's benefits in relation to any additional costs associated with the same activity. Businesses use this method when making decisions in an effort to maximize possible profits. It aids in determining the advantages of financial choices and business endeavors. When there are several possible investments but only a limited amount of money, experts employ marginal analysis. In these situations, professionals weigh the costs and benefits to decide which investment is more profitable.
2. **Trend Analysis:** Trend analysis is used in accounting to check financial statements for errors and determine whether any particular heads need to be adjusted. It is among the best management instruments available

for forecasting. Finding odd patterns and fixing underlying problems can be done with the help of trend analysis results. It makes use of historical data to comprehend the mood of the market. This facilitates the management's ability to make wiser business choices.

3. **Capital Budgeting:** The method by which management determines projects that will provide the highest returns on investment over time is known as capital budgeting. The management can assess the most profitable investment projects with the highest return on investment through this process. This method determines a profitable project by looking at IRR, NPV, and PB. Since this process provides an estimate of expected future cash flows, organizations can set long-term goals. The process of estimating cash flows aids management in planning profitable business strategies. Using this method also contributes to risk reduction.
4. **Constraint Analysis:** This entails analyzing the financial system's bottlenecks, which keep the company from operating at its best. Based on this analysis, the organization concentrates on making the most use of bottlenecks because they regulate the business's profitability. Here, problems brought on by principle bottlenecks are also examined, and the effects they have on revenue, profit, and cash flow are computed.
5. **Inventory Valuation and Product Costing:** It is the process used in accounting to give an organization's inventory a value. Since inventory makes up the majority of a company's assets, maximizing profitability may depend heavily on how well it is valued. Financial specialists can accurately determine a company's gross profitability by properly valuing its inventory.
6. **Standard Costing:** Standard costing involves updating accounting records with the actual cost instead of the anticipated cost. This is an alternative to a cost layering system, in which inventory items that are in stock are tracked down with their historical cost information. Estimates of costs for various company activities must be created for this. When it takes a while to determine the true cost, this method is used to approximate costs fairly.

Did you get it?

1. **What are some key performance indicators (KPIs) commonly used in managerial accounting, and how do they help measure organizational performance?**
2. **How does managerial accounting support budgeting, planning, and forecasting activities within an organization?**

FOCUS ON CAREERS

1. **Financial Manager:** A financial manager is responsible for managing the finances of an organization. They ensure the organization maintains adequate cash flow and liquidity through budgeting, accounting, and financial planning. Financial managers may also prepare reports on how well the organization meets its budget goals.

What Does a Financial Manager Do?

A financial manager has several responsibilities, including:

- Preparing financial reports and statements for upper management, executives, and company owners
- Evaluating the financial health of the organization based on trends and data
- Forecasting the financial needs and income of the business
- Discovering opportunities for the business to reduce costs, earn more and meet long-term financial goals
- Reviewing market trends to understand more about the industry and identify ways to expand the company
- Using financial reports and data to advise management on key financial decisions
- Overseeing the performance of other employees who work in accounting or finance for the organization
- Ensuring compliance with the accounting standards and financial reporting requirements of the organization

2. **Role of the Financial Manager:** The role of a financial manager is rapidly increasing due to advanced technology which has significantly reduced the amount of time that was occupied to produce financial reports.

- They analyze market trends to find opportunities for expansion or for acquiring companies.
- They have to do some tasks that are specific to their organization or industry
- They manage company credit
- Make some dividend pay-out decisions
- Keep in touch with the stock market if the company is listed
- Appreciate the financial performance concerning return investments
- They maximize the wealth of company shareholders
- To handle financial negotiations with banks and financial institutions

3. **Responsibilities of a Finance Manager:** Finance managers are responsible for maintaining financial records, managing budgets, and analyzing financial reports to help make financial decisions. If you are looking forward to starting

your career in finance you should be aware of the responsibilities of Finance Managers. Some of the critical responsibilities of a financial manager include:

- Fund Raising
- Allocation of Funds
- Profit Planning
- Understanding Capital Markets

4. **Fund Raising**: Finance managers help the organization raise funds through equity and debt. It is one of the primary responsibilities of finance managers to strike a balance between equity & debt and maintain the right amount of debt-equity ratio. It is necessary to keep enough cash and maintain liquidity to meet the organization's daily requirements. The finance manager should know how to operate on a strategic and tactical level to maintain financial stability.
5. **Allocation of Funds**: Once financial managers raise funds, the next step is to allocate the funds optimally. Diversification of assets and proper allocation of funds is a critical financial decision that influences the overall organizational activities. It is the responsibility of the finance managers to ensure the fund is allocated in the right manner across the various departments of the organization. The finance manager has to communicate effectively with other departments to avoid misappropriation of funds. The finance managers also have to take into consideration these factors for the allocation of funds:
   - The growth capability and size of the organization.
   - Long-term or short-term assets of the organization.
   - Mode of fundraising and the nature of stakeholders.

5. **Profit Planning**: Profit earning is essential for the survival of any organization. Profit is generated by various factors, including pricing, the competition between companies in an industry, the mechanism of supply and demand, and cost and output. It is the responsibility of the finance manager to find ways to boost the profitability of the organization by evaluating fixed factors of production and calculating opportunity costs.

6. **Understanding Capital Markets**: The capital market is a medium where savings and investments are channeled between suppliers and those in need. Financial managers need to have a clear understanding of the functioning of capital markets and should stay updated about the latest trends in the capital market while giving financial advice to the board of directors. It is the responsibility of the finance managers to set long-term and short-term financial goals for the organization by calculating the future risks and implementing strategies to mitigate those risks.

7. **How to Become a Financial Manager:** To become a financial manager, consider these steps:

i. **Complete High School:** A high school diploma or equivalent is the first step toward becoming a financial manager. As employers require a minimum of a bachelor's degree in a finance-related field, consider completing business and economics courses, as well as varying math classes. You may also have the opportunity to join investment or finance clubs in school, which can prepare you for the work you complete in a college major program.

ii. **Get a Degree:** Explore your degree options at the college or university of your choosing, and think of majoring in finance, accounting, business administration, economics or a related degree path. Employers often require one of these degrees for employment as a financial manager. When you share your education on your resume, consider including some of the most relevant courses for the role, which may include securities, financial planning, microeconomics, and general business.

iii. **Gain Experience in the Field:** Many financial managers begin their careers as accountants, auditors or financial analysts and gain experience by working directly with clients. Accountants work with companies to maintain books of record and prepare financial statements, while auditors examine the financial records of businesses, government agencies and other organizations to ensure that all transactions are properly recorded according to generally accepted accounting principles (GAAP).

Financial analysts help companies evaluate potential investments, manage assets and determine appropriate prices for assets like stocks and bonds. Working in these fields helps prepare you for working as a financial manager by teaching you how to analyze data and make predictions about future performance.

iv. **Consider a Master's Degree:** You may also opt to get your master's degree in one of these fields, which can make you feel more equipped for your chosen career and may qualify you for a variety of positions. By earning a master's degree, you're showcasing your advanced knowledge and proficiency in important subjects for the industry. Common courses for master's programs in a finance-related field include financial modeling, global markets, financial theory, and finance principles.

v. **Complete a Certification Program:** While the employers you apply with may not require that you hold any certifications, you may see this qualification under their preferred list of candidate experience. Certifications are a good idea if you want to make sure hiring managers know you have the competency to be successful in the role. There are a variety of certifications you can earn in this field, but some of the most popular are:

- Chartered Financial Analyst (CFA)
- Certified Treasury Professional (CTP)
- Certified Public Accountant (CPA)

To choose the best certification to pursue, research more about the requirements to sit for the exam and what career path is best served by the certification. For example, if you ultimately want to work for an investment firm as a finance manager, then the CFA certification may be one to strongly consider. Each certification comes with its own set of qualifications you must meet before attempting the exam. It's common to need at least a bachelor's degree in the field and a certain number of years of experience.

vi. **Explore Networking Opportunities:** Creating a strong network with other people in the finance industry is important for achieving career success. It allows you to meet others in your chosen field, which may help you learn about new job opportunities.

Networking can also often be a source of professional development, especially if you attend conferences or other training events. These types of events and online communities can be excellent beginnings for forming important connections in your career.

vii. **Advance Your Career:** As you progress in your career, you may consider pursuing advancement opportunities within financial management. For example, you may become a senior financial manager, which may involve supervising a team of financial managers within an organization. Seeking advancement opportunities may be a rewarding way to challenge yourself and enjoy new experiences within your career path.

8. **Critical Skills Required for Emerging Role of Finance Manager**

- **Numerical Skills**: Since finance managers are working with huge amounts of money on a daily basis, they should have strong numerical skills to monitor financial transactions. Errors in recording numbers could lead to huge losses and having strong numerical/ mathematical skills reduces the chance of errors and brings efficiency in financial operations.
- **Analytical Skills**: Finance managers should have analytical skills to evaluate the financial performance of the organization and in making financial decisions. Having strong analytical skills will help finance managers to think logically while implementing financial strategies.
- **Interpersonal Skills**: Finance Managers should have good interpersonal skills to maintain good communication flow with all the departments in the organization. Having effective communication skills and other interpersonal skills will help finance managers address financial constraints and ease the process of decision-making and budgeting.
- **Problem-Solving Skills**: Problem-solving skill is an inevitable skill required for finance managers. Having problem-solving skills will help in dealing with a wide range of information and financial documents effectively and in making sound financial decisions.
- **Leadership Skills**: Leadership skills help finance managers handle challenging situations and coordinate the team in a better way. Having financial managers with dynamic and solution-oriented mindsets will benefit organizations in overcoming risks.
- **Time Management Skills**: Time Management skills are essential to meet

deadlines. Excellent time management skills will help finance managers provide effective solutions and make crucial decisions on time.

9. **Work Experience:** Work experience for financial managers encompasses a range of roles and responsibilities across various industries and organizational settings. Entry-level positions often include financial analyst roles, where individuals analyze financial data, prepare reports, and assist in budgeting and forecasting processes. As they gain experience, financial managers may advance to roles such as finance manager, where they oversee financial operations, develop strategies to optimize financial performance, and provide insights to support decision-making.

Mid-level financial managers might take on responsibilities such as managing investment portfolios, assessing risk exposure, and developing financial policies and procedures to ensure compliance with regulations and organizational objectives. They may also be involved in mergers and acquisitions, conducting due diligence, and negotiating financial terms.

Senior-level financial managers, such as Chief Financial Officers (CFOs) or Finance Directors, are typically responsible for leading financial teams, setting overall financial strategy, and advising senior management and stakeholders on financial matters. They play a critical role in strategic planning, capital allocation, and driving organizational growth and profitability.

Work experience for financial managers often involves collaborating with cross-functional teams, including accounting, treasury, legal, and operational departments, to achieve financial goals and objectives. Effective communication, leadership, and problem-solving skills are essential for success in financial management roles, as is the ability to adapt to changing business environments and leverage technology to streamline processes and enhance decision-making.

Overall, work experience for financial managers is characterized by progressively challenging roles that require a combination of technical expertise, business acumen, and leadership capabilities to effectively manage financial resources, mitigate risks, and drive sustainable growth and profitability for organizations.

10. **Professional Development:** Most financial managers are qualified (or partly qualified) accountants. To become qualified, you need to pass (or be exempt from) a series of professional examinations and undergo a period of practical training.

Professional accountancy training is mostly on the job, and you will study for your examinations on a part-time basis. Employers usually support this activity and may help to fund the studies.

You may follow a structured graduate training scheme, which will give you exposure to a range of different functions. This will enable you to move into a financial management role at a later date. You may also be asked to complete a training log or portfolio to show evidence of your training and experience. Structured graduate training schemes are offered in large companies and in the public sector, although some financial managers gain their initial training in accountancy firms.

11. Career Prospects: Most financial managers start their career at a lower level and undertake professional accountancy qualifications, usually with the ACCA, CIMA or CIPFA, to become fully qualified.

Depending on the experience you gain, it may eventually be possible to step into the role of finance director or managing director. Knowledge about the day-to-day running of a company is essential in these roles.

Professional bodies such as ACCA and CIMA offer a Fellowship category of membership, which is awarded after a specific period of service and a certain level of competence and knowledge is demonstrated.

Financial management offers good opportunities to work overseas and professional qualifications from the major UK accountancy bodies are widely recognized around the world.

The expertise you offer as a financial manager is extremely transferable and it is therefore usually possible to move across into other areas of industry or commerce.

ROLE MODEL

J. P. MORGAN: THE MOST POWERFUL BANKERS OF ALL TIME

When John Pierpont Morgan arrived on Wall Street, it was a disorganized jumble of competing interests and one of the many financial centers in a country still struggling with the remnants of colonialism.

When he left Wall Street, it was a tightly knit group of big businesses leading one of the fastest-growing economies in the world. Much of the progress Wall Street experienced at the close of the 19th century and the beginning of the 20st was due to the influence of J.P. Morgan and the skill with which he wielded it.

1. **Early Life and Education:** When Morgan was born on April 17, 1837, in Hartford, Conn., there was very little doubt his future lay in banking. His father, Junius Spencer Morgan, was a partner in a bank run by another American, George Peabody.

Morgan was brought up knowing he would take his father's place, shuttling from the United States to Britain to peddle U.S. bonds to London investors. Most of these bonds were state and federal offerings and, at this period in history, a much higher risk than government bonds from European nations.

Upon his retirement, George Peabody left the bank completely in the hands of Junius, even removing his name from it. In 1864, J.S. Morgan & Co., the first Morgan bank, made its debut. By this time, J.P. Morgan had finished his European education and was learning his future trade as his father's New York agent while his father tended the more important London end of the business.

Morgan began to take over his father's responsibilities following the Drexel-Morgan merger. The Drexel-Morgan merger extended the scope of the business, strengthened international ties, and added to the capital the bank was able to loan.

As his father faded to the background, Morgan took an increasing role in underwriting companies for public offerings. He took a great interest in the railroad, holding shares, handling offerings, financing, and even placing Morgan employees on the company boards. With the importance of the railroad growing throughout the continent, Morgan picked an excellent time to expand both his bank's wealth and his personal power.

2. **Career:**
   - **Early Years:** Morgan entered banking in his father's London branch in 1856, moving to New York City the next year where he worked at the banking house of Duncan, Sherman & Company, the American representatives of

George Peabody & Company. From 1860 to 1864, as J. Pierpont Morgan & Company, he acted as agent in New York for his father's firm. By 1864–1871, he was a member of the firm of Dabney, Morgan & Company; in 1871, he partnered with the Drexels of Philadelphia to form the New York firm of Drexel, Morgan & Company.

In 1895, it became J. P. Morgan & Company, and retained close ties with Drexel & Company of Philadelphia, Morgan, Harjes & Company of Paris, and J. S. Morgan & Company (after 1910. Morgan, Grenfell & Company) of London. By 1900, it was one of the most powerful banking houses of the world, carrying through many deals especially reorganizations and consolidations. Morgan had many partners over the years, such as George W. Perkins, but remained in firm charge.

Morgan's ascent to power was accompanied by dramatic financial battles. He wrested control of the Albany and Susquehanna Railroad from Jay Gould and Jim Fisk in 1869, he led the syndicate that broke the government-financing privileges of Jay Cooke, and soon became deeply involved in developing and financing a railroad empire by reorganizations and consolidations in all parts of the United States. He raised large sums in Europe, but instead of only handling the funds he helped the railroads reorganize and achieve greater efficiencies. He fought against the speculators interested in speculative profits, and built a vision of an integrated transportation system. In 1885, he reorganized the New York, West Shore & Buffalo Railroad, leasing it to the New York Central. In 1886, he reorganized the Philadelphia & Reading, and in 1888, the Chesapeake & Ohio. After the United States Congress passed the Interstate Commerce Act in 1887, Morgan set up conferences in 1889 and 1890 that brought together railroad presidents in order to help the industry follow the new laws and write agreements for the maintenance of "public, reasonable, uniform and stable rates." The conferences were the first of their kind, and by creating a community of interest among competing lines paved the way for the great consolidations of the early twentieth century.

Morgan's process of taking over troubled businesses to reorganize them was known as "Morganization." Morgan reorganized business structures and management in order to return them to profitability. Morgan's reputation as a banker and financier also helped bring interest from investors to the businesses he took over.

In 1895, at the depths of the Panic of 1893, the federal treasury was nearly out of gold. President Grover Cleveland arranged for Morgan to create a private syndicate on Wall Street to supply the U.S. Treasury with $65 million in gold, half of it from Europe, to float a bond issue that restored the treasury surplus of $100 million. The episode saved the treasury but hurt Cleveland with the agrarian wing of his Democratic Party and became an issue in the election of 1896, when banks came under withering attack from William Jennings Bryan. Morgan and Wall Street bankers donated heavily to Republican presidential candidate William McKinley, who was elected in 1896 and reelected in 1900 on a gold standard platform.

In 1902, J. P. Morgan & Co. purchased the Leyland line of Atlantic steamships and other British lines, creating an Atlantic shipping combine, the International Mercantile Marine Company, which eventually became the owner of White Star Line, builder, and operator of RMS Titanic. In addition, J P Morgan & Co (or the banking houses that it succeeded) reorganized a large number of railroads between 1869 and 1899.

- **Later Years:** After the death of his father in 1890, Morgan took control of J. S. Morgan & Co (renamed Morgan, Grenfell & Company in 1910). Morgan began talks with Charles M. Schwab, president of Carnegie Co., and businessman Andrew Carnegie in 1900 with the intention of buying Carnegie's business and several other steel and iron businesses to consolidate them to create the United States Steel Corporation. Carnegie agreed to sell the business to Morgan for $480 million. The deal was closed without lawyers and without a written contract. News of the industrial consolidation arrived to newspapers in mid-January 1901. U.S. Steel was founded later that year and was the first billion-dollar company in the world with an authorized capitalization of $1.4 billion.

U.S. Steel aimed to achieve greater economies of scale, reduce transportation and resource costs, expand product lines, and improve distribution. It was also planned to allow the United States to compete globally with Britain and Germany. U.S. Steel's size was claimed by Schwab and others to allow the company to pursue distant international markets (globalization). U.S. Steel was regarded as a monopoly by critics, as the business was attempting to dominate not only steel but also the construction of bridges, ships, railroad cars and rails, wire, nails, and a host of other products. With U.S. Steel, Morgan had captured two-thirds of the steel market, and Schwab was confident that the company would soon hold a 75% market share. However, since 1901 the business' market share dropped, never reaching Schwab's dream of 75% market share.

Morgan also financed manufacturing and mining businesses and controlled banks, insurance companies, shipping lines, and communications systems. Through his firm came enormous funds from abroad to help develop American resources.

Enemies of banking attacked Morgan for the terms of his loan of gold to the federal government in the 1895 crisis, for his financial resolution of the Panic of 1907, and for bringing on the financial ills of the New York, New Haven & Hartford RR. In 1912, he appeared and publicly defended himself before a congressional committee headed by Arsène Pujo, which was investigating the "money trust" and which was aimed particularly at him.

In 1900, Morgan financed inventor Nikola Tesla and his Wardenclyffe Tower with $150,000 for experiments in radio. Tesla was unsuccessful and in 1904, Morgan pulled out. At the height of Morgan's career during the early 1900s, he and his partners controlled directly and indirectly assets worth $1.3 billion.

3. **Personal Life:** Morgan was a lifelong member of the Episcopal Church in the United States, and by 1890 was one of its most influential leaders.

In 1861, he married Amelia Sturges (1835–1862). After her death the next year, he married Frances Louise Tracy (1842–1924) on May 3, 1863, and they had the following children:

- Louisa Pierpont Morgan (1866–1946), who married Herbert Penny Livingston Satterlee (1863–1947)
- Jack Pierpont Morgan (1867–1943),
- Juliet Morgan (1870–1952), and
- Anne Morgan (1873–1952).

Morgan was physically large with massive shoulders, piercing eyes, and a purple nose, because of a childhood skin disease, rosacea. He was known to dislike publicity and hated being photographed; as a result of his self-consciousness of his rosacea, all of his professional portraits were retouched. He smoked large Havana cigars called Hercules' Clubs and often had a tremendous physical effect on people; one man said that a visit from Morgan left him feeling "as if a gale had blown through the house."

Morgan was scheduled to travel on the maiden voyage of RMS Titanic but canceled at the last minute.

Morgan died while traveling abroad in Rome. On March 31, 1913, just before his 76th birthday, Pierpont Morgan died in his sleep at the Grand Hotel. Nearly four thousand condolence letters were received there overnight and flags on Wall Street flew at half-mast. The stock market was also closed for two hours when his body passed through Wall Street. At the time of his death, he had an estate worth $80 million (approximately $1.2 billion today). His remains were interred in the Cedar Hill Cemetery in his birthplace of Hartford. His son, J. P. Morgan, Jr., inherited the banking business.

SUMMARY

- Managerial Finance is essentially a combination of economy and accounting.
- Financial services is the area of finance concerned with the design and delivery of advice and financial products to individuals, businesses, and governments.
- Managerial finance is concerned with the duties of the financial manager working in a business.
- The stockholders (owners) vote periodically to elect members of the board of directors and to decide other issues such as amending the corporate charter.
- Profit maximization is the short run or long run process by which a firm may determine the price, input and output levels that will lead to the highest possible total profit (or just profit in short).
- A sole proprietorship is a business owned by one person who operates it for his/her profit. The typical sole proprietorship is small, such as a bike shop, personal trainer, or plumber – most sole proprietorships operating in the wholesale, retail, service, and construction industries.
- A financial system is a system that allows the exchange of funds between financial market participants such as lenders, investors, and borrowers.
- The financial institutions are classified into term lending institutions, refinance institutions, investment institutions and state level institutions.
- A partnership consists of two or more owners doing business together for profit. Partnerships are typically larger than sole proprietorships and are common in the finance, insurance, legal and real estate industries.
- Financial service refers to services which are financial in nature offered by financial industries to its customer.
- Managerial accounting (also known as cost accounting or management accounting) is a branch of accounting that is concerned with the identification, measurement, analysis, and interpretation of accounting information so that it can be used to help managers make informed operational decisions.
- Managerial accounting assists managers in developing comprehensive plans and forecasts for future operations and financial performance.

REVIEW QUESTIONS

1. What is the goal of the firm and, therefore, of all managers and employees? Discuss how one measures achievement of this goal.
2. Which legal form of business organization is most common? Which form is dominant in terms of business revenues?
3. Describe the roles and the relationships among the major parties in a corporation: stockholders, board of directors, and managers.

4. What are the two primary activities of the financial manager that are related to the firm's balance sheet?
5. What is a financial market? Explain its role and function.

MULTIPLE CHOICE QUESTIONS

1. Which of the following is NOT a primary goal of financial management?
   a. Maximizing shareholder wealth
   b. Maximizing sales revenue
   c. Maximizing company value
   d. Minimizing cost of capital

2. The cost of capital is:
   a. The total expenses incurred by a company.
   b. The minimum return required by investors for providing funds to a company.
   c. The interest rate on the company's debt.
   d. The amount of cash available for investment.

3. Which of the following is a short-term source of financing?
   a. Common stock issuance
   b. Long-term bank loan
   c. Trade credit
   d. Bond issuance

4. Which financial statement shows a company's revenues and expenses over a specific period?
   a. Balance sheet
   b. Income statement
   c. Statement of cash flows
   d. Statement of retained earnings

5. The process of comparing financial ratios to industry averages or competitors is known as:
   a. Trend analysis
   b. Vertical analysis
   c. Horizontal analysis
   d. Ratio analysis

6. A company's inventory turnover ratio is calculated as:
   a. Cost of goods sold / Average inventory
   b. Average inventory / Cost of goods sold
   c. Sales / Average inventory

d. Average inventory / Sales

7. The payback period method is used to evaluate:

a. The profitability of an investment.

b. The risk associated with an investment.

c. The time it takes to recover the initial investment.

d. The present value of future cash flows.

8. The process of assessing the potential impact of various scenarios on a company's financial performance is known as:

a. Sensitivity analysis

b. Break-even analysis

c. Capital budgeting

d. Cash flow analysis

9. Which of the following represents a measure of a company's liquidity?

a. Debt-to-equity ratio

b. Return on assets (ROA)

c. Current ratio

d. Price-earnings (P/E) ratio

10. The weighted average cost of capital (WACC) is calculated as:

a. The average interest rate paid on the company's debt.

b. The average rate of return required by shareholders.

c. The average rate of return required by both debt and equity investors.

d. The average tax rate paid by the company.

Answer to Multiple Choice Questions

1. (b); 2. (b); 3. (c); 4. (b); 5. (d); 6. (a); 7. (c); 8. (a); 9. (c); 10. (c)

REFERENCES

1. Abor, J. & Biekpe, N. 2005. What determines the capital structure of listed firms in Ghana? African Finance Journal, 7(1): 37-48.
2. Bagchi B., Khamrui B. (2012), Relationship between Working capital management and profitability: A study of selected FMCG companies in India, Business and Economics Journal BEJ-60.
3. Baker M., Wurgler J. (2002), Market Timing and Capital Structure, Journal of Finance 57.
4. Baz J., Chacko G. (2004), Financial Derivatives. Pricing, Applications and Mathematics, Cambridge University Press, Cambridge.

5. Bennett, M. & Donnelly, R. 1993. The determinants of capital structure: some UK evidence. British Accounting Review, 25(1): 43-59.
6. Brigham, Eugene and Johnson, Ramon (2000), Issues in Managerial Finance, Holt Rinehart and Winston Publishers, Hindale Illinois
7. Cassimon, D., Engelen P.J. (2003), The New Frontiers of Corporate Finance, Global Business Review 5(1).
8. Clive Marsh (2009). Mastering Financial Management, Financial Times Prentice Hall.
9. Copeland T.E., Weston L.F., Shastri K. (2004), Financial Theory and Corporate Policy, Addison Wesley Publishing Company, Boston.
11. Darrell Duffie and Kenneth J. Singleton (2003). Credit Risk: Pricing, Measurement, and Management. Princeton University Press.
12. Deloof M. (2003), Does working capital management affect profitability of Belgian firms?, Journal of Business Finance & Accounting 30(3-4), pp. 573-588.
13. Dudycz T. (2000), Financial analysis (in Polish: Analiza finansowa), AE, Wroclaw, 2000.
14. Elvin M. (2004), Financial Risk Taking. An Introduction to the Psychology of Trading and Behavioural Finance, John Wiley & Sons.
15. Falope O.I., Ajilore O.T. (2009), Working capital management and corporate profitability: evidence from panel data analysis of selected quoted companies in Nigeria, Research Journal of Business management 3, pp. 73-84.
16. James Van Horne and John Wachowicz (2009). Fundamentals of Financial Management, 13th ed., Pearson Education Limited.
17. Lawrence Gitman and Chad J. Zutter (2019). Principles of Managerial Finance, 14th edition, Addison-Wesley Publishing.
18. W. F. Sharpe (1964). Capital asset prices: A theory of market equilibrium under conditions of risk. Journal of Finance 14, 3: 425–442.
19. W. F. Sharpe (1970). Portfolio Theory and Capital Markets. New York: McGraw-Hill.
20. W. F. Sharpe (1972). Risk, market sensitivity and diversification. Financial Analysts Journal 28, 1 (January/ February): 74–79.
21. W. F. Sharpe, G. J. Alexander, and J. V. Bailey (2000). Fundamentals of Investments, 3rd edition. Upper Saddle River, NJ: Prentice Hall.

CHAPTER

2

Financial Statement and Report

LEARNING OBJECTIVES

After studying this chapter, you will be able to:

- Understand the meaning of financial statements
- Discuss how to prepare financial statements
- Describe the vertical and horizontal analyzes of financial statements
- Define the financial reporting

INTRODUCTORY EXAMPLE

Monthly Financial Reports: Monthly financial reports are a management way of obtaining a concise overview of the previous month's status to have up-to-date reporting of the cash management, profit, and loss statements while evaluating future plans and decisions moving forward.

These financial reporting examples offer a more panoramic view of an organization's economic affairs, serving up elements of information covered in our daily and weekly explanations. By offering the ability to drill down into metrics over a four-week period, the data here is largely focused on creating bigger, more long-term changes, strategies, and initiatives.

These powerful documents offer detailed visual insights into the following areas:

- **Cash Management**: A comprehensive overview of your organization's liquidity and existing cash flow situation.
- **Profit and Loss**: A critical glimpse into your company's income statement and profits in a number of critical areas of the business.
- **The Bigger Pi**cture: A business financial report format offers a full overview of the company's core financing activities over a monthly period, providing data geared towards developing sustainable strategies and improvements that will foster growth and increased profitability.

Coupled with the insights delivered by daily and weekly reports, monthly ones in the form of online dashboards are pivotal to not only gaining an edge on your competitors but also getting a predictive vision that will ensure you meet – and even exceed – your financial targets indefinitely. As a result, your overall efficiency will become flawless, and you're likely to enjoy healthy growth in your year-on-year profits.

There is a wealth of KPIs to consider when looking at a monthly financial report sample. The best way to explain them in a practical context is by getting visual.

To help you understand how you can benefit from all of this, here are 5 monthly report examples, complete with explanatory insight and a deeper insight into their respective KPIs.

UNIT INTRODUCTION

Government laws mandate that specific entities, such as cooperatives, limited companies, and public utilities, keep accurate records and prepare financial statements. The financial statement provides the public with information about how well a company is fulfilling its social responsibility. Financial statements are required when issuing shares and bonds because they provide information about the financial soundness that potential buyers can use to determine whether to purchase shares or bonds. The union for workers may review the financial statement to see if they can make their demand. Financial statements help the management of a company make a variety of decisions. Globally, consumers are becoming more conscious of their rights and are increasingly using financial statements as a tool to assess the extent of industry exploitation. The tax legislation requires business entities to prepare fair and impartial financial statements. The financial statement serves as instruments to regulate equity and debentures issued by companies.

Financial reporting is a standard accounting procedure that typically occurs on an annual or quarterly basis and uses financial statements to reveal a company's financial data and performance over a specific time period. To put it simply, a financial report is essential to knowing how much money you have, where it's coming from, and where it needs to go. To make well-informed business decisions about the company's financial health, management needs access to accurate financial reporting. The financial reporting of your business will be a factor in the decisions of banks and potential investors regarding their loan and investment decisions. Financial reporting is sharing details about the company's performance over a given time period with management and the public (if the business is publicly traded). Typically, quarterly, and annual financial reports are released. This is not the same as management reporting, which provides financial data to individuals within the organization for use in internal decision-making. A public company's annual report contains financial reports.

Financial reporting has two main functions. First of all, it facilitates management's ability to make wise decisions about the goals and overarching plans of the business. The information provided in the reports can assist management in identifying the company's overall financial health as well as its strengths and weaknesses. Second, financial reporting gives all of the company's stakeholders—shareholders, prospective investors, customers, and government regulators—important information about the company's financial situation and operations. It serves as a way to guarantee that the business is being managed properly. It is important to remember that companies that are listed on a public exchange are bound by stringent reporting requirements that are upheld by the Securities and Exchange Commission (SEC).

2.1. MEANING OF FINANCIAL STATEMENTS

→Learning Objectives

- To define nature of financial statements
- To discuss the characteristics of financial statements
- To deal with the purpose of financial statement analysis
- To explain the personal financial statements

The primary goal of financial statement analysis, a judgmental process is to estimate the financial positions of an enterprise both now and in the past as well as its operational results. Its main goal is to come up with the most accurate estimates and predictions about the state of the enterprise going forward. Basically, it is gathering and evaluating data from financial statements to identify patterns and highlight a company's strong and weak points. This information can be helpful when making decisions that require comparing a company's performance over time (time series analysis) and with that of other companies (cross sectional analysis).

Analysis of financial statements aids in showcasing the business's financial performance. It is the process of correctly establishing the relationship between the items on the Balance Sheet and those on the Profit and Loss Account in order to determine the financial strength and weakness of a company. The process of gathering and analyzing data from financial statements to aid in management decision-making is known as financial statement analysis. Common techniques used in this process include budgeting, comparing current period to previous, and utilizing ratios. A financial appraisal is an objective assessment of a company's strength and profitability. It aims to draw attention to the important influences and connections between corporate effectiveness, managerial performance, financial strength and weakness, and the company's creditworthiness.

An in-depth analysis of the profitability and financial position's causes and effects is the goal of financial statement analysis. Financial analysis is the process of using accounting information and financial statements to identify a company's key operating and financial characteristics. Finding the management of the company's effectiveness and performance as seen in the financial records and reports is the aim of this kind of analysis. These documents and reports, which include the information needed for performance management, are financial statements. To determine the company's strengths and weaknesses, it is crucial to examine the financial statements.

A company's financial statements are meant to supply a large portion of the fundamental information needed for decision-making and, generally speaking, performance evaluation by different parties, including creditors, government agencies, present owners, possible investors, and, occasionally, rival businesses. The reports that the accountant uses to communicate and summarize the most basic financial data are called financial statements. The company's balance sheet, which shows the assets, liabilities, and capital as of a specific date, and the profit and loss account, which displays the operational results for a given period, are summarized in the financial statements. The financial statements are a set of information arranged in accordance with consistent and reasonable accounting practices. Financial statements serve the purpose of explaining certain financial facets of the business.

Analyzing financial statements entails evaluating an entity's financial statements and associated footnotes. Accountants, credit analysts, investment analysts, management, and other interested parties may perform this. Financial statements provide an evaluation of the past financial performance and future prospects of a company. A financial statement is analyzed in order to gain a deeper understanding of the performance and position of the company. The process of analyzing a financial statement involves assessing how its component parts relate to one another in order to better understand the performance and position of the company. Thus, the analysis of the financial statements used to assess the company's performance is known as the financial analysis. The main instruments used in financial analysis are ratio analysis, trend analysis, common size statement analysis, and comparative financial statement analysis.

Keyword

Investment analyst is a financial professional with expertise in evaluating financial and investment information, typically for the purpose of making buy, sell and hold recommend actions for securities.

Ratio calculations are made as part of financial statement analysis in order to assess a company's operating performance and financial status. Ratio is a crucial analytical tool for financial statements. The mathematical expression of the relationship between two accounting figures is called a financial ratio. Ratio is a measure that is used to assess a company's performance and financial status. It supports analysts' quantitative assessment of the company's performance and financial status. To evaluate financial performance, it compiles the most important relationships from financial reports and data. A business unit's financial and economic situation can be fully examined using ratio analysis, one of the most effective tools for financial analysis. Ratios are merely a practical means of condensing vast amounts of financial data and comparing the businesses' performances. When evaluating a company's financial performance over time, ratios are incredibly helpful metrics. An understanding of a bank's profitability, return on investment, capital sufficiency, and liquidity can be gained through performance ratios.

Depending largely on who the analysts are and why the firm is being evaluated, different analysts will want different kinds of ratios. Short-term creditors worry about the company's capacity to make on-time bill payments. The short-term ability to settle current liabilities is based on the quantity of liquid assets. They have a desire for liquidity. Bonds and debentures are held by long-term creditors; mortgages secured by the company are interested in both the immediate payment of interest and the final repayment of the principal. The business needs to make enough money over the long run and have enough liquidity in the short term. They look at profitability and liquidity. Aside from liquidity and profitability, stockholders also worry about the stock policy of the company. The company could not have paid the cash dividends without liquidity. The company would not be able to declare dividends in the absence of profits. The market price of the common stock would be lower if there were bad policies.

A company's financial statements for a year or less would not accurately represent the nature of its operations when analyzed. This means that the analysis must logically span a longer time frame. Trend analysis refers to the examination conducted over an extended duration. The ratio's trend analysis shows the direction of change. The percentage relationship that each item has to the same item in the base year is calculated using this method. One can determine whether the data reflect favorable or unfavorable tendencies by looking at trend percentages, which reveal changes in the financial and operating data between particular periods. An additional technique for assessing the company's performance is the Comparative Statement Analysis. It is used to compare the company's performance and standing to the industry average or to other companies. By doing this, weaknesses in the company's performance can be found and fixed.

2.1.1. Nature of Financial Statements

Financial statements are straightforward declarations that are derived from previously recorded data and facts. They are unwavering in their intentions, character, and sincerity. They are the result of a careful blending of documented facts, accounting concepts, rules, and conventions, as well as occasionally estimates and subjective opinions.

Thus, financial statements are affected by three factors i.e., recorded facts, accounting conventions and personal judgments.

- By recorded facts is meant the data contained in statements which have already recorded in accounting records. Example: Cash in hand and at bank, cost of fixed assets, amounts due from customers and due to suppliers of goods are all recorded facts represented numerically.
- Financial statements are prepared by adhering to certain concepts and established conventions.
- The role of personal judgments, estimates, and opinions is to be emphasized in accordance with the recorded facts and accounting concepts and conventions, particularly when two or more alternative procedures are available and equally acceptable. Example: an asset could be depreciated under several methods, and inventory could be valued under different methods. Under such circumstances, personal opinion and judgment play an important

role as to which of the methods are in closer conformity with the accounting standards and concepts in a particular circumstance or case.

2.1.2. Characteristics of Financial Statements

Financial statements are regarded as indices of an enterprises performance and position. As such, extreme care and caution should be exercised while preparing these statements. Financial statements generally reflect the following observable characteristics:

- **Internal Audience**: The people who are interested in a particular business enterprise are the target audience for financial statements. They must be prepared with the understanding that the user is generally conversant with business procedures and the definitions and implications of terms used in that context.
- **Articulation**: Since the fundamental financial statements are connected, they are referred to as articulated. Example: The profit and loss account displays the operational financial results and illustrates how the different balances on the balance sheet reflect changes in resources.
- **Historical Nature**: Financial statements typically provide historical data. They are not meant to offer projections of future economic activity and their impact on income and equity, despite the fact that they are increasingly used by creditors and potential investors as the foundation for the future.
- **Legal and economic consequences**: Economic and legal components are both evident in financial statements. Although they are conceptually focused on economics, a lot of the terms and practices have legal roots. Example: Conventions of disclosure and materiality.
- **Technical Terminology**: Financial statements use technical terms because they are byproducts of the technical accounting process. Therefore, it is crucial that those who use these statements are conversant with the various terms used in them as well as their definitions and interpretations.
- **Summarization and Classification**: The amount of business transactions that impact operations is so great that the reader can derive valuable insights only from the summary and categorization of business events and items.
- **Money Terms**: All business transactions are quantified, measured, and related in monetary terms. In the absence of this monetary unit of measurement, financial statements will be meaningless.
- **Various Valuation Methods**: There is variation in the methods of valuation for every item on a balance sheet. Example: Current exchange value is used to value cash; net realizable value is used to value accounts receivable; cost or market price is used to value inventories; and cost less depreciation is used to value fixed assets.
- **Accrual Basis**: Most financial statements are prepared on accrual basis rather than on cash basis i.e., taking into account all incomes due but not received, and all expenses due but not paid.

- **Need for Estimates and judgment**: Financial statements must include facts and figures that are based on estimates, subjective opinions, and judgments in multiple instances. Examples of situations where estimates and subjective judgments are needed include the rate of depreciation, the useful economic life of a fixed asset, and the provision for questionable debts.
- **Verifiability**: In order to increase the credibility of financial statements, it is imperative that the information they present be able to be independently verified.
- **Conservatism**: In order to prevent the possibility of overstating assets and incomes, estimates and personal judgments that are necessary during the preparation of financial statements should be based conservatively and moderately.

Keyword

Financial data consists of pieces or sets of information related to the financial health of a business. The pieces of data are used by internal management to analyze business performance and determine whether tactics and strategies must be altered.

2.1.3. Purpose of Financial Statement Analysis

The process of examining and assessing a company's financial statements, such as the profit and loss statement or balance sheet, in order to better understand its financial situation and make more informed decisions, is known as financial statement analysis. Financial data is recorded in financial statements; nevertheless, in order for investors, shareholders, managers, and other interested parties to find greater value in this information, financial statement analysis is required.

Every financial statement offers information spanning several years. When combined, financial statement analysis techniques such as vertical and horizontal analysis allow analysts to monitor performance metrics across financial statements. The financial statement's practice of listing each line item as a percentage of another is an illustration of vertical analysis. Each financial statement's line items are compared to prior time periods using horizontal analysis. Line items from one financial statement and line items from another are compared in ratio analysis. For instance, the number of times a company can pay off debt with current earnings is something that many analysts find useful. To do this, analysts can divide the debt, which is derived from the balance sheet, by the net income, which is derived from the income statement. Similar comparisons are made between the assets and stockholders' equity shown on the balance sheet and the company net income reported on the income statement by return on assets (ROA) and return on equity (ROE). Financial statement analysis involves the identification of the following items for a company's financial statements over a series of reporting periods:

- **Trends**: Create trend lines for key items in the financial statements over multiple time periods, to see how the company is performing. Typical trend lines are for revenues, the gross margin, net profits, cash, accounts receivable, and debt.
- **Proportion Analysis**: To determine how the sizes of different accounts in the financial statements relate to one another, a variety of ratios are available. A company's debt to equity ratio can be used to determine if it has taken on too much debt, and its quick ratio can be used to estimate its ability to pay its immediate liabilities. These analyzes typically compare the balance sheet's accounts for assets, liabilities, and equity with the income statement's revenue and expense listings.

Financial statement analysis is an exceptionally powerful tool for a variety of users of financial statements, each having different objectives in learning about the financial circumstances of the entity.

2.1.4. Personal Financial Statements

Financial statements are routinely prepared by businesses. This is due to the fact that these financial statements require an audit. These statements become official documents that can be used for taxation and loan applications after they are audited and confirmed to be accurate. However, the majority of people do not prepare personal financial statements because they are not required for taxation or loan purposes.

Making these kinds of statements, though, can be really beneficial. This is because the information these statements convey about a person's financial health is significant. This is why one of the habits that are ingrained during personal finance training sessions is creating personal financial statements.

Corporate financial statements are composed of three statements, i.e., the income statement, the balance sheet, and the cash flow statement. On the other hand, personal financial statements are also composed of three statements. Here too, the income statement and balance sheet are prepared. However, the cash flow statement is replaced by the budget.

- **Statement 1: The Income Statement**: An individual's income and expenses for a specified time period are listed on an income statement, as the name suggests. This statement must list the various sources of income that an individual receives. The next step is to make a list of the common expenses. It is necessary to list the fixed monthly expenses individually. However, monthly expenses that differ from one another should be kept separate. This can be attributed to the fact that fixed expenses are largely out of control. Variable costs, however, are controllable and measurable each month. Confusion is frequently caused by the way loan repayment must be documented. This is a result of some people's opinion that they ought to be exempt from liabilities. It's easier to add them as an expense, though. This is so because the income statement's final result—a surplus or deficit—rather than a profit or loss. The balance sheet is where the excess or deficit is subsequently carried over. It is imperative to acknowledge that the income statement solely depicts activities within a specific month. The amount resets to zero at the end of each month.

- **Statement #2: The Balance Sheet**: The balance sheet and corporate balance sheets are likewise fairly similar. People, however, need to be made aware of the reasoning. The inventory of a person's possessions is listed on the asset side. Considering the principle of conservatism, the assets should be valued at cost or market value, whichever is lower. In a similar vein, a list of all the debts must be made regarding liability. The same principle of valuation needs to be followed here. Net worth is the total after all assets and liabilities are listed. Every month, the excess is added to the assets and, in the event of a deficit, it is added to the liabilities. It is necessary to examine the balance sheet for solvency problems. For instance, if a person has too many current liabilities, i.e., credit card bills, mortgage payments, etc., and not enough current assets, i.e., cash on hand, a person may be falling into a debt trap.
- **Statement #3: The Budget**: Budgets are also created by corporations. Their budgets, however, are not included in the main statements. From a personal perspective, budgets are crucial because they serve as a control mechanism. The same format is used each time a budget is created, i.e., the balance sheet and the income statement. However, projections are filled in there rather than actual numbers. The budget statement looks ahead. Therefore, if a person notices that their monthly expenses are exceedingly high, they can cut back on some of their spending to reach their savings target.

Budgets can also be utilized for analysis as statements that look backward. It is possible to see the budgeted and actual expenditure amounts side by side. It is then possible to compute the difference between these figures. Next, the source of this variation can be identified. This enhances the planning process. It is obvious that the planner did not consider many factors if there is an excessive amount of variance.

Did you get it?

1. **What are the key components of each financial statement, and how are they interconnected?**
2. **How do businesses ensure the accuracy, reliability, and transparency of their financial statements?**

2.2. PREPARE FINANCIAL STATEMENTS

→Learning Objectives

- Describe the adjusted trial balance – closing the books
- Explain the adjusted trial balance – adjusting entries
- Know the translate the adjusted trial balance to financial statements
- Define the audit the financial statements
- Write the liquidity, solvency, profitability

Financial statement analysis is the process of assessing a business's worth or performance using its cash flow, income, or balance sheet. Investors can obtain a more comprehensive understanding of a company's financial profile by employing various methods such as ratio analysis, vertical analysis, and horizontal analysis. A financial statement is what happens when a company provides all the pertinent financial data in an organized and comprehensible way. Financial statements are meant to give both insiders and outsiders of the company a clear, concise picture of the company's current financial situation.

2.2.1. Adjusted Trial Balance – Closing the Books

The adjusted trial balance is the first step in the preparation of the financial statements. "Closing" the book and making the required adjusting entries to bring the financial records into line with the actual financial activity of the company are necessary steps in preparing the adjusted trial balance. Making sure that transactions that occur after the company's financial period are excluded from the financial statements is all that is required to close the books. For example, assume a business is preparing its financial statements with a December 31st year end. It acquires some property on January 14th. If the books are properly closed, that property will not be included on the balance sheet that is being prepared for the period on December 31st.

2.2.2. Adjusted Trial Balance – Adjusting Entries

A journal entry that is made at the conclusion of an accounting period to properly allocate income and expenses to the relevant years is known as an adjustment entry. Generally, prepayments, accruals, estimates, inventory, and prepaid expenses are the subjects of adjustment entries. A company might invest money or make erroneous assumptions about how an item or service will be used during the accounting period at any point during the year. Through adjusting entries, the business can go back and change those balances to accurately reflect what actually happened financially during the accounting period. In the end, understating expenses and overstating income could have an impact on the total amount of taxes paid if the adjusting entries are not recorded. For example, assume a company purchases 100 units of raw material that it expects to use up during the current accounting period. As a result, it immediately expenses the cost of the material. However, at the end of the year the company discovers it only used 50 units. The company must then make an adjusting entry to reflect that, and decrease the amount of the expense and increase the amount of inventory accordingly.

2.2.3. Translate the Adjusted Trial Balance to Financial Statements

Using the trial balance, the company then prepares the four financial statements. These statements are:

- **The Balance Sheet**: A summary of the company's assets, liabilities, and equity;
- **The Income Statement**: A summary of the business's income, expenses, and profits
- **The Statement of Cash Flows**: A report on a company's cash flow activities, particularly its operating, investing, and financing activities; and
- **The Statement of Changes in Equity**: A report that explains the changes of the company's equity throughout the reporting period Information flows from the unadjusted trial balance to the trial balance then to the income statement.

Keyword

Profitability is a measure of an organization's profit relative to its expenses. Organizations that are more efficient will realize more profit as a percentage of its expenses than a less-efficient organization, which must spend more to generate the same profit.

2.2.4. Audit the Financial Statements

The business will hire a third party from outside to audit its financial statements after they are prepared. In order to determine whether system controls are adequate, to verify that established policies and operational procedures are being followed, and to suggest any necessary modifications to controls, policies, or procedures, an audit is an impartial review and investigation of records and activities. The assurance that the statements' contents are accurate is provided to interested parties and outside investors by the audit.

2.2.5. Liquidity, Solvency, Profitability

How much cash a business has on hand or can produce quickly indicates how strong its finances are. High levels of cash on hand suggest that the company will have no trouble paying off debt when it comes due. The subject of financial liquidity is first raised in relation to the kinds of assets that a company possesses and their marketability.

The liquidity, solvency, profitability are follows:

1. **Liquidity:** The degree of liquidity that each asset possesses allows for additional asset classification. The capacity of an asset to be converted into cash is known as liquidity; certain things may be more liquid than others. For example, a stock can be sold in a matter of hours or days. However, it may take weeks, months, or even years to turn property—such as buildings or land—into cash. The term "liquid asset" is often used to describe financial instruments like stocks and bonds because of how simple it is to convert them and transfer ownership. All assets, though, have the potential to be liquidated—that is, traded for cash. A company's or an individual's current level of financial stability is referred to as their "solvency" in the business and finance domains. Additionally, a specific financial area, like property, cash flow, or insurance, may be covered by the term. A person who is solvent is one who has sufficient assets to pay off their debts and maintains the ability to fulfill all of their current financial obligations under the terms and conditions of each debt.

   Being financially stable is crucial for running both a household and a business. Families and individuals aim to accumulate reserves of assets that will sustain the household in the event that the primary source of income is temporarily disrupted or goes away entirely. When a household is solvent, its obligations can be met without going past due and it will still have some money left over at the end of the month.

2. **Solvency:** Similar to this, companies aim to be in a position where they always have resources available to manage debt for the company quickly and effectively. The concept of liquidity solvency is especially crucial for businesses. This essentially indicates that the company has enough cash on hand to pay its debts, or that it has assets that can be swiftly turned into cash without jeopardizing its capacity to operate. There's a strong likelihood that a company will be sold or shut down if it becomes insolvent and cannot renegotiate its current debt into manageable terms. In order to pay off at least some of the outstanding debt, any remaining assets are sold, and the proceeds are distributed among the different creditors.

   The solvency ratio, also referred to as the margin, is something that businesses typically monitor closely. This is just the relationship between assets and debt, where assets are defined as cash or assets that are easily convertible into cash. When a company has enough cash on hand to pay off its current debt without compromising other essential business operations, it has a good solvency margin or ratio. Different formulas exist for figuring out solvency ratios and margins, and many of them take into account elements specific to the industry the company operates. When evaluating solvency margins or ratios, one of the most crucial instruments is timely and accurate financial accounting. Maintaining current financial records makes it much simpler to spot patterns that could point a family or company toward insolvency and to take the necessary steps to bring things back to their previous state of stability.

3. **Profitability:** The ability of a business to turn a profit is referred to as profitability.

This can be evaluated prior to starting a business or it can be applied to an already-running enterprise. It may turn out that one set of circumstances is not likely to succeed or has not succeeded, but that doesn't always mean the project has to be abandoned. Altering operational elements like costs or pricing might be a more practical option.

The financial status of a business can be characterized by three fundamental scenarios. It has three possible operating states: profitable, break-even, and loss-making. The majority of the time, an organization wants to turn a profit. Determining profitability can be challenging in situations where cash flow is steady or plentiful. It is simple for someone to erroneously associate a large number of incoming and outgoing transactions with financial gain. However, receiving and spending money does not imply that a company is financially sound. It is essential to obtain the price of the products or services being provided in order to calculate profitability. When setting prices, a number of factors must be taken into account. This covers both fixed costs like the mortgage, repairs, and taxes as well as variable costs like gasoline, labor, and inventory. One must also take yield into account. This is the quantity of goods or services generated from a given quantity of raw materials in a given amount of time. For example, if a full tank of gas is only sufficient for two deliveries, the price is likely to be higher than it would be if a full tank of gas could accommodate six deliveries. If the price for two deliveries were priced the same as six deliveries, it is likely that profitability would be jeopardized. Tracking profitability may require two things. First, a business will likely need good and accurate records of its expenses. Second, depending on the size and complexity of the venture, a person with good accounting skills may be needed to ensure proper calculations. There may be a number of parties interested in the profitability of a particular venture. For example, sometimes people are owners of businesses but they are not operators, giving them a reason to be interested in the financial health and direction of the venture. Stakeholders who have money invested are also likely to be highly concerned with the profitability of a business. Employees, especially those at the managerial level, should also care because lack of profit can threaten job security and may damage a person's professional reputation.

Did you get it?

1. **How do businesses ensure compliance with regulatory requirements and reporting standards when preparing financial statements?**
2. **Write the statement of changes in equity.**

2.3. VERTICAL AND HORIZONTAL ANALYSES OF FINANCIAL STATEMENTS

→Learning Objectives

- Describe the interpret financial ratios

Investors and corporate management can examine a company's financials in great detail with vertical analysis, with a focus on the changes in financial statement items over time. This kind of review calls for attention to detail and accounting knowledge. In the business world, junior accountants are mentored by seasoned financial analysts who teach them the fundamentals of long-term investing. One benefit of vertical analysis is that it facilitates the preparation of comparisons between businesses of various sizes operating in the same industry. It also enables an organization to compare reports from the past with the current reports, identifying any patterns or areas in need of development.

Without a benchmark by which to compare the numbers, examining the raw data on a financial statement can be rather meaningless. This issue is resolved by vertical analysis, which creates what is referred to as a common-size balance sheet by connecting every item on a balance sheet to a single item. Common-size balance sheets facilitate easy comparisons with older sheets from the same company as well as with statements from other businesses.

When using vertical analysis on a balance sheet, all items on the sheet are measured in terms of the total assets. For example, imagine that a company has total assets of $1,000 US Dollars (USD) and inventory of $100 USD. Since the $100 USD comprises 10% of the $1,000 USD total assets, the inventory would be represented by the number 10 on the balance sheet. All of the different assets, whether it be cash, inventory, equity, or Accounts receivable, would have numbers that would add up to 100 on a common-size balance sheet.

Every item is shown as a percentage of total sales when performing a vertical analysis on income statements. This implies that 100 is the automatic representation of the total sales amount. Given that a company's interest expenses are $200 USD and its total sales are $4,000 USD, the interest would be represented by the number 5, as it represents 5% of the total sales. Businesses can rapidly ascertain trends, weaknesses, and strengths by utilizing vertical analysis. An organization may observe, for instance, a pattern where the proportion of cash is declining while the proportion of accounts receivable is increasing. This could be a sign of ineffective collection techniques. By applying the same level of analysis to an income statement, a company's decision-makers can determine precisely how every dollar is allocated among costs and expenses, resulting in a comprehensive financial picture. When a financial analyst utilizes specific financial data to evaluate a company's performance over time, the term "horizontal analysis" in business refers to a kind of fundamental analysis. In order to evaluate the growth of a given company over time, an analyst compares the same items or ratios for that company. Horizontal analysis can also be used to evaluate a company's performance in comparison to its rivals on a number of businesses in the same industry.

Keyword

Balance sheet is a financial statement that reports a company's assets, liabilities, and shareholder equity. The balance sheet is one of the three core financial statements that are used to evaluate a business.

A company can assess its economic evolution over time with the use of horizontal analysis. A horizontal review establishes the benchmark at a specific point in time, like the start of the year, as opposed to vertical analysis. Investors may be able to assess a company's cash balance over a five-year period, for instance, with the use of horizontal analysis. The balance sheet, income statement, and statement of cash flows are the financial statements that contain the data used in horizontal analysis for a company. It could be expressed as a ratio or as line items, like expense items. Comparing two or more items yields a ratio; for instance, the operating ratio is calculated by dividing expenses by net sales.

It is possible to conduct quarterly or annual horizontal analysis. In the case of quarterly analysis, performance can be compared to the same quarter last year or to the previous period. Quarter-to-quarter refers to an analyst comparing the same data from one quarter to the next; for example, "quarter-to-quarter sales increased 10%." Quarter-over-quarter refers to a comparison to the same quarter in the previous year, such as "earnings increased 3% from the previous quarter." The quarter-over-quarter comparison is typically more valuable in seasonal industries like retail because it shows the change from the same quarter a year ago. The benefit of horizontal analysis is that it can be used to compare a company's performance over time and assess whether its financial status is getting better. Comparing the outcomes of several businesses in the same sector to ascertain which one performs the best over time is another helpful application of it. Because metrics like gross margin can vary greatly between industries, it is most helpful when comparing companies in the same industry.

Vertical analysis, as opposed to horizontal analysis, describes how assets, liabilities, and equity are represented as a percentage of the total. Each of these three main balance sheet categories is expressed as a percentage of the total and is added up. When comparing businesses of varying sizes, vertical analysis can be helpful because it makes it simple to determine which company has more assets in relation to liabilities and equity or which has a higher percentage of liabilities as opposed to equity.

2.3.1. Interpret Financial Ratios

It makes sense to analyze and interpret financial ratios after taking the time to consider what the data actually indicates. A company's financial strength is correlated with its debt level; lower debt levels are associated with higher assets. A ratio of less than one is therefore stronger than a ratio of five. As long as debt is managed, taking on debt during expansionary times could be beneficial from a strategic standpoint. How successfully a business converts sales into actual cash is determined by its cash flow margin ratio. The computation involves dividing the operating cash flow by the net sales reported on the income statement. It is preferable if the operating cash flow ratio or percentage is higher.

The same is true with profit margin ratios. If it costs $20 to make a product and it is sold for $45, the gross profit margin is calculated by subtracting the cost of goods sold from revenue and dividing this result by the revenue [0.55 = ($45- $20) / $45]. The higher this ratio is, the more profit there is per product.

Remember

Vertical analysis is a method of analyzing financial statements in which each item in the statement is represented as a percentage of a single larger item. This method of analysis may be used with both balance sheets and income statements as a way of coherently comparing large monetary amounts and making sense of the data.

2.3.1.1. Current Ratio

A useful tool for accurately assessing a company's financial stability is the current ratio, which is straightforward yet highly effective. The value of the company's current assets and the total amount of its current liabilities are the only two accurate pieces of information needed to calculate a current ratio. Through a comparison of the two numbers, the company's current ratio can be found, allowing for future operations planning and the identification of strategies to enhance the industry as a whole.

The ability of a company to pay off short-term debt is one of the most significant details that this figure will disclose. A company with strong financials will typically have a high assets to liabilities ratio. This implies that the business won't expect any issues paying off any short-term debt that it might have taken on to upgrade a specific area of the production process or replace equipment. The straightforward calculation of dividing liabilities by assets, also known as a working capital ratio, can also help identify instances in which the business is not as secure as it ought to be. Even though the business might be paying its debts on schedule, a lower current ratio suggests that net profits are low and that adjustments are necessary if the business hopes to stay solvent in the long run. Therefore, a low current ratio can serve as a warning sign to start optimizing the use of available resources, boost overall operational efficiency, and perhaps even reorganize certain departments to complete necessary tasks more cheaply.

Businesses typically use the current ratio approach frequently. Businesses may decide to compute a current ratio every billing cycle, or at least every calendar quarter, in more volatile industries. Businesses operating in comparatively stable industries might find that a semi-annual current ratio is a good fit. Naturally, the ratio can be computed whenever a date is chosen for assessing the position of both assets and liabilities.

Keyword

Financial statements are written records that convey the financial activities of a company. Financial statements are often audited by government agencies and accountants to ensure accuracy and for tax, financing, or investing purposes.

2.3.1.2. Working Capital Ratio

A working capital ratio is a financial metric used to assess the short-term financial health of an organization. A company's assets are totaled and divided by the liabilities that the company currently owes to determine this ratio, which is also known as the current ratio. When a company has a negative working capital ratio, it indicates that it would not be able to pay off all of its debts at once and would not have any money left over for ongoing operations. The parameters of a good ratio are contingent upon the specifics of the enterprise and the degree of industry volatility in which it operates.

An investor needs to know more than just whether a business is making money; financial statements do not provide the whole story. The amount of capital a company has available to cover potential losses as well as make investments to grow the business is a more accurate indicator of its fiscal strength. One useful measure of this kind of strength in finances is the working capital ratio, which gives an instantaneous impression of how much cash a business has on hand when the ratio is computed. As an illustration, let's say that company A has $1,000 in assets total. These assets could be cash, stocks, inventory, or accounts receivable. Additionally, this business has accumulated debt totaling $800 USD, most of which is in the form of accounts payable. The $1,000 USD divided by the $800 USD yields a working capital ratio of 1.25. Investors should be wary of a company exhibiting a downward trend in its working capital ratio, as this suggests that the company may not be financially stable and could be on the verge of bankruptcy. A business may also examine its own ratio to identify any inefficiencies it may be experiencing. For instance, a business that reports strong profits but has a low current ratio might not be collecting payments effectively enough. It's also important to remember that a company may not necessarily benefit from an abnormally high working capital ratio. That might actually indicate that not enough of the company's excess capital is being allocated to potential investments. In the same vein, a low ratio is not always a bad thing, particularly for a young business that might be investing a larger portion of its capital than a more established one. The industry that the business serves also affects the criteria for a good current ratio. Companies in more unstable industries require more cash on hand to cover unexpected drops in sales than do companies in more stable industries.

2.3.1.3. Gross Profit Ratio

The relationship between gross profit and total net sales revenue is displayed by the gross profit ratio (GP ratio), a profitability metric. It is a well-liked instrument for assessing the company's operational performance. To calculate the ratio, divide the gross profit amount by the net sales amount. The percentage of profits made from the sale of goods or services before selling and administrative costs is displayed by the gross profit ratio. It is employed to assess a company's capacity to efficiently produce marketable goods. The ratio is significant in determining whether a company can continue to offer goods at a price that consumers are willing to pay, particularly when it is plotted on a trend line.

The following formula/equation is used to compute gross profit ratio:

$$\text{Gross profit Ratio} = \frac{\text{Gross profit}}{\text{Net sales}}$$

When gross profit ratio is expressed in percentage form, it is known as gross profit margin or gross profit percentage. The formula of gross profit margin or percentage is given below:

$$\text{Gross profit margin} = \frac{\text{Gross profit}}{\text{Net sales}} \times \mathbf{100}$$

Gross profit and net sales are the two fundamental ingredients in the gross profit ratio (GP ratio) formula. Net sales less the cost of goods sold equals gross profit. Net sales are calculated by deducting allowable discounts and returns from total gross sales. Typically, the company's income statement provides information on net sales and gross profit.

2.3.1.4. Net Profit Ratio

The ratio of after-tax profits to net sales is known as the net profit percentage. It displays the remaining profit following the recognition of income taxes and the deduction of all manufacturing, administrative, and financing costs from sales. As such, it is among the best indicators of a company's overall performance, particularly when paired with an assessment of how well it is allocating its working capital. In order to assess performance over time, the metric is typically presented as a trend line. It's also employed to contrast a company's performance with that of its rivals. A common profitability ratio that illustrates the connection between net profit after taxes and net sales is the net profit ratio (NP ratio). It is computed by dividing the net profit (after tax) by net sales.

$$\text{Net profit ratio} = \frac{\text{Net profit after tax}}{\text{Net sales}}$$

Net profit is calculated as gross profit less operating costs and income tax for the purposes of this ratio. The goal of this ratio is to assess the profitability of the company from its core operations; therefore, all non-operating revenues and expenses are excluded. Interest from investments and proceeds from the sale of fixed assets are two examples of non-operating revenue streams. Non-operating expenses include things like loan interest and asset sale losses.

The relationship between net profit and net sales may also be expressed in percentage form. When it is shown in percentage form, it is known as net profit margin. The formula of net profit margin is written as follows:

$$\text{Net profit margin} = \frac{\text{Net profit after tax}}{\text{Net sales}} \times 100$$

2.3.1.5. Receivables Turnover Ratio

A financial analysis tool used to assess a company's capacity to collect unpaid account receivable balances is the receivables turnover ratio. The speed at which a business collects unpaid cash balances from clients over the course of an accounting period is determined by this ratio. An elevated computed value derived from the receivables turnover ratio suggests that the company primarily conducts cash sales to clients. A high number can also be a sign that the business has a strict policy in place for collecting unpaid customer balances. Companies frequently sell their customers products or services on account. The business keeps track of outstanding amounts in its accounts receivable journal. While having a large amount of accounts receivable can be advantageous, businesses that are unable to promptly collect unpaid balances may experience cash flow problems. Furthermore, persistently providing account sales to clients with past-due balances may also lead to challenging cash flow circumstances. The owner or manager of the company can quickly review the amount of receivables by using the receivables turnover ratio. To ascertain the ef, this financial ratio is typically reviewed monthly or annually.

Net credit sales divided by average net accounts receivable is the traditional formula for the receivables turnover ratio. The amount of sales revenues less any discounts, returns, or other allowances recorded in the business's accounts receivable journal is known as net credit sales. The total amount of outstanding accounts receivable for the company less the allowance for bad debt expenses is the average net accounts receivable. The percentage of outstanding receivables that the business believes it will never be able to collect and will eventually write off is known as the bad debt expense. When businesses give credit to clients who have a bad credit history or who are unable to pay back sizable amounts of outstanding receivables, bad debt expenses frequently result.

Businesses frequently contrast their ratio computation with that of a rival business or the industry norm. Managers and owners of businesses can use this comparison to see how their firm compares to the receivables turnover ratios of other businesses. To raise this figure, managers and business owners might also need to enhance the company's collection practices. It's crucial to remember that this figure only serves as an average estimation for determining accounts receivable turnover. The actual operational performance of the company can be distorted when average numbers are used in financial or business ratios.

2.3.1.6. Inventory Turnover Ratio

The inventory turnover ratio is a commonly used financial metric that ascertains how frequently a business must replenish its inventory in order to maintain its current sales level over a specified duration, usually a year. The formal calculation is the average investment in the company's inventory divided by the cost of goods sold (COGS) for the year. By adding the value of the company's beginning and ending inventory for the year and dividing it by two, the average inventory is determined. By using the inventory turnover ratio, a business can effectively control its stock levels and ascertain the appropriate proportion of its cash to be invested in inventory at any given time.

In order to ensure stability and growth, managing a business requires a complex assessment of how to use available resources. A poor choice can swiftly spell the end for a company. When a company lacks liquidity, it is unable to respond to market opportunities or position itself to gain market share and boost sales.

A business can use the inventory turnover ratio to calculate how many times it can rotate its stock annually and maintain the same revenue levels as, say, if it bought all of the stock up front. From an operational standpoint, this implies that at the start of the year, the company would only need to allocate 25% of its inventory budget. As a result, the business has more working capital to pursue other projects rather than having cash stashed away on stockroom shelves.

2.3.1.7. Debt/Equity Ratio

The ratio of debt to equity indicates how much equity compared to debt is used to fund different aspects of a business's operations. It serves as a benchmark for assessing the financial health of an organization. By dividing the total liabilities by the shareholders' equity, this ratio is computed. The debt-to-equity ratio can be calculated using a variety of different scenarios. Liabilities, for instance, typically only comprise long-term debt, such as debt financed by bonds or other types of business loans. Another example is preferred stock. It can be included in the debt/equity ratio calculation as an asset or liability. For the purposes of determining a debt/equity ratio, a company's other liabilities, such as those recorded in an accounts payable ledger, may or may not be included. Due to their frequent changes, they may not always give a completely accurate picture of a company's liabilities. As a result, the company's decision to use them is entirely subjective.

Investors should exercise caution because not all companies compare the same things when presenting a debt/equity ratio. Even though one company might appear superior to another, it could all depend on the debt and equity that are stated. To genuinely comprehend how one company compares to another, one must be aware of this. The debt-to-equity ratio is a tool that investors use to assess the potential risk associated with investing in the company through stock purchases or bonds that it issues. Investors may view the company as riskier if the ratio indicates a higher level of debt relative to equity. As a result, they might be unwilling to invest in stocks or might need a higher interest rate before being persuaded to buy bonds.

Businesses that monitor their debt/equity ratio closely are those who may want to go to the bond market or maintain stock prices above a particular threshold. Businesses may occasionally be able to reduce their long-term debt commitments in an effort to raise this ratio. This may benefit the long-term circumstances of the business. Asset liquidation would be one method to achieve this. Although selling off some assets to pay off debt might be a zero-sum game, there could be advantages as well because debt and equity both decline. For instance, the company would profit from not having to pay interest on the debt, which might speed up the process of accumulating equity. On the other hand, significant changes to a debt/equity ratio take time to implement.

Did you get it?

1. **How does horizontal analysis aid in evaluating changes in financial statement data over time?**
2. **Define the net profit ratio.**
3. **Write the inventory turnover ratio.**

2.4. FINANCIAL REPORTING

→Learning Objectives

- To understand the objectives of financial reporting by business enterprises
- To discuss the importance of financial reporting
- To explain the purpose of financial reports
- To define the types of financial reports
- To describe the need of financial reports

For businesses and investors alike, financial reporting is essential because it offers critical data that illustrates financial performance over time. In order to guarantee fair trade, compensation, and financial activities, government and private regulatory bodies also keep an eye on financial reporting. Superior reporting standards are developed by general purpose financial reporting to support the effective operation of economies and the effective distribution of resources in capital markets. The focus of general purpose financial reporting is on meeting the needs of a broad spectrum of users who are unable to access the necessary financial data from the entity. It ought to be comprehensive enough for different users to understand the information. For this reason, they rely on the financial report as their source of information. Different users might need different information, perhaps beyond what general purpose financial reporting can provide. The entity, rather than the entity's capital providers, prepares the financial reports because it believes it has substance on its own, apart from that of its owners. An organization receives financial resources (its assets) in return for claims to those resources from capital providers (its liabilities and equity).

Capital providers include:

- **Equity Investors**: Economic resources are typically invested in an entity by equity investors with the expectation of receiving a return on their investment as well as a return on their initial investment. Because these factors impact the prices of their equity interests, equity investors are therefore concerned with the volume, timing, and uncertainty of an entity's future cash flows as well as the entity's competence in generating those cash flows. They also care about how well the entity's management and directors are carrying out their mandate to use invested funds profitably and efficiently.
- **Lenders**: Lenders usually expect to receive a return in the form of interest, repayments of borrowings, and increases in the prices of debt securities. Lenders

have similar interests as the equity investors.

- **Other Creditors**: Other creditors provide resources because of their relationship with the entity, instead of a capital provider; no primary relationship.
    - o Employee – salary or compensation
    - o Suppliers – extended credit
    - o Customer – prepay for goods and services
    - o Managers – responsible for preparing financial reports

Capital providers use relevant data from a specific entity's financial reporting to inform their decisions. The utility of financial reporting in evaluating the entity's potential for cash flow depends on its present cash resources and its capacity to raise enough money to pay back its capital providers. The usefulness of financial reporting in evaluating stewardship also encompasses the management's obligations to safeguard the entity's assets, or financial resources, from adverse consequences. In order to ensure that the entity's assets are protected in accordance with legal requirements, contractual obligations, and other legal frameworks, management's performance is crucial to the decision-making process.

2.4.1. Objectives of Financial Reporting by Business Enterprises

Poor financial reporting is a common cause of small businesses not making the profits they could be making or eventually going out of business. Maintaining operational efficiencies that produce steady cash flows and long-term profits requires more than just knowing your sales figures, bank balance, and expense breakdown. Establishing a financial reporting system will assist you in establishing guidelines, keeping tabs on your operations, and maximizing your earnings.

Financial reporting has different purposes and meanings depending on the size and kind of business. In the context of nonprofit organizations, this means revealing to the public the sources and purposes of funding, the salaries of officers and key employees, and other financial data. Financial reporting at small businesses gives managers access to a range of continuous reports that help them comprehend how every aspect of the company's operations impacts its bottom line. The reports also give managers the ability to plan long-term business strategies and create and track budgets. Financial reporting at publicly traded companies is the process of making data available to the public for review by interested parties, including the media, the Securities and Exchange Commission, and shareholders.

1. **Helps with Pricing:** Financial reporting aids in the best price setting for businesses. The computation of your overhead and production expenses at various levels should be included in your business's financial data so you can see how different sales volumes will impact your costs. With this knowledge in hand, you can set your prices wisely. Pricing for various distribution channels, like online sales, print catalog sales, and in-store sales, can be determined with the aid of a financial report that displays the cost of sales for each channel.
2. **Reduces Cash Flow Problems:** Typically, a budget outlines your expected sales date and cost, with the latter usually being recorded in

the month of the anticipated sale. Cash shortages may result from this, as your expenses to complete the sale may come before you get paid for the sale, which could take up to 30 days. A cash flow report is an essential financial document for any business as it indicates the timing of receiving funds and the payments due for debts, taxes, and other obligations. Your ability to plan for credit and cash reserves is enhanced by this report.

3. **Effective Production and Labor Planning:** Understanding your labor and production costs will enable you to more effectively plan your workforce requirements and production schedule, preventing significant spikes in costs that you might have otherwise dispersed if you had been aware of possible issues. You can take steps to make part of an order earlier, reducing labor costs with better scheduling, if you know that a large order might increase your costs because you need to add temporary workers, pay overtime, increase training, or add a shift.
4. **Improved Cost Containment:** Monitoring your expenses and identifying areas for cost reduction to optimize profitability can be facilitated by having precise knowledge of your production and overhead expenses. You might be unaware, for instance, of the extent to which credit card interest reduces your earnings. The knowledge of that could encourage you to allocate a portion of your surplus funds towards debt repayment and revenue growth.
5. **Better Money Access:** Lenders frequently request internal financial reports along with your bank statement when you apply for credit. A balance sheet, which is a list of your assets and liabilities, may indicate that your net worth is actually negative even though your bank statement may indicate that you have $25,000. The ability to demonstrate your cash flow, net worth, and receivables to prospective lenders, investors, and creditors could mean the difference between receiving their money or not.

2.4.2. Importance of Financial Reporting

Financial statements offer a variety of crucial financial data that analysts, creditors, and investors use to assess the financial performance of a business. Many of the financial data in financial reports are mandated by legal requirements or accepted accounting standards. Financial reporting facilitates management's communication of the company's goals for the future as well as its past achievements.

Here are a few reasons why financial reporting is important to your business:

- **Tax Purposes**: The primary justification for utilizing financial reports is that it's mandated by law. These reports are used by the Internal Revenue Service to verify that you are paying your fair share of taxes. Profit-driven businesses are required to pay a hefty amount in taxes. Precise financial reporting assists them in minimizing their tax liability and guarantees that their resources do not run out quickly.
- **Showing Financial Condition**:

Before making an investment, potential investors want to know how well the business is doing. The financial reporting of a business is used by creditors, investors, and other capital providers to determine the security and return on their capital. Investors are curious about the whereabouts and current status of their money. Financial statements, such as the balance sheet address, offer comprehensive details about the assets, outstanding debt, and equity components of the company. This information can be used by creditors and investors to better understand the capital structure and position of the company.

- **Evaluating Operations**: A balance sheet's data represents an organization's assets, liabilities, and total assets at the conclusion of a given financial period. A balance sheet, however, does not reveal what operational modifications may have taken place to affect a company's financial situation. Investors should also take operating results during the period into account. An income statement, which is used for financial reporting, presents data on sales, costs, and profits or losses. Investors can analyze a company's historical income performance and projected cash flow by using the income statement.
- **Examining Cash Flow**: The income statement of a company shows its profits, but it doesn't give any specific details about its cash exchange. Investing and financing are examples of non-operating activities that cause a company to experience cash inflows and outflows over time. Investors are paid back with cash from all sources, not operating income. For this reason, a cash flow statement is crucial to examine for investors. The cash flow statement displays the amount of money that is exchanged over time between the business and outside contractors. Investors can determine whether a company has enough cash on hand to cover costs and purchases by looking over this statement.
- **Sharing Shareholder Equity**: For equity investors, the statement of shareholders' equity is crucial. It displays how different equity components, such as retained earnings, have changed over time. A company's net worth can be calculated as follows: shareholder equity is the total assets less the total liabilities of the company. Higher investment returns for current equity shareholders result from a company's shareholders' equity growing steadily as a result of rising retained earnings rather than a growing shareholder base.
- **Mitigate Errors**: Businesses can identify costly errors and inter-errors early in the process with the aid of accurate financial reporting. Financial statement discrepancies are the best way to identify illicit financial activity. Errors that have occurred can be located by a reconciliation procedure. In order to determine whether there has been an accounting error or whether someone has tampered with any aspect of the business, companies invest a lot of time in reconciling their books of accounts and confirming each journal entry.

Did you know?

Financial reporting information is based on estimates, judgments, and models of the financial effects on an entity of transactions and other events in which, is only ideal for preparers and standard setters to strive.

2.4.3. Purpose of Financial Reports

A business's cash flows, financial position, and operational results are all disclosed through financial reporting. In order to allocate resources, readers evaluate the statement. Financial reporting is a way of following standard accounting practices to give an accurate depiction of a company's finances, including:

- Revenues
- Expenses
- Profits
- Capital
- Cash flow

Financial reporting is the process of creating documents that inform management, investors, and the government about a company's financial situation.

Financial reporting includes:

- external financial statements (income statement, statement of comprehensive income, balance sheet, statement of cash flows, and statement of stockholders' equity)
- notes to the financial statements
- communication regarding quarterly earnings and related information through press releases and conference calls
- quarterly and annual reports to stockholders
- financial information posted on a business's website
- financial reports to governmental agencies including quarterly and annual reports to the Securities and Exchange Commission (SEC)
- documentation pertaining to the issuance of common stock and other securities

2.4.4. Types of Financial Reports

A number of financial reports are available to shed light on the company's past, present, and future financial situations. Having an annual report with this financial data is essential for business owners like you because it will help you make better business decisions and run your company more efficiently. It will also help you analyze operations. Out of all the financial reports, the following five are the most crucial accounting reports that any business owner should review annually and on a regular basis to better understand the financial performance of the company.

1. **Balance Sheet**: The balance sheet is a financial statement that, at a given point in time, typically at the conclusion of an accounting period, summarizes a company's total assets (current, non-current, and intangible assets), liabilities (financial obligations), and shareholders' equity (investments and retained earnings). It offers a quick overview of a company's financial situation, outlining the assets and liabilities as well as the sources of funding for those assets. To spot patterns and make better financial accounting decisions, consult the balance sheet. Lenders

will utilize it to assess a company's creditworthiness, so it is also crucial to them.

2. **Income Statement**: The Profit and Loss Statement (P&L), Statement of Operations, or Statement of Income are some other names for the Income Statement. The Income Statement presents the profitability (net income or net loss) for the business over a given time period, typically a month, quarter, or year, by summarizing all of the revenues and expenses incurred. Both internal and external stakeholders—investors and creditors—use the income statement to analyze profitability and determine the degree of risk associated with investing or borrowing money. Examples of internal stakeholders include the management group and board of directors. Revenues must exceed expenses for a business to be both viable and valuable.

Remember

The Cash Flow Statement is presented with three sections: operating, financing and investing activities, and indicates which areas of the business are generating and using the most cash. One of the best uses for the Cash Flow Statement is to estimate future cash flow which will assist with budgeting and decision making.

3. **Cash Flow Statement**: The Cash Flow Statement is a summary of a company's total cash inflows and outflows over a given time period. Because it solely accounts for cash-related transactions—non-cash activities like sales or credit purchases or depreciation—this statement differs from the balance sheet and income statement. Together, the Income Statement, Balance Sheet, and Cash Flow Statement comprise the typical financial statement package. Once the month-end close procedures have been completed, your accounting team should prepare these financial statements each month. Key performance indicators can (and ought to) be computed and tracked over time using them.

4. **Accounts Receivable Aging Report**: The outstanding accounts receivable are grouped by the Accounts Receivable (A/R) Aging Report according to the invoice due date, which is usually current, as well as 1–30, 31- 60, 61–90, and >90 days past due. Idle accounts receivable are a common source of cash flow issues, particularly for small and mid-sized businesses. You have less money available to run your business the more money you have locked up in receivables from late payments and slow-paying clients. Companies can improve the proactive management of the receivable collections process by reviewing the A/R Aging report as soon as an invoice is sent. This will also increase accountability for the person in charge of collections. Most accounting systems have the ability to generate the A/R Aging Report, which can be viewed at any time. If your company is having trouble collecting accounts receivable, you might need to review this report once a week to help identify past due accounts. To enhance business cash

flows, collection procedures can be started as soon as these accounts are located.

5. **Budget vs Actual**: The actual results, mostly from the Income Statement, are compared to the budgeted amounts that were anticipated at the start of the period in this report. The reader will be able to evaluate the degree to which a company's revenue and spending align with the financial forecasts that are part of the budget by using this report. It can assist in determining which areas were over and under budget, suggesting areas where more staff could be hired, or drawing attention to a gross profit margin that does not meet financial reporting standards.

2.4.5. Need of Financial Reports

We saw some powerful financial statement templates to empower your business, but before finishing our journey through financial reports, we are going to do one last stop to show you some of the main ways in which your business could benefit from them.

Financial reports created with professional business analytics tools offer a clear snapshot of your business's financial health and they will give you the answers you need to plan strategies and tackle any issues that might arise with your finances. Here are the top 5 benefits.

1. **Financial Performance Tracking**: As a devoted reader of this blog, you are aware of how critical data is to the success of any business. CFOs and other pertinent stakeholders can obtain a fast and precise overview of every financial aspect of a company by utilizing contemporary financial reports. They will be better able to plan strategies, anticipate future outcomes, and identify growth opportunities as a result of making more informed decisions.
2. **Mitigating Errors**: Every detail matters when discussing finances. Inaccurate financial reporting can harm your company's profitability and put it in legal jeopardy if disparities are discovered in your financial statements. You will be able to continuously monitor the performance of your finances in every area and address any errors before they become more serious problems because many BI finance tools on the market guarantee accurate financial reports with the most recent data available.
3. **Showing Financial Condition to Investors and Stakeholders**: A financial report that provides an overview of your company's performance will be an essential tool if you currently have investors or are searching for new ones in order to grow your enterprise. It will assist you in demonstrating to your investors where their money has gone and where it is currently, as well as convince prospective new investors and other pertinent stakeholders that your company is worthwhile.
4. **Debt Management**: As we mentioned in one of our examples of financial statements, wrong debt management can damage a business to the point of no return. Investing in innovative BI solutions to generate professional financial reports that contain a detailed balance sheet of your assets

and liabilities can help you understand your liquidity and manage your debts accordingly.

5. **Staying Compliant with Tax Laws**: Maintaining legal compliance is one of the main advantages of using financial reports. Regardless of the size of your business, taxes must be paid, and tax agents will review your financial records to ensure that you are paying the correct amount. You can lessen your tax liability and keep your financial records consistent by tracking this data in an expert financial report.

Did you get it?

1. **What do you understand by balance sheet?**
2. **Define the income statement.**
3. **Evaluate the debt management.**

FOCUS ON CAREERS

1. **Financial Reporting Analyst:** A finance and reporting analyst is an individual who prepares financial documentation that reflects the financial standing of an organization. To ensure accurate financial reports, finance and reporting analyst must work closely with various departments and use the Generally Accepted Accounting Principles (GAAP) to create financial statements. They are required to analyze the organization's income and expenses and reconcile accounts. Finance and reporting analysts also provide financial information to auditors and issue data used in Securities and Exchange Commission (SEC) filings.
2. **What a Financial Analyst Does?**

Analysts have many duties and responsibilities, depending on the organization they work for, the industry they are in, and their seniority.

i. **Gather data and information:** The work of a financial analyst starts with gathering data and information about whatever they need to analyze. Examples include historical financial reports, accounting data from the general ledger, stock price information, statistics and macroeconomic data, industry research, and just about any other type of quantitative data. The information will be gathered from sources such as the company's internal databases, third-party providers such as Bloomberg or Capital IQ, and government agencies such as the Securities and Exchange Commission (SEC).

ii. **Organize information:** Once the data is gathered it's typically entered into Excel or some other type of database. Once inputted, the next task is to organize it, clean it up, and get it into a format it can be made sense of. This typically means sorting the numbers by data, or by category, adding formulas and functions to make sure it's dynamic, and using consistent formatting styles so that it's easy to read and understand.

iii. **Analyze financial results:** With the data all cleaned up and organized in Excel, it's time for the financial analyst to start analyzing past information and historical results. This typically includes looking at ratios and metrics like gross margin, net margin, fixed vs. variable costs, year-over-year (YoY) growth rates, return on equity (ROE), return on assets (ROA), debt/equity ratio, earnings per share (EPS), and many others. The analyst will look for trends and benchmark the performance against other companies in the same industry.

iv. **Make forecasts and projections:** Now that historical information has been analyzed, it's time to make projects and forecasts about how the company will perform in the future. There is both an art and a science to predict how a company will perform, and many assumptions and even leaps of faith have to be made. Common forecasting methods include regression analysis, year-over-year growth rates, as well as bottom-up and top-down approaches.

v. **Develop recommendations:** A good financial analyst is not only good with numbers but actually generates insights and recommendations on how to improve the operations of a business. Examples of helpful recommendations and insights include ways to cut costs, opportunities to grow revenue, ways to increase market share, operational efficiencies, customer satisfaction, and much more. This is what truly separates a world-class financial analyst from the rest. These recommendations will be presented to the CEO, the CFO, other executives, and/or the board of directors.

vi. **Build Excel models:** For analysts working in investment banking, equity research, corporate development, financial planning & analysis (FP&A), and other areas of corporate finance, financial modeling will be a big part of the job. These models typically start by linking the 3 financial statements and then layering on more advanced types of financial models such as discounted cash flow analysis (DCF models), internal planning models, and more arcane models such as LBO models and M&A models.

vii. **Make presentations:** When someone asks, what does a financial analyst do, the answer will always include something to do with making presentations (often in PowerPoint). The analysis that's completed in Excel then has to be turned into charts and graphs, which can then be inserted into pitchbooks and management presentations.

viii. **Generate reports:** Internal reports and dashboards are a part of the daily life of an analyst. Whether it's presenting key performance indicators (KPIs) or tracking actual vs. budgeted results, it's imperative to the company or the client that information be clearly presented, timely, easy to understand, accurate, and insightful.

3. **Compliance:** All employees are accountable for compliance with all laws, regulations, and adherence to established internal controls and procedures when performing their job duties. Each employee is expected to be familiar with the legal and regulatory requirements and internal controls affecting his or her job responsibilities. It is the affirmative duty of each employee to carry out these responsibilities at all times in a manner that complies with all applicable legal and regulatory requirements and internal controls. All employees shall be responsible for communicating upward, problems in operations, noncompliance with the code of conduct, or other policy violations or illegal actions. Employees must participate in required training on pertinent compliance laws and regulations as required by the Bank of the Pacific.

4. **Financial Reporting Analyst Job Duties:** A financial reporting analyst typically has a wide range of responsibilities, which can include:
   - Implementing new accounting standards to ensure compliance with regulations
   - Reviewing financial statements to determine whether they are accurate and meet accounting standards
   - Reviewing transactions to identify any possible errors or indications of fraudulent activity

- Analyzing data to identify trends in spending or revenues that could indicate future problems
- Reviewing reports generated by other departments within the company to ensure that they are accurate
- Calculating taxes owed based on taxable income and filing tax forms such as Form 1040 or Form 1120
- Providing analysis of financial data from multiple sources including financial statements, accounting records, tax returns, and bank statements
- Preparing financial statements for public release based on company requirements
- Communicating with investors, analysts, and regulators about financial issues such as risks or opportunities related to the company's industry, geographic area, or other sector

5. **Financial Reporting Analyst Salary & Outlook:** Financial reporting analysts' salaries vary depending on their level of education, years of experience, and the size and industry of the company. They may also earn additional compensation in the form of bonuses.
   - Median Annual Salary: $82,500 ($39.66/hour)
   - Top 10% Annual Salary: $125,000 ($60.1/hour)

The employment of financial reporting analysts is expected to grow at an average rate over the next decade.

Demand for financial reporting analysts depends largely on the state of the economy. As the economy grows, companies will need to evaluate their assets and liabilities and ensure that their financial records are accurate. In addition, as firms expand globally, they will need to evaluate their international operations and ensure that their financial records are in compliance with international accounting standards.

6. **Financial Reporting Analyst Job Requirements:** A financial reporting analyst typically needs to have the following qualifications:
   - **Education:** Most employers require financial reporting analysts to have a bachelor's degree in accounting, finance or a related field. Some employers prefer candidates who have a master's degree in accounting or finance. Relevant coursework includes accounting, business law, economics, finance, mathematics, statistics, and tax accounting.
   - **Training & Experience:** Many employers require candidates to complete a training program before taking on a role as a financial reporting analyst. These programs are typically part-time and last between six and 12 months. They provide students with the necessary skills and knowledge to succeed in the role. Training programs may include courses in accounting, finance, business, and computer skills.
   - **Certifications & Licenses:** Certifications enable professionals to prove

their qualifications to current and future employers. There are several certifications available to financial reporting analysts who want to increase their earning potential and further their career advancement opportunities.

7. **Financial Reporting Analyst Skills:** Financial reporting analysts need the following skills in order to be successful:
   - **Accounting:** Accounting is the foundation of financial reporting, and accounting skills are necessary for a career as a financial reporting analyst. Accounting skills include knowledge of bookkeeping, budgeting, taxes, and other financial topics.
   - **Communication:** Communication is another skill that can be very helpful for a financial reporting analyst. This is because they often need to communicate with a variety of people, including other financial analysts, company executives and investors. Effective communication can help a financial reporting analyst convey their ideas and information to others in a clear and understandable way.
   - **Data Analysis:** Data analysis is the ability to interpret large amounts of data and draw conclusions from it. Data analysis is an important skill for financial reporting analysts because they often need to analyze large amounts of financial data to draw conclusions about a company's financial health.
   - **Financial Knowledge:** A background in finance can help you learn accounting and other financial skills more quickly. Having a basic understanding of financial concepts can help you interpret financial statements and other financial documents.
   - **Problem-Solving: P**roblem-solving skills are essential for financial analysts, as they are often tasked with finding solutions to financial problems. For example, if a company's revenue is decreasing, a financial analyst may be tasked with finding a solution to the problem. This may involve analyzing the company's expenses and finding ways to reduce them, or finding ways to increase revenue.

8. **Financial Reportin**g Analyst Work Environment: Financial reporting analysts work in a variety of settings, including corporate offices, banks, and accounting firms. They typically work regular business hours, although they may occasionally work overtime to meet deadlines. Financial reporting analysts typically work on teams with other financial professionals, such as accountants and auditors. They may also interact with other departments within their company, such as marketing, sales, and production. Financial reporting analysts must be able to work well under pressure and meet deadlines. They must also be able to pay close attention to detail and have excellent analytical and problem-solving skills.

CASE STUDY

FINANCIAL ETHICS: THE BERNIE MADOFF CASE

On December 11, 2008, as the arrest of Benard Madoff, the former non-executive chairman of NASDAQ and chairman of Bernard L. Madoff Investment Securities LLC, many investors, big firms, banks, charities, universities and even governments were in panic, realizing that they were involved in a giant financial fraud, 'all just one big lie.' According to an official document on March 12, 2009 from the Department of Justice of United States, Madoff pleaded guilty to eleven felony counts related to a massive Ponzi scheme and faced a statutory maximum sentence of 150 years in prison.

Source: https://www.mbaknol.com/business-ethics/case-study-on-financial-ethics-the-bernie-madoff-case/.

Actually, what Mr. Madoff did was simple; He continually paid high returns to existing clients with the funds injected by new investors without engaging in any form of legitimate investment activity and this is what people call 'the Ponzi scheme,' named after Charles Ponzi who did such kind of financial fraud in 1920's. However, it is easily understanding financial fraud that tricked investors billions of dollars, not just because of the golden reputation of Madoff and the greediness of investors for 'high return,' but mainly because of the lack of regulation of the financial markets. Even Madoff said, he could have been caught in 2003, but the investigators of the Securities and Exchange Commission (SEC) overlooked the problems and missed the chance again and again. Besides, a federal prosecutor said the fraud could be dated back to at least the 1980s.

1. **Key Stakeholders and Their Involvement:** When the Madoff case was revealed, large numbers of stakeholders were involved and its victims are now scattered from Hollywood to Zurich to Abu Dhabi. Mr. Madoff has said, the losses of his clients might be $50 billion. Among the stakeholders, many of them are prominent and famous executives and organizations while many of them are hidden victims.

In the list of big losers, some of them are familiar organizations like Bank Santander ($3.1 billion), Bank Medici ($2.1 billion), HSBC ($1 billion) and Korea Life Insurance ($50 million) while others are not known by many people but still are quite big multinationals, for example, Tremount Group ($3.3 billion), Ascot Partners ($1.8 billion), the world's largest sovereign wealth fund Abu Dhabi Investment Authority ($400 million) and the biggest loser in the whole case, Fairfield Greenwich Group ($7.5 billion) which worked with Madoff's company for 20 years.

Other than firms and banks, some charities and universities were involved in the case. For instance, Elie Wiesel Foundation and Charities for Humanity ($15.2 million) has been an investor since at least 1998 and nearly all of its assets were in Madoff's fund. Picower Foundation ($958 million), the largest foundation that has announced its closure due to Madoff's fraud, had its founder Jeffry Picower (a noted philanthropist) found dead at the bottom of his own swimming pool in October, 2009. Universities like Yeshiva University and Tufts University lost $120 million in total.

In terms of the amount of money, the losses of many other ordinary clients seem not as much as the big stakeholders listed above but these clients and victims actually suffered severe loss. For example, a retired soldier Mr. Fox, who invested nearly $1 million in Madoff's fund, killed himself after realizing that all his life savings were gone. Many foundations of charities closed down due to the fraud and as a result, scientific projects, healthy care campaigns supported by those charities were forced to close. For example, Innocent Project, a justice organization using advanced DNA detecting technology to help those wrongly imprisoned people, could not do more because its backer JEHT Foundation lost all of its money in Madoff's Ponzi scheme.

2. **Ethics and Value**s: While many people were still in the despair of the financial crisis, the revelation of the case of Madoff not long after the crisis, undoubtedly gave another shock to the world. Just like The Wall Street Journal (2009) said 'Mr. Madoff's decline and fall added to national crisis of confidence and distrust of financial system. And the human cost has also been severe, with some investors losing all their money and at least one committing suicide.' It is obviously that a financial fraud ran by a major figure (former NASDAQ chairman) from market regulation and administration boards would yield many ethical issues/debates and distrust of the financial system.

SUMMARY

- Financial statement analysis is a judgmental process which aims to estimate current and past financial positions and the results of the operation of an enterprise, with primary objective of determining the best possible estimates and predictions about the future conditions.
- The financial statements of a business enterprise are intended to provide much of the basic data used for decision making, and in general, evaluation of performance by various groups such as current owners, potential investors, creditors, government agencies, and in some instance, competitors.
- Financial statement analysis is the process of reviewing and evaluating a company's financial statements (such as the balance sheet or profit and loss statement), thereby gaining an understanding of the financial health of the company and enabling more effective decision making.
- Financial statement analysis is the process of evaluating a company's performance or value through a company's balance sheet, income statement, or statement of cash flows.
- Working capital ratio is a financial calculation designed to measure a company's financial strength in the short term. Also known as the current ratio, this ratio is calculated by taking the sum total of a company's assets and dividing them by the liabilities that the company currently owes.
- Gross profit ratio (GP ratio) is a profitability ratio that shows the relationship between gross profit and total net sales revenue. It is a popular tool to evaluate the operational performance of the business.
- The net profit percentage is the ratio of after-tax profits to net sales. It reveals the remaining profit after all costs of production, administration, and financing have been deducted from sales, and income taxes recognized.
- Debt/equity ratio is a measure of the proportion of equity versus debt that is used to finance various portions of a company's operations.
- Financial reporting is a crucial process for companies and investors, as it provides key information that shows financial performance over time. Government and private regulatory institutions also monitor financial reporting to ensure fair trade, compensation and financial activities.
- Financial reporting provides information about the results of the operation, financial position and cash flows of a business.
- The Balance Sheet is a financial statement summarizing a company's total assets (current, non-current and intangible assets), liabilities (financial obligations), and shareholders' equity (investments and retained earnings) at a specific point in time, usually at the end of an accounting period.

REVIEW QUESTIONS

1. What are personal financial statements? Explain.
2. How to audit the financial statements?
3. How do you interpret financial ratios?
4. Define the importance of financial reporting.
5. Clarify the purpose of financial reports.

MULTIPLE CHOICE QUESTIONS

1. What do we understand from financial statements?

a. A group of reports regarding the organization's various financial aspects.
b. A group of reports regarding the employee's data.
c. A collection of reports pertaining to the organization's vision and mission.
d. None of the above

2. What does a balance sheet indicate out of the following options

a. The demographic details of the employees
b. The overall organization's liabilities, assets as well as stockholders' equity
c. The report regarding the weekly work progress of the organization
d. None of the above

3. Which of the following is not a part of the financial reports of the organization

a. Balance sheet
b. Income statements
c. Report with the vision and mission of the organization
d. Report regarding the flow of cash

4. Which of the following can be a part of financial reports?

a. The report regarding the financial result of the organization
b. The report with details about the financial position of the organization
c. The report regarding the flow of cash of the organization
d. All of the above

5. In a balance sheet report, the total value of assets should be able to match the worth of the following

a. The total sum of equity and liabilities
b. Total number of employees in the organization
c. The total earnings of the organization in the past week
d. The total number of new employees hires in the organization during the past year

6. **Which of the following is the most suitable statement for explaining the statement of cash flows**
    a. Report regarding the assets, equity, and liabilities
    b. Report explaining the purpose of business
    c. Report regarding the changes in the flow of cash for a particular time
    d. Report regarding the working and functioning of the organization
7. **Which of the following can be a part of liabilities in the balance sheet**
    a. Debts
    b. Dividends payable
    c. Wages that are payable
    d. All of the above
8. **What are the limitations of the financial statements**
    a. There can be subjective interpretations of the financial statements as per the investors
    b. There may be manipulation done in the financial statements such that the real profit-loss of the organization is not shown to the investors
    c. The financial statements give a detailed description of the cash flow of the organization
    d. Both A and B
9. **Which of the following can be called very important in terms of the financial statements**
    a. The report regarding ethics of the organization
    b. The list of holidays in the organization
    c. Cash flow statement, balance sheet and the income statement
    d. List of investors for the organization
10. **What can be some of the commonly depicted items in the financial statement of an organization**
    a. Cost of goods
    b. Debts
    c. Taxes
    d. All of the above

Answer to Multiple Choice Questions

1. (a); 2. (b); 3. (c); 4. (d); 5. (a); 6. (c); 7. (d); 8. (d); 9. (c); 10. (d)

REFERENCES

1. Aziz, A. Performance Appraisal-Accounting and Quantitative Approaches (Jaipur: Pointer Publishers, 2003) 22.
2. Costigan, M.H. and Lovata Linda, (2002). Empirical Analysis Adopters of Economic Value Added, Management Accounting Research, Vol.13, No.2, pp. 40-46.
3. Khustrokhan, H.R, (2002). Tata Tea Ropes in Stern Stewart & Company to Better EVA, Business Standard, p. 7.
4. Moyer, Stephen. Distressed Debt Analysis: Strategies for Speculative Investors. Ft. Lauderdale, FL: J. Ross Publishing, 2004.
5. Parmar, S.J. Financial Efficiency Modern Methods, Tools and Techniques (Jaipur: Raj Book Enterprises, 2004).
6. Abbott, L. J., S. Parker and T. J. Presley. 2012. Female board presence and the likelihood of financial restatement. Accounting Horizons (December): 607-629.
7. Abdelsalam, O. H., S. M. Bryant and D. L. Street. 2007. An examination of the comprehensiveness of corporate internet reporting provided by London-listed companies. Journal of International Accounting Research 6(2): 1-33.
8. Aboody, D., M. E. Barth and R. Kasznik. 2004. Firms' voluntary recognition of stock-based compensation expense. Journal of Accounting Research (May): 123-150.
9. Acito, A. A., J. J. Burks and W. B. Johnson. 2009. Materiality decisions and the correlation of accounting errors. The Accounting Review (May): 659-688.
10. Baird, J. E. and M. S. Rolfes. 2011. Onesource Corporate Consulting, Inc: Tax and financial reporting considerations. Journal of Accounting Education 29(4): 250-264.
11. Ball, R., A. Robin and G. Sadka. 2008. Is financial reporting shaped by equity markets or by debt markets? An international study of timeliness and conservatism. Review of Accounting Studies 13(2-3): 168-205.
12. Gajewski, J. and L. Li. 2015. Can internet-based disclosure reduce information asymmetry? Advances in Accounting: Incorporating Advances in International Accounting 31(1): 115-124.

CHAPTER

3

Cost of Capital

LEARNING OBJECTIVES

After studying this chapter, you will be able to:

- Discuss on concept of cost of capital
- Focus on cost of long-term debt
- Explain the cost of preferred stock
- Identify the cost of equity share capital

INTRODUCTORY EXAMPLE

Cost of Capital: Cost of capital is a fundamental concept in finance that represents the minimum return a company must generate on its investments to satisfy its investors' expectations and maintain the market value of its equity and debt. It comprises the cost of equity, which is the return required by equity investors for bearing the risk of owning shares in the company. The cost of equity is influenced by factors such as the company's beta, dividend policy, and overall market conditions. Additionally, the cost of debt represents the interest rate the company pays on its debt obligations. This rate is influenced by prevailing interest rates, the company's credit rating, and the terms of the debt agreements. The weighted average cost of capital (WACC) combines the cost of equity and the cost of debt, adjusted for the respective weights of equity and debt in the company's capital structure. Companies use the WACC as a discount rate to evaluate the feasibility of potential investments and determine whether the expected returns exceed the cost of capital. By understanding and effectively managing their cost of capital, companies can make informed decisions about capital budgeting, financing, and overall strategic direction, ultimately maximizing shareholder value and long-term profitability.

UNIT INTRODUCTION

The cost of capital is a crucial factor in investment decisions because it is used to assess the value of the business concern's investment proposal. When calculating the present value of upcoming cash flows related to capital projects, it serves as a discount rate. The terms cut-off rate, target rate, hurdle rate, and required rate of return are alternative terms for cost of capital. Because the cost of capital is directly related to the firm's value and earning potential, the finance manager must exercise caution when making decisions regarding it when the firms are using different sources of funding.

3.1. CONCEPT OF COST OF CAPITAL

→Learning Objectives

- To discuss assumption of cost of capital
- To understand determination of the cost of capital
- To explain importance of cost of capital
- To describe classification of cost of capital
- To define cost of capital applications: valuation and project selection

The rate of return a company needs to achieve on project investments in order to retain its market value and draw in funding is known as its cost of capital. The required rate of return on its investments, which include debt, equity, and retained earnings, is known as the cost of capital. The market value of a company's shares will decrease if it is unable to generate returns at the anticipated rate, thereby decreasing the total wealth of its shareholders.

"The minimum required rate of earnings or the cutoff rate of capital expenditure is the cost of capital." The term "cost of capital" refers to "a cut-off rate for the allocation of capital to project investment." It is the project's rate of return that will maintain the stock's market price steady. "The rate that must be earned on the net proceeds to provide the cost elements of the burden at the time they are due" is one way to define cost of capital.

3.1.1. Assumption of Cost of Capital

When determining and quantifying the cost of capital, a number of closely related assumptions are used. It is to be considered that there are three basic concepts:

1. It is not a cost as such. It is merely a hurdle rate.
2. It is the minimum rate of return.
3. It consist of three important risks such as zero risk level, business risk and financial risk.

Cost of capital can be measured with the help of the following equation.

$K=r_j + b + f.$

Where;

K = Cost of capital.

r_j = The riskless cost of the particular type of finance.

b = The business risk premium.

f = The financial risk premium.

3.1.2. Determination of the Cost of Capital

Cost is more accurately defined as stakeholders' expectations than as the amount the company actually pays or plans to pay. Here Stakeholders include providers of capital (shareholders, debenture holder, money lenders etc.), intermediaries (brokers, underwriters, merchant bankers etc.), and Government (for taxes). In the event that the company issues debentures with a 9% coupon, but investors anticipate a 10% coupon, investors will subscribe for the debentures at a discount rather than par. Therefore, rather than 9%, the company's cost will be 10%. In addition to providing investors with a return, the company must also pay commissions, brokerage fees, and other costs. To middlemen for the issuance of debentures. The cost of capital will rise by more than 10% as a result. However, interest payments are tax deductible under the Income Tax Act, which lowers the company's cost of capital. The annual percentage rate is used to express the cost of any financing source.

To calculate cost first of all we should identify various cash flows like:

1. Inflow of amount received at the beginning
2. Outflows of payment of interest, dividend, redemption amount etc.
3. Inflow of tax benefit on interest or outflow of payment of dividend tax.

After that, we can find a rate where the present value of outflows and inflows equals one another by using the trial and error method. In essence, that rate is IRR. Since there is an initial outflow followed by a number of inflows, the internal rate of return (IRR) in investment decisions indicates income. We also have the option of using shortcut formulas. These shortcut formulas are simple to use, but they only provide an approximation of the answer.

3.1.3. Importance of Cost of Capital

A crucial component of financial management is calculating the cost of capital in order to determine the capital structure of the company (Figure 3.1).

Figure 3.1. *The cost of capital is an indication of the cost a business incurs to finance itself, and it's an important metric for a business.*

Source: https://blog.insight-experience.com/what-is-the-cost-of-capital-and-why-is-it-important.

Importance to Capital Budgeting Decision: The choice of capital budget is primarily influenced by each source's cost of capital. The present value of cash inflow must exceed the present value of cash outflow in accordance with the net present value method. As a result, capital budgeting decisions are made using the cost of capital.

- **Importance to Structure Decision:** The arrangement of the various types of long-term securities is known as the capital structure. If the cost of capital is acceptable, a company will use a specific kind of source. Therefore, consideration of the cost of capital aids in structuring decisions.

- **Importance to Evolution of Financial Performance:** Cost of capital is one of the important determine which affects the capital budgeting, capital structure and value of the firm. Hence, it helps to evaluate the financial performance of the firm.
- **Importance to Other Financial Decisions:** Apart from the above points, cost of capital is also used in some other areas such as, market value of share, earning capacity of securities etc., hence, it plays a major part in the financial management.

3.1.4. Classification of Cost of Capital

Cost of capital may be classified into the following types on the basis of nature and usage:

- Explicit and Implicit Cost.
- Average and Marginal Cost.
- Historical and Future Cost.
- Specific and Combined Cost.

1. **Explicit and Implicit Cost:** Depending on how the cost of capital is calculated, the cost of capital can be either explicit or implicit. The price the company pays to obtain financing is known as the explicit cost. This may be calculated with the help of the following equation;

$$CI_0 = \sum_{t=1}^{n} \frac{CO_t}{(t+C)^t}$$

Where;

CI_o = initial cash inflow

C = outflow in the period concerned

N = duration for which the funds are provided

T = tax rate

The rate of return associated with the best investment opportunity for the company and its shareholders that would be lost if the projects the company is currently considering were approved is known as the implicit cost.

2. **Average and Marginal Cost:** The average cost of capital

Keyword

Marginal cost is the change in the total cost that arises when the quantity produced is incremented, the cost of producing additional quantity.

is the weighted average of the costs of all the capital components that the business uses. The weighted average cost of all forms of financing, including debt, equity, and retained earnings, is taken into account. The weighted average cost of new financing raised by the business is known as the **marginal cost**. When a business seeks out additional funding, there is an additional cost of capital.

3. **Historical and Future Cost:** The costs that have already been incurred to finance a specific project are known as historical costs. It is predicated on the real expenses spent on the prior project. The projected cost of financing for the suggested project is known as the future cost. The computation of expected cost is based on past performance.
4. **Specific and Combine Cost:** A source of capital's specific cost is the price associated with each type of capital source, including debt, equity, loans, and retained earnings. Finding each and every unique source of funding is highly beneficial. The total cost of capital from all sources combined is known as the composite or combined cost of capital. It also goes by the name "total cost of capital." It helps to comprehend the overall costs related to the company's entire financing.

Keyword

Capital investment is the amount invested in a company to enhance its business objectives. Also, the individual/entity can earn an income or recover the invested capital from earnings generated by the company over the years.

3.1.5. Cost of Capital Applications: Valuation and Project Selection

There are numerous uses for cost of capital, the two most popular being capital investment project selection and valuation.

1. **Net Cash Flow is the Preferred Economic Income Measure:** We will assume that net cash flow, also known as free cash flow, will be the economic income measure to which the cost of capital is applied. Discretionary cash that can be distributed to capital stakeholders is known as net cash flow (e.g., dividends, withdrawals, discretionary bonuses) without jeopardizing the projected ongoing operations of the business.

   For the purpose of capital investment project selection and valuation, the majority of financial analysts today prefer to concentrate on net cash flow as a measure of economic income. Money available to stakeholders is represented by net cash flow. Because it eliminates owners' discretionary spending of business funds, the majority of analysts favor this income metric. Even though the majority of recent corporate finance literature favors net cash flow as the appropriate economic income variable to which to apply cost of capital for valuation and decision-making, some analysts continue to prefer accounting income.

2. **Cost of Capital is the Proper Discount Rate:** It was stated that the cost of capital is typically applied as a discount rate to present value in order to convert projected future returns. Value today always equals future cash flow discounted at the opportunity cost of capital.

Let us keep in mind critical characteristics of a discount rate:

- A discount rate is a yield rate used to convert anticipated future payments or receipts into present value (i.e., a cash value as of today or as of a specified valuation date).
- The discount rate represents the total rate of return that the investor expects to realize on the amount invested.

The use of the cost of capital to estimate present value thus requires two sets of estimates:

- **The Numerator**: The expected amount of return on the investment in each future period over the life of the investment.
- **The Denominator**: The discount rate, which is the cost of capital.

Typically, analysts and investors apply the same cost of capital to each increase in expected future return, based on the simplifying assumption that the cost of capital remains constant throughout the investment life. However, in certain exceptional circumstances, analysts may decide to calculate a discrete cost of capital to apply to the projected return for each subsequent period.

3. **Present Value Formula:** Converting the foregoing concepts into a mathematical formula, we have the following, which is the essence of using cost of capital to estimate present value:

$$PV = \frac{NCF_1}{(1+k)} + \frac{NCF_2}{(1+k)^2} + \ldots + \frac{NCF_n}{(1+k)^n} \quad (1)$$

Where;

PV = Present value

NCF_1 ... NCF_n = Net cash flow (or other measure of economic income) expected in each of the periods 1 through n, n being the final cash flow in the life of the investment

k = Cost of capital applicable to the defined stream of net cash flow

- **Example: Valuing a Bond:** A simple example of the use of Formula 1 is valuing a bond for which a risk rating has been estimated. Let us make five assumptions:

1. The bond has a face value of $1,000.
2. It pays 8% interest on its face value.
3. The bond pays interest once a year, at the end of the year. (This, of course, is a simplifying assumption. Some bonds and notes pay only annually, but most publicly traded bonds pay interest semiannually.)
4. The bond matures exactly three years from the valuation date.
5. As of the valuation date, the market yield to maturity (i.e., total rate of return, including interest payments and price appreciation) for bonds of the same risk grade as the subject bond is 10%.

Note three important implications of this scenario:

1. Although the market cost of capital at the valuation date is 10%, the issuing company's embedded cost

of capital for this bond is only 8%. The difference could have resulted from a drop in interest rates generally at the time this bond was issued, or it could have been caused by an increase in the market's assessment of the bond's risk between the bond's issue date and valuation date.

2. The issuing company would presumably have to offer investors a 10% yield, the current market-driven cost of capital for bonds of that risk grade, in order to entice investors to buy the bonds if it wanted to issue new debt on comparable terms as of the valuation date.

3. When we talk about "cost of capital," we mean market cost of capital, not embedded cost of capital, for the purposes of valuation and capital budgeting decisions. (Embedded cost of capital is sometimes used in utility rate-making only on valuation and capital budgeting applications of cost of capital.) Substituting numbers derived from the preceding assumptions into Formula 1 gives us:

Remember

The equity ratio calculates the proportion of a company's total assets financed using capital provided by shareholders. The equity ratio, or "proprietary ratio", is used to determine the contribution of shareholders to fund a company's resources, i.e. the assets belonging to the company.

$$PV = \frac{\$80}{(1+.10)} + \frac{\$80}{(1+.10)^2} + \frac{\$80}{(1+.10)^3} + \frac{\$1{,}000}{(1+.10)^3}$$

$$= \frac{\$80}{1.10} + \frac{\$80}{1.21} + \frac{\$80}{1.331} + \frac{\$1{,}000}{1.331}$$

$$= \$72.73 + \$66.12 + \$60.11 + \$751.32$$

$$= \underline{\underline{\$950.28}}$$

In this example, the fair market value of the subject bond as of the valuation date is $950.28. That is the amount that a willing buyer would expect to pay and a willing seller would expect to receive (before considering any transaction costs).

3. **Relationship of Discount Rate to Capitalization Rate:** It is important to distinguish between a discount rate and a capitalization rate and to understand the relationship between the two. Critical characteristics of a capitalization rate include:

   - A discount rate is used to convert all expected future payments to a present value; a capitalization rate, on the other hand, is a yield rate used to convert a single payment or measure of economic income into present value.
   - The capitalization rate represents only the current rate of return, that is, the return received in a single

period (as opposed to a discount rate, which represents the total rate of return).

4. **Applications to Businesses, Business Interests, Projects, and Divisions:** An equity interest in a business or all of the capital that a business has invested can be valued using the same construct. A cost of capital discount rate that accounts for the risk involved in realizing the targeted cash flows is applied when projecting the cash flows accessible to the interest that has to be valued.

Analyzing a capital budgeting choice, like constructing a plant or purchasing equipment, can also be done using the same framework. If so, the cash flows that need to be discounted are incremental cash flows—that is, cash flows that would not have happened in the absence of the decision. Early in the cash flow stream, while money is being invested in the project, it might not be positive.

The most important relationship to keep in mind is that investment, not investor, determines cost of capital. As a result, the analyst needs to assess the risk associated with each project. When a project's risk is compared to the company's overall risk, the project's cost of capital should be adjusted accordingly, either higher or lower, to reflect the differences in risk.

The corporate finance literature generally agrees that the risk of an investment should be the basis for evaluating it, rather than the company's overall risk, which determines the cost of capital for the company. This is despite the fact that some companies apply a single "hurdle rate" to all proposed projects or investments. The cost of capital for the company will increase as a result of the market recognizing and pricing this increased risk. The stock price will drop and shareholder value will be lost if the returns on the riskier new investment are insufficient to generate higher returns commensurate with this higher cost of capital.

Divisional cost of capital, or cost of capital estimation for a division of a company, lies in the middle of cost of capital estimation for a company as a whole and cost of capital estimation for a particular project. Estimating the cost of capital for a division is similar to estimating the cost of capital for a privately held company overall in many ways.

Did you get it?

1. **Describe the cost of capital is the proper discount rate.**
2. **What are the relationship of discount rate to capitalization rate?**
3. **Define the average and marginal cost**

3.2. COST OF LONG-TERM DEBT

→Learning Objectives

- Understand the net proceeds
- Discuss the before-tax cost of debt
- Write the cost of irredeemable debentures
- Define the cost of convertible debenture

Long-term debt cost refers to the financing expense linked with raising fresh capital via long-term borrowing. The money is usually raised by selling corporate bonds.

3.2.1. Net Proceeds

The money that the company gets from the sale of a bond, or any other security, is known as the net proceeds. The flotation costs, or the total cost of issuing and selling securities, are deducted from the total proceeds. These fees are applicable to debt, preferred stock, and common stock offerings made to the public.

They include two components: (1) underwriting costs, or compensation earned by investment bankers for selling the security; and (2) administrative costs, or issuer expenses such as legal and accounting costs.

3.2.2. Before-Tax Cost of Debt

The rate of return the company must pay on new borrowing is known as the before-tax cost of debt, or r_d. There are three methods to determine a company's before-tax cost of debt for bonds: calculation, approximation, or quotation.

1. **Using Market Quotations:** The **yield to maturity (YTM)** on the company's current bonds or bonds with comparable risk issued by other companies can be used to quickly determine the before-tax cost of debt. Current bonds' yield to maturity (YTM) indicates the rate of return that the market demands. For example, if the market requires a YTM of 9.7% for a similar-risk bond, this value can be used as the before-tax cost of debt, r_d, for new bonds. Bond yields are widely reported by sources such as the Wall Street Journal.
2. **Calculating the Cost:** Using the net proceeds that the company receives from the bond's issuance, this method determines the before-tax cost of debt by computing the yield to maturity (YTM) of the bond's cash flows. This value is

the cost to maturity of the debt's associated cash flows, as seen from the issuer's perspective. An electronic spreadsheet or a financial calculator can be used to calculate the YTM. It shows the debt's annual percentage cost before taxes.

3. **Approximating the Cost:** Although not as precise as using a calculator, there is a method for quickly approximating the before-tax cost of debt. The before-tax cost of debt, r_d, for a bond with a $1,000 par value can be approximated by

$$r_d = \frac{I + \frac{\$1,000 - N_d}{n}}{\frac{N_d + \$1,000}{2}}$$

Keyword

Yield to maturity (YTM) is yield to maturity which means the total return you expect from your investment in bonds/debt mutual funds if the same is held till maturity.

Where;

I = annual interest in dollars

N_d = net proceeds from the sale of debt (bond)

n = number of years to the bond's maturity

4. **After-Tax Cost of Debt**: The interest expense on debt lowers the company's taxable income and, consequently, its tax liability because, in contrast to dividends paid to equity holders, interest payments to bondholders are tax deductible for the company. In order to determine the net cost of debt for the company, we need to solve for the after-tax cost of long-term debt and take into consideration the tax savings that come with debt. The after-tax cost of debt, ri, can be found by multiplying the before-tax cost, r_d, by 1 minus the tax rate, T:

$$r_i = r_d \times (1 - T)$$

3.2.3. Cost of Irredeemable Debentures

Debentures that have not been redeemed by the debenture issuer are referred to as irredeemable debentures. Cost of debentures not redeemable during the life time of the company is calculated as below:

$$K_d = \frac{I}{NP}(1 - t)$$

Where;

K_d = Cost of debt after tax

I = Annual interest payment

N_P = Net proceeds of debentures or current market price

t = Tax rate

Net proceeds means issue price less issue expenses. If issue price is not given then students can assume it to be equal to current market price. If issue expenses are not given simply assume it equal to zero.

In absence of any specific information, students may use any of the above formulae to calculate the Cost of Debt (K_d) with logical assumption. Above formulas give approximate value of cost of debt. In these formulas higher the difference between RV and NP, lower the accuracy of answer. Therefore, one should not use these formulas if difference between RV and NP is very high. Also these formulas are not suitable in case of gradual redemption of bonds.

3.2.3.1. Cost of Redeemable Debentures (Using Approximation Method)

The cost of redeemable debentures will be calculated as below:

$$\text{Cost of Redeemable Debenture } (K_d) = \frac{I(1-t) + \frac{(RV-NP)}{n}}{\frac{(RV+NP)}{2}}$$

Where;

I = Interest payment

N_P = Net proceeds from debentures in case of new issue of debt or Current market price in case of existing debt.

RV = Redemption value of debentures

t = Tax rate applicable to the company

n = Remaining life of debentures.

The above formula to calculate cost of debt is used where only interest on debt is tax deductable. Sometime, debts are issued at discount and/ or redeemed at a premium. If discount on issue and/ or premium on redemption are tax deductible, the following formula can be used to calculate the cost of debt.

$$\text{Cost of Redeemable Debenture } (K_d) = \frac{I + \frac{(RV-NP)}{n}}{\frac{(RV+NP)}{2}}(1-t)$$

3.2.3.2. Cost of Debt Using Present Value Method [Yield to maturity (YTM) Approach)]

The relevant cash flows are discounted using the internal rate of return (IRR) to determine the cost of redeemable debt (K_d). Here YTM is the annual return of an investment from the current date till maturity date. So, YTM is the internal rate of return at which current price of a debt equals to the present value of all cash-flows.

The relevant cash flows are as follows:

Year	Cash flows
0	Net proceeds in case of new issue/ Current market price in case of existing debt (NP or P_0)
1 to n	Interest net of tax [I(1-t)]
n	Redemption value (RV)

Steps to calculate relevant cash flows:

Step-1: Identify the cash flows

Step-2: Calculate NPVs of cash flows as identified above using two discount rates (guessing).

Step-3: Calculate IRR

- **Amortization of Bond:** Amortization of a bond may occur annually i.e. instead of repaying the principal at maturity, it is done annually. Under such circumstances, interest will be calculated on the outstanding amount and the principal will decrease with yearly payments. The bonds' cash flows will be inconsistent.

The formula for determining the value of a bond or debenture that is amortized every year is as follows:

$$V_B = \frac{C_1}{(1+K_d)^1} + \frac{C_2}{(1+K_d)^2} + \ldots\ldots + \frac{C_n}{(1+K_d)^n}$$

$$V_B = \sum_{t=1}^{n} \frac{C_t}{(1+K_d)^t}$$

3.2.4. Cost of Convertible Debenture

Convertible debenture holders may choose to have their debentures redeemed for cash or to receive a certain number of company shares in lieu of cash. The computation of convertible debentures' cost bears a strong resemblance to that of redeemable debentures. It is assumed that each debenture holder will select the option with the higher value when determining the debenture redemption value, and this assumption is taken into account when calculating the cost of debt.

Did you know?

Dutch investors were the first to trade their shares at a regular stock exchange. The process of buying and selling these shares of stock in the VOC became the basis of the first official (formal) stock market in history.

Did you get it?

1. **How is the cost of long-term debt determined in financial analysis?**
2. **What factors influence the interest rate a company pays on its long-term debt?**

3.3. COST OF PREFERRED STOCK

→Learning Objectives

- Define the preferred stock dividends
- Discuss how to calculating the cost of preferred stock
- Write the cost of redeemable preference shares
- Focus on cost of irredeemable preference shares

A company's cost of preferred stock is essentially the amount it pays in exchange for the revenue it receives from the issuance and sale of the stock. Put another way, it's calculated by dividing the company's annual payout by the total amount of stock they issued.

This metric is frequently used by management to assess the most efficient and cost-effective methods of capital raising. To raise money for operations or expansions, corporations can issue debt, common shares, preferred shares, and a variety of other instruments. The preferred dividend is divided by the market price per share to determine the cost of preferred stock. After they've ascertained that rate, they can contrast it with alternative financing options. The Weighted Average Cost of Capital is also computed using the cost of preferred stock (Figure 3.2).

Figure 3.2. *Cost of preferred stock.*

Source: https://corporatefinanceinstitute.com/resources/valuation/cost-of-preferred-stock/.

3.3.1. Preferred Stock Dividends

The stock is frequently referred to as "x-dollar preferred stock" when dividends are declared as "preferred stock dividends." Therefore, on each share of preferred stock owned, a "$4 preferred stock" is expected to pay $4 in dividends to preferred stockholders annually. Dividends on preferred stocks are occasionally expressed as an annual percentage rate. The percentage of the stock's par, or face, value that corresponds to the yearly dividend is represented by this rate. For example, an annual dividend of $4 per share would be expected from an 8% preferred stock with a $50 par value (0.08 × $50 par = $4). Any dividends expressed as percentages should be converted to annual dollar dividends prior to determining the cost of preferred stock.

Keyword

Weighted Average Cost (WAC) method of inventory valuation uses a weighted average to determine the amount that goes into COGS and inventory.

3.3.2. Calculating the Cost of Preferred Stock

The ratio of the preferred stock dividend to the net proceeds of the preferred stock sale for the company is known as the cost of preferred stock, or r_p. The amount to be received less any flotation expenses is known as the net proceeds. The following equation gives the cost of preferred stock, r_p, in terms of the annual dollar dividend, D_p, and the net proceeds from the sale of the stock, N_p:

$$r_p = \frac{D_p}{N_p}$$

Duchess's preferred stock (10.6%) is significantly more expensive than the company's long-term debt (5.67%). This discrepancy results from the fact that preferred stock carries a higher risk than long-term debt and that the cost of long-term debt (the interest) is tax deductible.

3.3.3. Cost of Redeemable Preference Shares

Redeemable preference shares are company-issued preference shares that can be redeemed at maturity. With the exception of the dividends paid to preference shareholders not being tax deductible, the cost of redeemable preference shares is comparable to that of redeemable debentures. Cost of preference capital is calculated as follows:

$$\text{Cost of Redeemable Preference Shares } K_p = \frac{PD + \frac{(RV - NP)}{n}}{\frac{(RV + NP)}{2}}$$

Where;

PD = Annual preference dividend

RV = Redemption value of preference shares

NP = Net proceeds on issue of preference shares

n = Remaining life of preference shares.

Net proceeds are the issue price minus the issue costs. Students can assume that the issue price is the same as the current market price if it is not stated. If issue expenses are not given simply assume it equal to zero. The discount rate used to compare the net proceeds from the sale of preference shares to the present value of the future principal and dividend payments can also be used to determine the cost of redeemable preference shares.

3.3.4. Cost of Irredeemable Preference Shares

The price of irredeemable preference shares is comparable to the perpetual cost calculation. The preference dividend is divided by the issue's net proceeds or current market price to determine the cost. The cost of irredeemable preference share is as below:

$$\text{Cost of Irredeemable Preference Share } (K_{P}) = \frac{PD}{P_0}$$

Where;

PD = Annual preference dividend

P_0= Net proceeds in issue of preference shares

3.4. COST OF EQUITY SHARE CAPITAL

→Learning Objectives

- Explain the dividend price approach
- Discuss on earning/ price approach
- Identify the growth approach or Gordon's model
- Define the realized yield approach
- Describe the capital asset pricing model (CAPM) approach

The expectation of equity shareholders is the cost of equity, just like it is for any other source of funding. Value, as we all know, is calculated by dividing performance by expectations. It is possible to compute expectation as a balancing factor if we are aware of value and performance. Performance in this context refers to the sum that the business pays investors, such as interest, dividends, redemption prices, etc. The amount of interest or dividend on debentures and preference shares is fixed, but it is unknown for equity shares.

Therefore, there is no single method for calculation of cost of equity.

1. If dividend is expected to be constant then dividend price approach should be used.
2. If earning per share is expected to be constant then earning price approach should be used.
3. If dividend and earning are expected to grow at a constant rate then growth approach, which is also named as Gordon's model should be used.
4. If it is difficult to forecast future then realized yield approach should be used, which looks into past.
5. All above methods calculate cost of equity as a balancing figure. While the cost of equity or expectation of investors is dependent on risk. Higher the risk higher the expectations and vice versa. Capital asset pricing model calculates cost of equity based on risk.

Different methods are employed to compute the cost of equity share capital.

3.4.1. Dividend Price Approach

The Dividend Valuation Model is another name for this. It is assumed by this model that the dividend per share will always remain the same. Here, cost of equity capital is computed by dividing the expected dividend by market price per share as follows:

$$\text{Cost of Equity } (K_e) = \frac{D}{P_0}$$

Keyword

Capital asset is defined as property of any kind held by an assessed, whether connected with their business or profession or not connected with their business or profession.

Where;

K_e = Cost of equity

D = Expected dividend

P_0 = Market price of equity (ex- dividend)

3.4.2. Earning/ Price Approach

Supporters of this strategy link the market price of the company's shares to its earnings. As a result, the expected rate of a company's earnings would determine the cost of equity share capital. It is argued that every investor, whether or not they receive a payout from the company whose shares they invest in, anticipates receiving a specific amount of earnings. Therefore, the cost of equity share capital can be interpreted based on an investor's expectation that the company in which he plans to subscribe for shares should have at least a 20% rate of earning. Suppose the company is expected to earn 30% the investor will be prepared to pay \$150 $\left(\frac{30}{20} \times 100\right)$ for each share of \$100.

Earnings/ Price Approach:

$$\text{Cost of Equity } (K_e) = \frac{E}{P}$$

Where;

E = Current earnings per share

P = Market share price

This approach assumes that earning per share will remain constant forever. The Earning Price Approach is similar to the dividend price approach; only it seeks to nullify the effect of changes in the dividend policy.

3.4.3. Growth Approach or Gordon's Model

As per this approach the rate of dividend growth remains constant. Where earnings, dividends and equity share price all grow at the same rate, the cost of equity capital may be computed as follows:

$$\text{Cost of Equity } (K_e) = \frac{D_1}{P_0} + g$$

Where;

D_1 = [D0 (1+ g)] i.e. next expected dividend

P_0 = Current Market price per share

g = Constant Growth Rate of Dividend.

In case of newly issued equity shares where floatation cost is incurred, the cost of equity share with an estimation of constant dividend growth is calculated as below:

$$\text{Cost of Equity } (K_e) = \frac{D_1}{P_0 - F} + g$$

Where; F = Flotation cost per share

Remember

The GGM works by taking an infinite series of dividends per share and discounting them back to the present using the required rate of return.

3.4.4. Realized Yield Approach

Traditionally, "expected return" refers to the average rate of return that has been realized over the last few years. The equity cost is calculated by referencing historical records of dividends that equity shareholders have actually received. While this method offers a unified method for figuring out equity costs, it is based on implausible assumptions such as the company's risks remaining constant, shareholders' expected rate of return remaining constant, and the shareholders' reinvestment opportunity cost (rate) equal to the realized yield. This strategy is impractical if the earnings do not stay consistent.

3.4.5. Capital Asset Pricing Model (CAPM) Approach

The risk-return trade-off for securities is described by the CAPM model. It explains how risk and return on securities have a linear relationship. The risks, to which a security is exposed, can be classified into two groups:

1. **Unsystematic Risk**: Because the risk is associated with the performance of the company, it is also known as company-specific risk. The portfolio of securities can be diversified to minimize or completely eliminate this kind of risk. Another name for this is diversifiable risk.
2. **Systematic Risk:** It's the general risk that a business operates

under, either macroeconomic or market-specific. This kind of risk is non-diversifiable since diversification cannot remove it. Examples include interest rates, government policies, and inflation. According to the CAPM approach, a business should only be concerned with non-diversifiable risk because, unlike diversifiable risk, which can be eliminated by an investor through diversification, non-diversifiable risk cannot be eliminated.

The non-diversifiable risks are assessed in terms of beta coefficient (b or ⍰) through fitting regression equation between return of a security and the return on a market portfolio.

Thus, the cost of equity capital can be calculated under this approach as:

Cost of Equity $(K_e) = R_f + ß (R_m - R_f)$

Where;

K_e = Cost of equity capital

R_f = Risk free rate of return

ß = Beta coefficient

R_m = Rate of return on market portfolio

$R_m - R_f$ = Market risk premium

Therefore, Required rate of return = Risk free rate + Risk premium

- The idea behind CAPM is that investors need to be compensated in two ways time value of money and risk.
- The time value of money is represented by the risk-free rate in the formula and compensates the investors for placing money in any investment over a period of time.
- The other half of the formula represents risk and calculates the amount of compensation the investor needs for taking on additional risk. This is calculated by taking a risk measure (beta) which compares the returns of the asset to the market over a period of time and compares it to the market premium.

According to the CAPM, a security's or portfolio's expected return is equal to the rate on a security that carries no risk plus a risk premium. The investment should not be made if the expected return is not greater than or equal to the required return.

- Estimation of betas with historical data is unrealistic; and
- Market imperfections may lead investors to unsystematic risk.

Even in cases where the company is losing money, the CAPM can be used to calculate cost of equity. Measuring investors' expectations from that specific company's equity shares is the fundamental component in calculating the cost of equity share capital. As a result, the entire issue of figuring out the price of equity shares depends on the elements that influence the expectations of a specific investor group in a business that falls within a given risk category.

Did you get it?

1. **What factors influence the cost of equity for a company?**
2. **Why is the cost of equity share capital important in financial decision-making?**

A CLOSER LOOK

The concept of cost of capital is a fundamental principle in finance that plays a crucial role in investment decision-making. It represents the minimum return that a company must earn on its investments to satisfy its investors and maintain the value of its stock. In simple terms, the cost of capital is the cost of financing the company's operations through a combination of debt and equity.

Calculating the cost of capital involves evaluating the cost of debt and the cost of equity. The cost of debt is relatively straightforward as it represents the interest rate that the company pays on its debt. On the other hand, the cost of equity is more complex and requires considering the return expected by shareholders and the risk associated with the company's stock.

To calculate the cost of equity, a commonly used approach is the capital Asset Pricing model (CAPM). This model considers the risk-free rate, the expected market return, and the company's beta, which measures the stock's sensitivity to market movements. The cost of equity is then determined by adding a risk premium to the risk-free rate.

Beta is a measure of a stock's volatility in relation to the overall market. It quantifies the sensitivity of a stock's returns to fluctuations in the market. A beta of 1 indicates that the stock's price moves in line with the market, while a beta greater than 1 suggests that the stock is more volatile than the market. On the other hand, a beta less than 1 indicates that the stock is less volatile than the market. By analyzing beta, investors can assess the level of risk associated with a particular stock or portfolio.

Determining the cost of capital is crucial for businesses as it helps in evaluating investment opportunities and making informed financial decisions. Beta plays a significant role in calculating the cost of equity, which is a crucial component of the overall cost of capital.

The cost of equity represents the return that shareholders require for investing in a company's stock. Beta is used to estimate the systematic risk associated with a stock, which reflects the risk that cannot be diversified away. The higher the beta, the higher the systematic risk, and consequently, the higher the cost of equity.

When analyzing beta, it is important to consider a few key points:

- **Industry Comparison:** Comparing the beta of a stock to the beta of its industry peers can provide valuable insights. A stock with a higher beta than its peers may indicate higher risk, while a lower beta may suggest lower risk.
- **Time Horizon:** Beta is not a static measure and can vary over time. It is essential to consider the time period used to calculate beta and ensure it aligns with the investment horizon being considered.
- **Market Conditions**: Beta is influenced by market conditions, and it may not accurately reflect the stock's risk during periods of extreme market volatility. It is important to consider the current market environment while interpreting beta.

ROLE MODEL

BENJAMIN GRAHAM: FATHER OF VALUE INVESTING

Benjamin Graham, widely known as the 'father of value investing,' was an American investor, economist and academic. Born in United Kingdom towards the end of the nineteenth century he moved with his parents to the USA at the age of one, losing his father at nine. Thereafter, he grew up under extreme poverty, which motivated him to earn enough money and make his family comfortable. Always a bright student, he earned his bachelor's degree from Columbia University and then took up a job at the Wall Street as a Chalker. Quickly climbing the ladder and earning enough, he formed his own partnership firm at the age of 32 and started teaching at Columbia University at 34. Although he lost substantial chunk of his asset in the stock market crash of 1929 it failed to dampen his enthusiasm and learning from his mistake, he wrote two widely acclaimed books on investment. His concepts in managerial economics have led to development of value investing within different investment vehicles like mutual funds, hedge funds, diversified holding companies. He had many disciples, among whom Warren Buffet is most notable.

1. Childhood and Early Years: Benjamin Graham was born as Benjamin Grossbaum on May 9, 1894, in London, England into a Jewish family. His parents, Isaac M. and Dorothy Grossbaum, migrated to the USA when he was one year old, eventually settling down in New York, where Isaac started an export import business. In 1903, Isaac Grossbaum passed away, leaving his wife to take care of nine year old Benjamin and his two younger siblings, Leon and Victor. While she could still manage, the Bank Panic of 1907 robbed her of her savings, forcing the family to move in with Dorothy's brother, Maurice Gerad. A brilliant student at school, Benjamin entered Columbia University on a scholarship, graduating in 1914 as salutatorian of his class. At that time, he was just 20 years old and ready to make his fortune, taking a bold and unorthodox step.

Few weeks before his graduation, the University offered him teaching positions in three different faculties: Greek and Latin philosophy, English, and mathematics. Although the job would have given him financial security he declined the offer and joined the Wall Street.

2. Early Career: In 1914, Benjamin Grossbaum began his career as a messenger at the Newburger, Henderson and Loeb, a brokerage firm at the Wall Street. In those days, it was deemed a revolutionary step because at that time university graduates did not consider stock broking as a career option. Initially, his main job was to write scores on the blackboard; but with the passage of time, as he won the confidence of the proprietors with his natural intelligence he was given other responsibilities. Very soon, he was doing financial researches for the firm. Rising through the ranks exceptionally quickly, he became a partner of Newburger, Henderson, and Loeb in 1920. He was soon earning $50,000 per year. Sometime now, he changed his surname to suit the Wall Street ambience, becoming Benjamin Graham instead of Grossbaum.

3. Forming Partnership: In 1926, Benjamin Graham formed Graham Newman Co with Jerome Newman, another Wall Street broker. It was indeed a revolutionary partnership as they adopted some radical strategies, which not only safeguarded their clients' investments, but also enabled them to provide a 670% return over a period of ten years. While putting a bet that a particular stock price was going to rise, they would place simultaneous bet that the price of another stock was going to fall. This way, they could fully use the available resources, without having to keep cash cushions, outperforming leading mutual funds by 40%.

4. Northern Pipeline Affair: Also in 1926, Graham made an astonishing discovery, which helped him to establish his position in the stock market. Back in 1911, Standard Oil, owned by the Rockefellers, was broken up into 34 independent entities. However, knowing little about their financial status, Wall Street paid hardly any attention to them. In 1926, all pipeline companies were asked to file financial statements to the Interstate Commerce Commission, which they did very superfluously. While going through these reports, Benjamin Graham was instinctively drawn to one Northern Pipeline Company. Wanting to know more about its financial status, he immediately took a train to Washington. To his astonishment he found that while the Northern Pipeline was trading at $65 per share, the company held railroad bonds at $95. He also realized that the nature of its holding, which included other liquid assets, was such that the company could distribute its assets without affecting the operators. Graham now began to pick up the company's stock, acquiring 5% of it within 1926. He now went to meet the top boss of Northern Pipeline, demanding that they distribute the excess asset to the shareholders because they were its rightful owners. But they refused to entertain the idea. In 1927, during the shareholders' meeting, Graham took his proposal directly to his shareholders. As required, he put his proposal in the form of a motion; but none of the present shareholders agreed to second it and therefore, it was discarded. Undeterred, Benjamin Graham decided to take his battle to the next stage via proxies. Hiring a law firm, he now began to solicit proxies. He also visited Rockefeller's Foundation; but did not receive much encouragement. However, by January 1928, he had acquired proxies for roughly 37.50% of the company's shares. The shareholder's meeting in 1928 was a turning point in Graham's career. In this meeting, he not only had 37.50% proxies with him, the Rockefeller Foundation, which gave their proxies to the company management, sent a directive that the company should distribute as much cash as the business can spare. Northern Pipeline was now forced to accept Graham's election to its board. Shortly, they distributed $70 per-share of excess liquid assets to its shareholders. Impressed, Rockefeller invited him for a meeting, eventually reaching out to other affiliates, who had excess liquid cash, urging them to distribute it among its rightful owners. At the urging of Rockefeller, many other former associates began offloading their excess liquid cash, distributing them among the shareholders. Known as 'Northern Pipeline Affair, the ripple effect established Benjamin Graham as a brilliant analyst and a shareholder activist.

5. After Stock Market Crash: Graham's success in the Northern Pipeline Affair opened another avenue for him. In 1928, he joined Columbia Business School of Columbia University as a faculty member, a position he held until 1955. In 1929, as the stock market experienced a major crash, setting in the Great Depression, Graham Newman Partnership lost major portion of their stock; but still managed to remain afloat. Eventually they regained their assets; never to lose again, enjoying an average annual return of 17% until 1956.

The stock market crash also set him thinking, resulting in the publication of his first book, 'Security Analysis' in 1934. Co-written with David Dodd, it was the first book to systematically deal with the study of investments. In 1948, Graham Newman Co bought Government Employees Insurance Co. In spite of the world 'Government' in its name it was a private firm. Since an investment funds could not own an insurance company, they turned it into a public company, distributing shares among investors. In 1949, he published his seminal work, 'The Intelligent Investor.' Concurrently, he continued to play an important role in the stock market, buying shares that traded far below the companies' liquidation value and thus he continued to make profit in stocks while minimizing downside risk.

6. Noted Disciples: Over the years, Benjamin Graham's performance in the stock market attracted the attention of many young would-be investors. One of them was Warren Edward Buffet. In1949, the nineteen year old would-be business magnet and investor enrolled at the Columbia University only to study with him. Upon graduation in 1951, Buffet approached Graham for a job in his company, wishing to work in the stock market. He had such an enormous respect for Graham that he was willing to work without salary. Although initially Graham discouraged him he later relented. Buffet joined the Graham Newman Corporation in 1954 at an annual salary of $12,000, remaining there until Graham retired in 1956. He later remembered Graham to be a tough, but accommodating boss. It is not known when, but Graham also took classes at New York Stock Exchange Institute, where American investor and fund manager, Walter J. Schloss, was one of his students. Eventually, he also went to work for Graham, learning from him the tricks of the trade. Graham also yielded enormous influence on Irving Kahn, his teaching assistant at the Columbia Business School at Columbia University. Few other noted investors, who considered themselves to be Graham's disciples and employed his value investing techniques, were William J. Ruane, Seth Klarman, Bill Ackman and Charles H. Brandes.

7. Later Years: In 1956, Benjamin Graham dissolved his partnership with Newman and retired from stock market. Thereafter, he moved to California, teaching at the University of California, Los Angeles and also at Anderson School of Management, New Mexico. Concurrently, he also kept his home in New York and traveled frequently to France.

Although he dissolved the partnership, his interest in the stock market did not diminish. He spent a large part of his retired life devising simplified formulas, which would help average investors to invest in stocks. He also wrote extensively about monetary policies. Over the time, he became disillusioned with average stockholders as they failed to demand their rights as the true owner of the company. However, he saw a light of hope in takeovers as that forced the companies to function properly. During his later years, he also started taking Sunday classes for children not belonging to any church or temple. He told them about history of religion, discussing the topic in general. The children loved these classes.

8. Major Works: Benjamin Graham is best remembered for his two books, 'Security Analysis' and 'The Intelligent Investor.' While in 'Security Analysis,' he clearly distinguished between investment and speculation, in 'The Intelligent Investor,' he mainly dealt in value investing. He is also famous for devising, what we now call 'Benjamin Graham formula.' Published in 'The Intelligent Investor,' the formula helps the investors to quickly determine if their stocks were priced rationally. His two other popular concepts were 'Mr. Market' and 'margin of safety.'

9. Personal Life and Legacy: Benjamin Graham married thrice; but little is known about his spouses or his children. His first wife, whose name remains unknown, was initially a dance teacher. Although she later gave up her career to look after her family she had to resume teaching after the 1929 stock market crash. Graham divorced her first wife in 1937, marrying a young actress in the following year. But this marriage was also short lived. He shortly divorced her to marry his secretary, Estelle Messing Graham. Estelle, also called Estie, had been described as "a warm, giving and non-judgmental person." With Estelle, he had one son, Benjamin Graham Jr. From his previous two marriages, he had at least two more sons; Newton, who died of meningitis of the spine at the age of eight and Newton II, who served in the U.S. Army. In 1954, his second son Newton II, while posted in France, committed suicide. On receiving the news, Graham traveled to France to make arrangement for his last rites. There, he met Marie Louise Amigues, who though twenty years senior to Newton, was in relationship with him.

Eventually Graham and Amigues developed a relationship and Graham began to spend more time with her. In 1965, he told Estelle that he would stay with her in California for six months and spend the other six months with Amigues in France. When Estelle rejected the offer he left home. On September 21, 1976, Graham died in Aix-en-Provence, France, at the age of 82. His concepts on investor psychology, minimal debt, buy-and-hold investing, fundamental analysis, concentrated diversification, buying within the margin of safety, activist investing, and contrarian mindsets are still being used by the serious investors all over the world.

SUMMARY

- Cost of capital is an integral part of investment decision as it is used to measure the worth of investment proposal provided by the business concern. It is used as a discount rate in determining the present value of future cash flows associated with capital projects.
- Cost of capital is one of the important factors which affects the capital budgeting, capital structure and value of the firm.
- The cost of debentures which are not redeemed by the issuer of the debenture is known as irredeemable debentures.
- The cost of preferred stock to a company is effectively the price it pays in return for the income it gets from issuing and selling the stock. In other words, it's the amount of money the company pays out in a year divided by the lump sum they got from issuing the stock.
- The cost of preferred stock, r_p, is the ratio of the preferred stock dividend to the firm's net proceeds from the sale of the preferred stock.
- Cost of redeemable preference share is similar to the cost of redeemable debentures with the exception that the dividends paid to the preference shareholders are not tax deductible.

REVIEW QUESTIONS

1. Discuss various uses of the concept of cost of capital.
2. Mention the importance of cost of capital.
3. Why is the cost of capital the minimum acceptable rate of return on an investment?
4. How is the cost of debt capital ascertained? Give examples.
5. Critically examine the different approaches for computing cost of equity.

MULTIPLE CHOICE QUESTIONS

1. The cost of equity share or debt is known as ________.

a. The specific cost of capital
b. The related cost of capital
c. The burden on the shareholder
d. None of the above

2. Which of the following methods involves computing the cost of capital by dividing the dividend by market price/net proceeds per share?

a. Adjusted price method
b. Price earning method
c. Dividend yield method
d. Adjusted dividend method

3. In weighted average cost of capital, an organization can affect its cost of capital through ____________.

a. The policy of investment

b. The policy of capital structure

c. The policy of dividends

d. All of the above

4. _______ is the rate of return for the most viable investment opportunity for a company that they will forgo by selecting any other project.

a. Implicit cost

b. Specific cost

c. Explicit cost

d. None of the above

5. What is Marginal Cost?

a. It is the cost of raising an additional unit of capital

b. It is the additional cost of capital when the company decides to raise finance for its operations

c. It is the weighted average cost of raising finance

d. All of the above

6. The premium that is considered to be the difference between the current yield on treasury bonds and the expected return on common stock is ___________.

a. Current risk premium

b. Past risk premium

c. Expected premium

d. None of the above

7. Which among the following figures is not relevant while calculating the cost of the redeemable preference shares?

a. Earnings per share

b. Flotation cost

c. Discount

d. None of the above

8. Which of the following factors affecting the cost of capital can be controlled by the firm?

a. Tax rates

b. Dividend policy

c. Level of interest rates

d. All of the above

9. Which of the following is an uncontrollable factor that affects the cost of capital for a firm?

a. Capital structure policy

b. Debt service charges

c. Investment policy

d. None of the above

10. _________ is the cost that is used to raise the common equity of a firm by reinvestment of the internal earnings.

a. Cost of reserve assets

b. Cost of stocks

c. Cost of mortgage

d. Cost of common equity

Answer to Multiple Choice Questions

1. (a); 2. (c); 3. (d); 4. (a); 5. (a); 6. (a); 7. (a); 8. (b); 9. (d); 10. (d)

REFERENCES

1. Brealey, R., Myers, S., & Allen, F., (2017). *Principles of Corporate Finance*. McGraw-Hill Education.
2. Brigham, E. F., & Houston, J. F., (2018). *Fundamentals of Financial Management*. Cengage Learning.
3. Copeland, T. E., Weston, J. F., & Shastri, K., (2004). *Financial Theory and Corporate Policy*. Pearson Education.
4. Damodaran, A., (2012). *Investment Valuation: Tools and Techniques for Determining the Value of Any Asset*. Wiley.
5. Fernandez, P., (2014). *Valuation Methods and Shareholder Value Creation*. Academic Press.
6. Harris, R. S., & Raviv, A., (2006). The capital asset pricing model: Theory and evidence. *Journal of Economic Perspectives, 10*(1), 3–22.
7. Modigliani, F., & Miller, M. H., (2008). The cost of capital, corporation finance, and the theory of investment. *The American Economic Review, 48*(3), 261–297.
8. Myers, S. C., & Majluf, N. S., (2004). Corporate financing and investment decisions when firms have information that investors do not have. *Journal of Financial Economics, 13*(2), 187–221.
9. Pratt, S. P., & Grabowski, R. J., (2018). *Cost of Capital: Applications and Examples*. Wiley.
10. *PricewaterhouseCoopers Risk Premium Study,* (2000). p. 12. Now the Standard & Poor's Corporate Value Consulting Risk Premium Reports.

12. Ross, S. A., Westerfield, R. W., Jordan, B. D., & Roberts, G. S., (2019). *Fundamentals of Corporate Finance.* McGraw-Hill Education.

13. *Stocks, Bonds, Bills & Inflation, Valuation Edition 2001 Yearbook* (p. 123), (2001). Chicago: Ibbotson Associates.

CHAPTER

4

Cash Management and Cash Analysis

LEARNING OBJECTIVES

After studying this chapter, you will be able to:

- Describe the cash management
- Focus on management of cash flows
- Identify the cash flow analysis

INTRODUCTORY EXAMPLE

POS Transaction: A POS transaction, or point of sale transaction, is a financial transaction that occurs at the point where a customer makes a purchase from a business. It involves the transfer of funds from the customer's payment method, such as a credit card or debit card, to the merchant's account.

These transactions typically take place in physical retail stores, but they can also occur online or through mobile payment systems. The purpose of a POS transaction is to facilitate the sale of goods or services and provide a record of the transaction for both the customer and the business.

To manage these transactions, businesses deploy a comprehensive system encompassing both software and hardware components, commonly referred to as POS or Point of Sale systems.

POS hardware typically includes elements such as a credit card reader, a cash register, or even a tablet. Simultaneously, the accompanying software diligently records transaction data and effectively integrates these sales into a company's financial records.

Here's a simplified breakdown of how a typical POS transaction works:

- **Step 1:** A customer shops for goods/products from a seller. Whether it's a retail store, restaurant, or online marketplace, the customer selects the items they wish to purchase.
- **Step 2:** The seller scans the goods/products and shares price information with the customer. Using a barcode scanner or manually entering the item details, the seller determines the total purchase amount and communicates it to the customer.
- **Step 3:** The buyer makes the payment. The customer selects their preferred payment method, such as a credit or debit card, mobile wallet, or cash. They provide the necessary information or physically hand over the payment to the seller.
- **Step 4:** A POS transaction is recorded. The point of sale system captures all the transaction details, including the purchase amount, payment method, date, and time. This information becomes a vital part of your financial records and provides insights for analysis and reporting.

It's important to note that while this is a simplified overview, the actual process may vary based on the specific point of sale system and payment methods used.

UNIT INTRODUCTION

The most crucial resource for business firms' operations is cash. It is both the final result for business operations and the fundamental input required to keep the business operating continuously. A business should always have enough cash on hand to cover its expenses because surplus cash will sit idle and deficiency cash will cause operational disruptions. Normally, every business firm holds 1 to 3 percent of its assets in the form of cash to enable itself to discharge its routine obligations such as payment of salaries, bills, day-to-day expenses, repayment of loans, dividends, interest, etc. A vital component of financial stewardship for any organization is cash management, which includes the tactics used to maximize the processing, application, and oversight of cash flows. Sustaining sufficient liquidity to fulfill immediate obligations and looking for ways to invest excess money for better returns are both essential components of effective cash management. It necessitates a careful examination of cash inflows and outflows, projection of cash requirements, and the application of policies to guarantee the best possible use of the available resources. In cash analysis, past cash flow data is examined closely in order to spot patterns and trends. Financial ratios like the current ratio and quick ratio are used to gauge liquidity. Businesses can build resilience and sustainable growth in dynamic economic environments by minimizing financing costs, capitalizing on investment opportunities, and enhancing their financial stability through the implementation of strong cash management practices and routine cash analysis.

4.1. CASH MANAGEMENT

→Learning Objectives

- To understand the objectives of cash management
- To discuss the scope of cash management
- To explain the importance of cash management
- To describe the motives for holding cash
- To define the factors determining level of cash
- To write the compensating balances
- To identify the cash management models

A broad area of finance that deals with the acquisition, handling, and application of cash is called cash management. It entails evaluating investments, cash flow, and market liquidity. Since cash is the most liquid form of current assets, managing it is one of the most crucial aspects of working capital management as a whole. Therefore, the finance function's job is to ensure that the business's various functional areas always have enough cash on hand when they need it. In addition, it must be made sure that the money is not blocked in the form of idle cash, as this incurs costs in the form of missed opportunities and interest. Therefore, the goal of cash management is to strike a balance between idle cash and these two extremes of cash shortage.

4.1.1. Objectives of Cash Management

To keep the organization's liquidity position appropriate, the main goal of cash management is to direct cash flow from surplus to deficit units. Furthermore, the goals of cash management can be broadly separated into two categories: preserving the organization's cash position to meet its present obligations and regulating the organization's cash inflow and outflow.

Other important objectives of cash management are discussed as follows:

- **Planning of Cash Flows**: refers to planning an organization's cash inflow and outflow over a given length of time. Cash flow planning aids in preserving a sufficient level of capital to support the organization's daily operations.
- **Synchronizing Cash Flows:** refers to creating a balance between the business's cash inflow and outflow. There would be no need to retain excess cash if the

amount of cash payments (outflow) equaled the amount of cash receipts (inflow).

- **Optimizing Cash Holding**: refers to figuring out how much cash the company should hold on hand to cover unforeseen expenses. The finance manager is responsible for determining the ideal cash holding to prevent either an excess or a shortage of cash.
- **Investing Idle Cash**: refers to making short-term investments with the idle cash held in the company. For a brief period of time, an organization can earn a respectable rate of return by investing its excess cash in marketable securities. Marketable securities have a high degree of liquidity and are readily convertible into cash at any time.

4.1.2. Scope of Cash Management

The term "cash management" describes an organized approach to managing the inflows and outflows of cash that arise from operating a business. Comprehending the fundamental principles of cash management can aid businesses in making plans for the unanticipated events that almost all companies encounter.

Keyword

Cash inflow is the money going into a business which could be from sales, investments, or financing. It's the opposite of cash outflow, which is the money leaving the business.

1. **Cash Planning**: Cash planning is a methodical approach to projecting the amount of money needed for a specific time frame, with the goal of keeping a healthy cash balance on hand to cover obligations and payments as they become due. Consequently, it involves projecting both cash inflows and outflows. A company needs to have positive cash flow, which is the opposite of negative long-term cash inflows.
2. **Managing Cash Flows**: The goal of cash planning is to keep a sufficient cash balance on hand to meet obligations and payments as they become due. It is a methodical approach to projecting the amount of money needed for a specific time frame. Forecasting of cash inflows and outflows is thus included. The job of putting policies and procedures regarding the inflow and outflow of cash into practice is known as managing cash inflows. It consists of short-term investment plans for times when there is a cash surplus and borrowing programs for times when there is a cash shortage.
3. **Optimum Cash Level**: "Cash optimization" refers to making something as flawless or efficient as feasible. Most businesses concentrate on cash flows, but they are challenging to manage. The ability to optimize and manage cash flows associated with the daily operations of the

business is more problematic than forecasting investments and payments to creditors and owners. Sound business practices, profitability, and survival all depend on efficient cash flow.

4. **Investing Idle Cash**: The company should think about investing in short-term marketable securities if it has excess cash balances available at specific times. However, if a company is regularly turning a profit, it ought to think about making longer-term, higher-yielding investments. But, as was already mentioned, a company must exercise caution and keep some cash on hand in case of unanticipated expenses or to benefit from discounts for on-time payments.

Remember

Cash is used as investment capital to be allocated to long-term assets, such as property, plant, and equipment (PP&E) and other non-current assets. Excess cash after accounting for expenses often goes towards dividend distributions.

4.1.3. Importance of Cash Management

The most liquid asset used to meet the firm's obligations is cash, which makes it one of the most important aspects of working capital management. However, because cash yields nothing, it is a sterile asset. In order to preserve the company's liquidity position without endangering profitability, the finance manager must manage cash. The difficulty in accurately projecting cash flows and the lack of perfect timing between cash inflows and outflows highlight the importance of cash management. In view of the above, at one time a firm may experience dearth of cash because payments of taxes, dividends, seasonal inventory, etc., build up while at other times, it may have surfeit of cash stemming out of large cash sales and quick collections of receivables. Interestingly, a finance manager in real life has to spend a lot of time managing cash, which makes up a small amount of the current assets of the company. This is the reason why several new methods have emerged in recent years to reduce the company's cash holdings.

4.1.4. Motives for Holding Cash

The businessmen hold cash for 3 motives, which are as follows:

1. **Transactions motive**: The cash manager's job is to set aside the appropriate amount of money at the appropriate time to pay for the appropriate purpose. In actuality, there will never be a synchronization between cash obligations and cash receipts. Therefore, in order to meet expenses on time, a company must maintain a comfortable level of cash on hand and hold the maximum amount of cash. The amount of cash balance that must be maintained increases with the size of business transactions, and vice versa.
2. **Precautionary motive**: Sometimes businesses need money

right away. In case of emergencies like machine failure, fire, theft, accidents, etc., they require cash; otherwise, they risk facing severe penalties. In these situations, financially strong companies can survive rather than failing. Thus, injuries, mishaps, theft, equipment failure, etc., demand cash right away in most organizations. The businesses must keep cash on hand to cover the aforementioned scenarios. We refer to this balance as the precautionary cash balance. They must therefore raise money quickly, sometimes even on their own. Only financially sound businesses with excellent credit will be able to endure the extreme circumstances mentioned above at that point.

3. **Speculative motive**: Of course, not every company engages in commerce for speculative purposes. Every company faces speculative conditions from time to time, like sharp and abrupt changes in raw material prices and interest rates that drive up the demand for goods. The abrupt increase in demand for the goods as a result calls for the quick availability of cash. Therefore, the speculative environment offers the potential to create profitable opportunities. Businesses that are able to turn a profit quickly will seize these uncertain business opportunities.

4.1.5. Factors Determining Level of Cash

The factors affecting or determining the cash requirements of a business are as follows:

1. **Timing of Cash Flows**: The requirement to maintain a cash balance results from the timing differences between cash inflows and outflows. When cash inflows and outflows are exactly equal, i.e., if they occur simultaneously, there wouldn't be a need to maintain a cash balance. When outflows of cash exceed inflows of cash, a cash balance must be maintained. Therefore, by projecting cash inflows and outflows, the amount of cash needed can be ascertained. A cash budget is used to forecast.
2. **Cash Shortage Costs**: The amount and times of cash shortages would be disclosed by the cash budget. There are costs associated with any cash shortage, which vary depending on the amount and length of the shortfall. Cash shortage costs are expenses incurred as a result of a cash shortage.

Examples of cash shortage costs are:

- Transaction cost relating to raising cash to tide over the shortage such as brokerage etc., for sale of marketable securities.
- Borrowing costs like interest etc., for borrowing to cover the shortage,
- Penal interest charged by banks due to shortfall in compensating or minimum balances in the bank.
- Costs due to deterioration of credit rating like shortage in the supply of raw-material, less favorable terms offered by suppliers and so on.
- Loss of cash discount because of non-payment in time due to shortage of cash. Cash shortage costs should also be considered along with cash shortage itself in determining cash needs.

3. **Cash Excess Costs**: A company will lose out on opportunities to invest its excess cash if it holds more than it needs. It will consequently lose interest that it could have made by investing extra money somewhere else. The amount of cash that should be on hand shouldn't be decided upon excessively because this factor should also be taken into account.
4. **Cash Management Costs**: Costs associated with cash management include salary and other clerical expenses of employees in cash management. This factor should also be taken into account when determining cash need.
5. **Uncertainty**: Cash flows are never entirely predictable, and there is always some degree of uncertainty in the forecast due to things like unanticipated debtor delays. A firm must always have some extra cash on hand to cover these unforeseen expenses.
6. **Firm's Capacity to Borrow in Emergent Situations**: A company can maintain a low level of cash if it can borrow money quickly in an emergency. Numerous factors, including the company's relationship with banks, credit standing, and other factors, affect its ability to borrow money.
7. **Attitude of Management**: The level of cash is influenced by the management's perspective on profitability and liquidity. The amount of cash on hand will be large if management values liquidity over profitability. Conversely, there won't be as much cash on hand if profitability takes precedence over liquidity.
8. **Efficiency of Management**: The management can maintain a low level of cash if it can speed up customer cash collection and slow down cash disbursement.

4.1.6. Compensating Balances

Compensating balances are the cash in bank accounts that are required to make up for the services that banks provide to businesses. Any bank requires a minimum balance to be kept in the account in order to operate and maintain a current account or savings account. To a business concern, that is referred to as compensating balances. A bank will typically determine the compensating balance after taking into account the account's operating expenses and revenue. The bank charges a minimum balance for a number of services it provides to its customers in order to earn interest and partially offset the cost of the free services the bank provides to its customers. "Relate the cash balance to the amount needed to keep one's banker happy" is one way to calculate the compensating balance from a business perspective. This brings to mind a simple procedure of trial and error to determine minimum cash level. Every three months reduce the average bank balance by 5%. Keep doing this until a bank officer calls to find out what has happened. At that point you know you have a working cash level which if not maintained, will cause you to be unpopular at the bank.

4.1.7. Cash Management Models

Several mathematical models, including the operating cycle model (a), inventory model (b), stochastic model (c), and probability model (d), have also been developed to determine the ideal cash balance. However, the Inventory Model as developed by William J. Baumol and the Stochastic Model of M. H. Miller and Daniel Orr are mainly used to determine the optimum balance of cash. William J. Baumol developed a model which is usually used in inventory management but has its application in determining the optimal cash balance also. Baumol discovered that cash management and inventory management are similar. In inventory management, the optimal cash balance is the trade-off between the transaction cost and the opportunity cost, or the cost of borrowing or holding cash. This is because Economic Order Quantity (EOQ) involves a trade-off between carrying costs and ordering costs. (i.e., the cost of converting marketable securities into cash etc.) The optimal cash balance is reached at a point where the total cost is the minimum.

Keyword

Economic order quantity (EOQ) refers to the ideal order quantity a company should purchase in order to minimize its inventory costs.

The Baumol model is based upon the following assumptions:

- The cash needs of the firm are known with certainty.
- The cash disbursements (usage) of the firm occur uniformly over a period of time and is known with certainty.
- The opportunity cost of holding cash is known and it remains constant.
- The transaction cost of converting securities into cash is known and remains constant.

The Baumol model can also be represented algebrically:

$$C = \sqrt{\frac{2A \times F}{O}}$$

Where;

C = Optimum balance

A = Annual (or monthly) cash disbursements

F = Fixed cost per transaction

O = Opportunity cost of holding cash.

Did you get it?

1. **Write the cash shortage costs.**
2. **Identify the cash excess costs.**

4.2. MANAGEMENT OF CASH FLOWS

→Learning Objectives

- Evaluate the methods of accelerating cash inflows
- Focus on methods of slowing cash outflows
- Describe the factors determining cash flow
- Discuss on advantages of ample cash

A finance manager must make sure that cash is coming in and going out according to plan in order to effectively manage cash. This calls for comparing actual performance to pre-established plans and objectives, identifying any discrepancies, examining variations in those discrepancies to identify the root causes, and then implementing corrective action to address the anomaly. A cash budget report makes all of this possible. In addition, effective cash management calls for faster cash inflows and slower cash outflows.

There are various methods of speeding cash collections and delaying payments. We shall now discuss each of these methods below:

4.2.1. Methods of Accelerating Cash Inflows

1. **Prompt Payment by Customers**: The prompt collection of payments from customers is necessary to boost cash flows. Prompt billing will make this feasible. It is better if a self-addressed envelope is sent with the bill and a prompt response is requested. Customers should be promptly informed about the amount payable and the deadline for payment. Offering a cash discount to clients is another way to encourage them to make an early payment. The customer saves money when a discount is available, and they pay quickly out of a sense of urgency to receive it.
2. **Quick Conversion of Payment into Cash**: Enhancing the cash collection procedure can speed up cash inflows. Early collection can expedite the collection process once the customer writes a check payable to the concern. The amount collected against the customer's check and the check itself are not the same thing. This is due to many factors, (i) mailing time, i.e. time taken by post office for transferring check from customer to the firm (ii) time taken in processing the check within the organization and sending it bank for collection, (iii) collection time within the bank, i.e. time taken by the bank in collecting the payment from the customer's bank, called bank float.

3. **Decentralized Collections**: By employing the decentralized collections system, a large company with a broad geographic reach can expedite collections. Instead of gathering receipts in one location, several collecting centers are opened in various locations. The goal of setting up multiple collection points is to shorten the time it takes for a customer's check to be sent, for it to be received by the company, and for it to be collected. The check is sent for collection as soon as it is received.
4. **Lock Box System**: A lock box system is an additional method to cut down on the time spent mailing, processing, and collecting. The company chooses a few collection points at various locations under this system. The number of customers and the amount of remittances expected from each location are taken into consideration when choosing the locations. It is requested of the parties to send their checks to the post office box number that the firm rents. The post box can only be used by a local bank. The bank will begin the check collection process by picking up the mail several times a day. The sum thus obtained is credited to the business's account. For the purpose of processing the checks, the bank will compile a thorough record of all the checks it has received. Cheque collection is accelerated by this method, which also prevents delays from the accounting department's processing and mailing times.

4.2.2. Methods of Slowing Cash Outflows

A company can maintain cash flow by managing payments well. Slowing down payments as much as possible is the goal of cash outflow control. Following methods can be used to delay disbursements:

1. **Paying on Last Date**: Payments may be withheld until the very last day of the due date. Only the tenth day should be used for payment if the credit is for ten days. Short-term use of the funds can be beneficial, and the company can take advantage of cash discounts.
2. **Payments through Drafts**: Through the use of drafts rather than checks, a business can postpone payments to its suppliers. In order to ensure that the check is paid when it arrives, the business must maintain a balance in its account at the time of issuance. However, a draft can only be paid upon presentation to the issuer. For presentation to the buyer's bank, the receiver will deliver the draft to its bank. Prior to being deposited into the bank, it takes several days. If it is able to accurately estimate this float, the company can utilize it.
3. **Adjusting Payroll Funds**: Payroll funds can also be used more sparingly. This can be accomplished by extending the payment period to one month if the payments are currently made on a weekly basis. The finance manager has the ability to schedule the issuance and distribution of salary checks. Only a small number of the checks may be presented for payment if they are issued on a Saturday; in fact,

not all of the checks may be presented on Monday. The **Finance Manager** can deposit the funds in the bank based on his prior experience, as he may be aware of the typical time taken by staff members to cash their paychecks.

4. **Centralization of Payments**: Payments ought to be made via drafts or checks, and they ought to be centralized. The process of having checks cleared by the mail takes time when they are issued from the main office. One benefits from the time allotted for collecting checks.
5. **Interbank Transfer**: Interbank transfers also provide for an effective use of cash. Amounts can be transferred to the bank where payments are to be made if the company has accounts with multiple banks. It will assist in preventing too much money in one bank.
6. **Making use of Float**: Float is the difference between the balance in the bank's pass book and the balance displayed in the company's cash book (Bank column). The amount in the bank's cash book is deducted each time a check is written. The recipient of the check is not required to present it for payment right away. The check will arrive by mail if the party is at a different station, and it might take several days for it to be presented. There will be money in the bank until the checks are not presented to the bank for payment. If the business can accurately estimate this float, it can utilize it.

Keyword

Financial Manager is a key decision-maker in an organization. They use data analysis and advise senior managers on profit-maximizing ideas, which can help optimize company profits over time by making intelligent decisions for investments or spending funds to have the greatest return on investment.

4.2.3. Factors Determining Cash Flow

The Cash flow depends upon on the following factors:

- **Operating Decisions**: Managerial decisions regarding all the attributes of profit affect cash flow.
- **Capital Expenditure Decisions**: The acquisition or disposal of long-lasting assets results in depreciation charges against profits.
- **Inventory Decisions**: Changes in the amounts tied up in stocks increase or decrease the cash flow.
- **Customer Credit Policies**: An increase in customer credit delays the cash inflow, but reduction in credit accelerates it.
- **Supplier Credit Policies**: An increase in supplier credit creates a positive cash flow, for it decelerates the cash outflow. Reduction in supplier credit accelerates the cash outflow.

- **Financial Obligations**: Interest and dividend payments and other contractual repayments have an impact on cash flow.
- **Investing Decisions**: The utilization of surplus funds or, conversely, the liberation of funds, affects cash flow.
- **Financing Decision**: The acquisition of additional capital on a long term or short term basis has an impact on the cash flow.

Did you know?

In 1992, the International Accounting Standards Board issued International Accounting Standard 7 (IAS 7), Cash Flow Statement, which became effective in 1994, mandating that firms provide cash flow statements.

4.2.4. Advantages of Ample Cash

We are aware that operating a business requires cash flow. The foundation of any business is cash. Without money, no business can thrive. Therefore, one of a financial manager's main duties is cash planning. A firm having sufficient cash balance can drive the several advantage some of them are listed below:

1. **Increase in Goodwill**: A company's goodwill or reputation is largely dependent on its ability to pay off all of its debts and retire all obligations as they become due. It is only feasible if the company keeps a healthy cash balance.
2. **Cash Discount**: Cash discounts are obtained when we pay with cash, and only businesses with sufficient cash on hand are eligible to take advantage of these deals from suppliers. Both the cost of production and the cost of raw materials will decrease. Therefore, a decrease in production costs will inevitably result in an increase in profit margin.
3. **Good Bank Relations**: Commercial banks prefer to have positive relationships with businesses that have a lot of cash on hand. These businesses can obtain bank credit facilities at fair interest rates.
4. **Encouragement to Investors**: The dividends are typically paid out in cash. Only cash dividends are preferred by investors. An adequate cash balance is also necessary for a company to pay a high cash dividend. A company can continue to have a sound cash dividend policy if it has a healthy cash position. Because shareholders are drawn to cash dividends, this encourages investors to purchase shares of these companies.
5. **Exploitation of Favorable Market Conditions**: Only businesses with sufficient cash on hand can take advantage of advantageous market circumstances, such as buying necessities in bulk at a discount and holding onto inventory for a future increase in price.
6. **Ability to Face Crisis**: Since working capital is typically under a lot of strain during business crises like depression, having enough cash on hand helps an organization weather such storms. Therefore, a company with adequate working capital can deal with challenging business circumstances with ease.
7. **High Efficiency and Morale**: A sufficient flow of cash is necessary for production to proceed efficiently.

Labor efficiency rises when the production process runs uninterrupted. Sufficient funds also boost morale. A business with an adequate cash balance feels secure, confident, and has high morale, all of which contribute to overall efficiency. As was already mentioned, having enough money allows us to pay salaries and wages on schedule, which will boost employee morale as well.

Did you get it?

1. **How do businesses monitor and analyze their cash flows?**
2. **What are the key components of cash flow management strategies?**
3. **How do businesses optimize cash inflows and outflows to ensure liquidity and financial stability?**

4.3. CASH FLOW ANALYSIS

→Learning Objectives

- To understand statement of cash flow in a business's financial statements
- To describe uses of cash flow
- To execute the process of replacement projects
- Analysis with reference of project's net cash flows
- Write the sunk costs
- Define opportunity costs
- Discuss on externality in economics
- Define the tax rate
- Understand tax depreciation procedures and the effect of depreciation on the firm's cash flows.
- Identify the cash flow analysis techniques

Cash flow analysis is a vital financial tool that provides insights into the inflows and outflows of cash within an organization over a specific period. By scrutinizing cash flow statements, businesses can gain a comprehensive understanding of their liquidity, solvency, and overall financial health. The analysis typically involves categorizing cash flows into three main activities: operating, investing, and financing. Operating cash flows represent the cash generated or used in the core operations of the business, including revenue from sales, payments to suppliers, and operating expenses. Investing cash flows pertain to the purchase or sale of long-term assets, such as property, equipment, or investments in securities, which can significantly impact the organization's capital structure and future growth prospects. Financing cash flows encompass transactions related to the company's capital structure, including proceeds from issuing stock or debt, repayment of loans, and payment of dividends to shareholders. Through cash flow analysis, businesses can evaluate their ability to generate cash from core operations, assess their investment and financing decisions, and identify potential cash flow constraints or opportunities. Furthermore, comparing cash flow trends over multiple periods allows companies to identify patterns, assess the effectiveness of financial strategies, and make informed decisions to enhance cash flow management and optimize resource allocation. Ultimately, a thorough cash flow analysis enables businesses to maintain adequate liquidity, support strategic initiatives, mitigate financial risks, and navigate economic uncertainties with resilience and confidence, thereby fostering long-term sustainability and success in today's dynamic business landscape.

4.3.1. Statement of Cash Flow in a Business's Financial Statements

A company's estimated net cash flow is shown in its statement of cash flows. When a company's cash balance changes over a given period of time (usually a quarter or a year), its net cash flow is equal to that change. It is positive when the cash balance rises because more cash is available, and it is negative when it falls.

Remember

Just because you may have the cash for a new purchase doesn't mean that you can afford it. For example, if you hire new employees, you must be able to pay them while paying your bills, loan payments, and upkeep.

- **Operational cash flows**: Money obtained or spent as a consequence of internal business operations for the company. This covers adjustments to working capital in addition to cash earnings. If the company is to stay solvent, this needs to be net positive over the medium term.
- **Investment cash flows**: Money received from the sale of long-term assets or used to finance capital purchases like long-term assets, investments, and acquisitions.
- **Financing cash flows**: Money received through debt and equity issuance, or distributed as debt repayments, dividends, or share buybacks.

4.3.2. Uses of Cash Flow

Cash flow factors can be used for calculating parameters, such as:

- to ascertain the value or rate of return of a project. Financial models like net present value and internal rate of return utilize the cash flows into and out of projects as inputs.
- to identify liquidity issues within a company. Being liquid does not always equate to profitability. Even a profitable business can fail due to a cash flow crisis.
- as a substitute indicator of a company's profitability in cases where accrual accounting principles are thought to be inaccurate in representing the state of the economy. For instance, a business that barters its goods rather than selling them for cash may be conceptually profitable but producing little operating cash flow. In this scenario, the business might be raising more debt financing or issuing shares to generate operating cash.
- can assess the "quality" of revenue produced by accrual

accounting. It is deemed low quality when a significant portion of net income comes from non-cash items.

- to evaluate the risks within a financial product (e.g., matching cash requirements, evaluating default risk, re-investment requirements, etc.)

The term "cash flow" is generic and can be used in a variety of contexts. Users may define it according to their own needs. It can be used to describe predicted future flows or real past flows. It can be used to describe a subset of the involved flows or the total of all involved flows.

4.3.3. Replacement Projects

A replacement project is an endeavor in which the business replaces an investment with a project that is being phased out at the end of its life. The process of capital budgeting and subsequent project management requires consideration of replacement project possibilities. An endeavor known as a replacement project is one in which the business ends a project and replaces it with a new investment. This replacement project can be used to replace an investment that is about to expire with a new one that is exactly the same or to replace an investment that is currently in place but isn't working well with one that management thinks will work better. The projected cash flows of a project are the main consideration when evaluating it and, in the end, determining whether or not to invest in it. These cash flows serve as the foundation for the project's value, typically following the application of a discounted cash flow analysis technique. A project's useful life is usually limited. Analysis can be done to ascertain whether replacement is a feasible option at all and to ascertain when the best time to replace will be. This is achieved by comparing the projected cash flows from the replacement project to the cash flows of the ongoing project.

4.3.4. Analysis

A project's net cash flows include project-generated income and expenses as well as more indirect effects like opportunity costs, sunk costs, and project-related depreciation costs. When management takes into account all of these factors, it can evaluate the project's incremental cash flows, or the inflows and outflows the project generates over predictable time periods.

Discounted cash flow analysis ought to be done for the prospective replacement project as well as the current one. These analyzes can then be used to compare the projected profitability of the two projects, which should help management decide which investments to make. As a general rule, there will be a cash inflow to start the new project and an outflow to conclude the previous one. An example of this would be the terminal value realized upon selling the current equipment.

The loss of expected future cash flows from the previous project, or opportunity cost, must also be taken into account. A general form that can be used to analyze these cash flows is:

Increase in Net Income + (Depreciation on New Investment – Depreciation on Old Investment)

4.3.5. Sunk Costs

Sunk costs are expenses incurred after the fact that are not recouped and are therefore not relevant when making decisions about future investments in the project that incurred them. Sunk costs are costs incurred in retrospect that are unrecoverable because they have already occurred. Prospective costs, or future expenses that might be incurred or altered in the event that a decision is made, are occasionally contrasted with sunk costs.

1. **Impact on Investment Decision:** Sunk cost analysis is a common tool used in business decision analysis. According to conventional microeconomic theory, an investment decision should only take prospective (future) costs into consideration. When it comes time to market a pharmaceutical product, for instance, the research and development are done after the fact. Such expenses are sunk once incurred and ought not to influence pricing decisions in the future. The company will charge market prices whether R&D had cost one dollar or one million dollars. Therefore, the costs of R&D are considered sunk once they are retrospective and irrecoverable. At that point, they have no rational bearing on further investment decisions.

Keyword

Sunk cost is a cost that has already been incurred and cannot be recovered. Sunk costs are contrasted with prospective costs, which are future costs that may be avoided if action is taken.

2. **Difference from Economic Loss:** Economic loss is not the same as the sunk cost. For instance, after being bought, an automobile can be sold again, but most likely not for the original asking price. The difference between these values (including transaction costs) represents the economic loss. Regardless of the car's resale value, the amount originally paid shouldn't influence any sane decisions made about it in the future. Notwithstanding the amount received, the car should be sold if the owner can gain more value from doing so than from keeping it unsold. In this sense, the term "sunk cost" refers to an economic amount paid in the past that is no longer significant for making decisions about the future, rather than a precise figure. Either the initial cost or the anticipated financial loss may be referred to as the "sunk cost." It can also be used as shorthand for irrational decision-making, irrelevant data, or an analysis error brought on by the sunk cost fallacy.

4.3.6. Opportunity Costs

Opportunity cost is the value that is lost when deciding between two options that are mutually exclusive. Opportunity cost is any activity's cost expressed as the value of the next best option lost (that is not chosen). Put another way, it refers to the giving up of the second-best option accessible to an individual or group that has selected one of several options that are mutually exclusive.

1. **Economic Concept:** An important idea in economics is opportunity cost, which connects the mutual exclusion of choices and the scarcity of resources. Making sure that

limited resources are distributed effectively depends heavily on the idea of opportunity cost. The true cost of output lost, lost time, pleasure, or any other benefit that provides utility are all regarded as implicit opportunity costs, so they are not limited to monetary or financial costs or chance, expenses. Opportunity cost in cash flow analysis refers to the cash flow that the organization could have from its existing assets if they are not utilized for the project at hand. Determining how to allocate assets always involves some trade-offs.

2. **Assessing Opportunity Cost:** Opportunity cost is evaluated in terms of anything that has value to the decision maker in addition to money or material considerations. For instance, someone who wants to watch both of the concurrently airing television shows but is only able to record one can only watch the desired program. As a result, missing out on a college football game could be the opportunity cost of watching an NFL football game, or vice versa.

4.3.7. Externalities

An externality is a result of an economic activity where someone not involved in the transaction bears the expense or benefit. An externality in economics is a cost or benefit that is borne by a party other than the buyer or seller of the goods or services and is not transferred through prices.

The cost of an externality is a negative externality, or external cost, while the benefit of an externality is a positive externality, or external benefit.

1. **Relation to Prices:** Prices in a competitive market do not fully reflect the costs or benefits of producing or consuming a good or service, in the case of both positive and negative externalities. It is not possible for producers and consumers to split the entire cost and benefit of an economic activity.

2. **Over- and Under-Production:** Any voluntary exchange is advantageous to both parties involved, according to standard economic theory. This is due to the fact that if either party believed trading was not advantageous, neither would engage in it. On the other hand, an exchange might have unintended consequences for other people. Individuals who incur external expenses do so willingly, whereas those who gain benefits from external sources do so for free. If there are external costs, a voluntary exchange could lower the overall economic benefit. When someone is impacted by negative externalities like air pollution, they may experience lowered utility in the form of explicit costs like increased medical costs or subjective discomfort. Conversely, a positive externality would enhance third parties' utility at no additional expense to them. Less of the good will be produced than would be ideal for society as a whole since the welfare of society as a whole is increased but the providers are unable to profit from it. For instance, air pollution-causing manufacturing costs society as a whole, but public education benefits society as a whole. A competitive market will cause the good to be overproduced if there are external costs, such as

pollution, since the producer will not account for these costs when producing the good. Too little of the good would be produced by private markets if there are external benefits, such as in the field of education, since producers and buyers do not account for the benefits to other parties. The total of all parties' economic gains and expenses is what is referred to as the overall cost and benefit to society in this context.

Keyword

Competitive market is a theoretical economic term to define a market where there is a large number of buyers and sellers and none has the ability to affect the market individually.

3. **"Free Rider" Problem:** Positive externalities are often associated with the free rider problem. For example, individuals who are vaccinated reduce the risk of contracting the relevant disease for all others around them, and at high levels of vaccination, society may receive large health and welfare benefits. Conversely, any one individual can refuse vaccination, still avoiding the disease by "free riding" on the costs borne by others.
4. **Market Correction:** The market-driven method of addressing externalities is to "internalize" the costs and benefits to third parties. One way to do this is by making polluters pay for any harm they cause. However, internalizing costs or benefits is frequently impractical, particularly when it is impossible to ascertain their true monetary values.

4.3.8. Tax Rate

The amount of tax stated as a percentage is known as the tax rate. The tax rate in a given system denotes the proportion at which an individual or business is subject to taxes.

- *Methods*

There are several methods used to present a tax rate:

i. statutory
ii. average
iii. marginal
iv effective

i. Statutory: The tax rate imposed by law is known as the statutory rate. In contrast to sales taxes, which may have a flat statutory rate, income taxes may have multiple statutory rates for various income levels.

ii. Average: The ratio of taxes paid to the tax base (taxable income or spending) is known as the average tax rate. Divide the total tax liability by the taxable income to determine the average tax rate on an income tax.

iii. **Marginal:** A marginal tax rate is the tax rate that is applied to the final dollar of the tax base, which can be spending or taxable income. It is frequently used to explain how one's tax obligation changes as income increases. This rate can be ascertained for an individual by altering their income earned or spent and computing the resulting change in taxes due. The range of income for which a specific marginal tax rate is applicable is known as an individual's tax bracket. Although the tax rate is generally progressive in most nations, the marginal tax rate may change as income or consumption rises. The average tax rate will be less than the marginal tax rate in these circumstances. For example, a person may pay half as much in average taxes even though their marginal tax rate is 45%. Every taxpayer, regardless of income or consumption, pays the same percentage of income in a jurisdiction with a flat tax on earnings. Proponents of this system suggest removing the flat tax from an initial $10,000 or other fixed amount of earnings. In addition to the corresponding tax brackets, marginal tax rates can be found explicitly in published tax tables that breakdown taxes by income. It can be computed by observing the relationship between tax and changes in pre-tax income as opposed to taxable income.

iv. **Effective:** When used by different sources or in different contexts, the term "effective tax rate" can mean quite different things. In general, it means that a certain amount of income or other tax base is divided by a certain amount of tax. In U.S. income tax law, the term is used in relation to determining whether a foreign income tax on specific types of income exceeds a certain percentage of U.S. tax that might apply on such income. The term "tax divide" has been used inconsistently by the popular press, the Congressional Budget Office, and think tanks to refer to different tax measures divided by different income measures. An effective tax rate can be entirely derived from simulations or assumptions, or it can include econometric, estimated, or assumed adjustments to actual data. It also includes tax exemptions or breaks.

4.3.9. Depreciation

Depreciation is the method by which an asset's value is dispersed over time and used up. Depreciation is a term used to describe two very different but related concepts: the reduction in asset value (fair value depreciation) and the distribution of asset cost over the life of the asset (depreciation with matching principle).

i. **Fair Value Depreciation:** The values of entities and businesses are impacted by fair value depreciation. A reasonable and objective assessment of the potential market price of a good, service, or asset that takes into consideration the price at which the asset could be purchased or sold in a current transaction between willing parties is what is meant to be understood by this concept, which is used in accounting and economics.

ii. **Allocation of Cost with Matching Principle:** Net income is impacted by how an asset's cost is distributed among its use periods. Any enterprise or source of revenue that relies on material assets has expenses associated with those assets. The appropriate costs must be deducted from the activity's receipts in order to calculate the net income. The cost of assets used in the activity but not yet consumed is one example of such a cost. These expenses need to be broken down by the time of use. The matching principle of accrual accounting requires that costs be deferred rather than recognized as current expenses when assets generate benefits in later periods. The depreciation expense is documented by the business for the purpose of financial reporting. The expenses are logically and methodically distributed as a depreciation expense to each of the asset's use periods, starting from the point at which it is put into service.

Generally, this involves four criteria:

- the cost of the asset
- the expected salvage value, also known as residual value of the asset
- the estimated useful life of the asset
- a method of apportioning the cost over such life. The cost of an asset so allocated is the difference between the amount paid for the asset and the salvage value.

Methods: Any technique for distributing net cost to the times when the asset is anticipated to be used is called depreciation. Usually, the cost is divided among the anticipated use periods of the asset as a depreciation expense. Businesses recognize this kind of expense for tax and financial reporting purposes. For the same business, different depreciation methods may apply to different assets. Techniques may be outlined in a nation's tax or accounting regulations.

Several standard methods of computing depreciation expense may be used, including:

- fixed percentage
- straight line
- declining balance method

Depreciation expense generally begins when the asset is placed in service. For instance, a depreciation expense of 100 dollars per year for 5 years may be recognized for an asset costing 500 dollars.

4.3.10. Cash Flow Analysis Techniques

The income statement and statement of cash flows are two financial statements that companies prepare as part of their monthly accounting cycle. A company's profit or net income is displayed on the income statement, and its cash position is displayed on the statement of cash flows. The difference between a company's cash available at the start and end of an accounting period is its cash flow at any given point in time. The cash is used to cover operating costs, direct expenses, principal debt service, and the acquisition of assets like equipment. It also comes from loan proceeds, investment income, and asset sales. Money is everything when running a small business. On paper, you could be profitable, but financially strapped. Should that be your situation, you may be at risk of losing your clientele.

- **How to Do a Cash Flow Analysis:** Cash is the gasoline that makes your business run. A cash flow analysis is a method for checking up on your firm's financial health. It is the study of the movement of cash through your business, also called a cash budget, to determine patterns of how you take in and pay out money.

- **The Difference between a Cash Budget and a Statement of Cash Flows:** Keeping track of cash flow is essential for the survival of your small business. However, accountants sometimes speak about the cash budget and a more comprehensive statement of cash flows.
- **Preparing and Analyzing a Statement of Cash Flows:** Analyzing a statement of cash flows involves looking at the sources and uses of funds from the comparative balance sheets, which allows a company to better see its future cash needs.
- **Calculate Your Company's Free Cash Flow:** One of the most significant findings from the examination of the cash flow statement for a small business owner is the free cash flow calculation. In short, free cash flow is the amount of money left over after a business pays for any capital expenses, such as purchasing new machinery or plants. The benchmark for the financial stability of your business is free cash flow. To strengthen your cash flow analysis, include a review of your company's free cash flow.

Did you get it?

1. **How does cash flow analysis differ from other financial analyzes, such as income statement or balance sheet analysis?**
2. **What are the primary components of cash flow analysis, and how are they calculated?**

A CLOSER LOOK

"Maintaining free access to cash for the community demands robust strategies to mitigate the escalating costs incurred by banks and ATM operators in handling cash. A pivotal step in this direction is modernizing cash management systems to foster efficiency and reduce operational costs. To reconcile the demand for free access to cash with the requisite cost reductions, banks are increasingly turning towards tech-driven solutions in cash management that elevate service levels while driving down expenses.

Source: https://www.financederivative.com/the-future-of-banking-streamlined-cash-management-or-atms/.

Operating a vast ATM network can be a double-edged sword for banks, simultaneously offering customer convenience and engendering considerable challenges, including substantial cash handling, management, transit, and security costs. Each ATM embodies a multifaceted operation involving numerous cash transfer operatives, necessitating a coordinated strategy to forestall costly inefficiencies.

The remedy is a holistic, data-centric approach to streamline the management of intricate ATM networks and counter the escalating costs associated with cash access. The merits of such an approach, grounded in continuous data collection and analysis across ATM networks, encompass:

- **Strategic Planning**: Leveraging real-time data to craft bespoke strategies for individual branches or regions, assuring optimal cash flow management and averting superfluous cash loading orders.
- **Operational Transparency**: Facilitating stakeholders with instantaneous access to accounting and operational data relating to cash supply chains, thereby enabling timely interventions and adaptations.
- **Enhanced Customer Experience**: Minimizing ATM downtimes to guarantee uninterrupted cash access to customers, enhancing their banking experience.

The answer lies in a series of sophisticated features that employ cutting-edge predictive analytics, automation, and data-driven decision-making:

- **Predictive Analysis**: Forward-thinking solutions predict cash necessities of distinct units, offering precise demand and cash flow projections by considering variables such as seasonal fluctuations, holidays, and daily usage trends.
- **Automation and Monitoring**: Swapping manual processes or basic mathematical functions with modern software solutions for cash management ushers in real-time monitoring and efficient intervention planning, which can potentially diminish order management costs by a significant margin, whilst improving precision and operational fluidity.
- **Optimized Cash Transit Management**: Utilizing predictive analytics to strategically plan cash restocks, thereby reducing the likelihood of ATMs depleting their cash reserves and improving customer satisfaction.
- **Data-Driven Decision** Making: Availing a comprehensive dashboard to generate timely reports and monitor critical metrics facilitates strategic decision-making grounded in accurate data, substantially reducing residual cash stock in ATMs.

As the financial landscape evolves, banks and financial institutions are impelled to adapt and innovate. Traditional cash management approaches are increasingly becoming outdated, paving the way for modern, data-driven solutions. These not only embody a commitment to technological advancement but also signify a strategic movement towards future readiness.

CASE STUDY

EFFECTIVE CASH FLOW MANAGEMENT IN THE B2B SEGMENT

In the competitive landscape of the B2B segment, managing cash flow effectively is paramount to the success and stability of businesses. Today, we present a compelling case study of a company that not only conquered its cash flow challenges but also experienced remarkable growth in collections and the ability to pay advance salaries on EID ul Adha, a significant religious holiday. By implementing a comprehensive cash flow management plan, they achieved a 30% increase in collection rates. This case study serves as a shining example for other companies facing similar cash flow obstacles.

Source: https://imageio.forbes.com/specials-images/imageserve/6495e772d91603578e8f46c2/0x0.jpg?format=jpg&height=900&width=1600&fit=bounds.

1. **The Cash Flow Challenge:** Many businesses in the B2B segment face the hurdle of extended credit periods, which strain cash flow and create financial crunches. Our featured company, a pest control and cleaning business, was no exception. Operating on a credit period of 60 to 90 days, they encountered difficulties in meeting financial obligations, especially when faced with the need to pay advance salaries due to EID Ul Adha.
2. **The Cash Flow Conundrum: Understanding Cash Flow Dynamics:** Cash flow represents the movement of money into and out of a business. It is the lifeblood that sustains a company's operations and determines its financial health. When cash flows smoothly, businesses thrive; however, challenges arise when cash flow becomes irregular or insufficient.
   - **The Importance of Cash Flow Management:** Effectively managing cash flow is vital for a business's financial health. It ensures that the company

has enough cash on hand to meet its financial obligations, such as salary payments and supplier invoices. Additionally, proper cash flow management allows businesses to capitalize on growth opportunities while providing a safety net for unexpected financial hurdles.

- **The Challenge: Extended Credit Periods:** Extended credit periods pose a significant challenge in the B2B segment. Although businesses provide services upfront, they often experience delays in receiving payments for a considerable duration, ranging from 60 to 90 days. This delay in cash inflow creates a cash flow crunch, forcing businesses to cover operational expenses, including salaries, before receiving payment for their services.
- **The Additional Challenge: Early Salary Payments:** In the case of the pest control and cleaning company, they faced an extra challenge of paying salaries almost 10 days earlier than usual due to the religious holiday, EID ul Adha. This further intensified the pressure on their cash flow, demanding sufficient funds to cover these early salary payments.

3. **The Solution: Effective Cash Flow Management:** Thankfully, businesses can implement several strategies and techniques to manage cash flow effectively. By addressing the challenges head-on, businesses can enhance their cash flow, achieve greater financial stability, and steer themselves towards success. The following approaches can help:

- **Understanding Credit Terms: The First Step to Improved Cash Flow:** Credit terms refer to the conditions under which lenders extend credit to borrowers. In the B2B segment, these terms typically dictate the period within which clients must pay for the services provided.

Extended credit periods create a strain on cash flow since businesses have to rely on their own funds to cover operational expenses until payments are received. Renegotiating credit terms can significantly alleviate this pressure and improve cash flow.

- **Implementing a Rolling Forecast: Your Crystal Ball into the Future:** A rolling forecast is an invaluable financial tool for predicting future cash flow based on existing and projected transactions. By examining historical data, businesses can anticipate and prevent cash flow crunches proactively.
- **Leveraging Technology: Your Best Friend in Cash Flow Management:** In today's digital age, technology plays a crucial role in streamlining financial processes and optimizing cash flow management. By adopting accounting software that automates invoicing and collections, businesses can expedite cash conversion cycles and access real-time financial data.
- **Establishing a Cash Reserve: Your Safety Net in Times of C**ash Flow Crunches: Establishing a cash reserve acts as a financial safety net for businesses. By setting aside a portion of profits to cover unexpected expenses or financial challenges, businesses gain stability and flexibility in managing their cash flow effectively.

SUMMARY

- Cash management refers to a broad area of finance involving the collection, handling, and usage of cash. It involves assessing market liquidity, cash flow, and investments.
- Cash management refers to a systematic way of handling cash inflows and outflows resulting from business operations.
- Cash planning is a systematic way of forecasting the cash requirements for a given period with an objective to maintain adequate cash balance in hand, sufficient to meet the payments and obligations as and when they mature.
- Cash management is one of the critical areas of working capital management and assumes greater significance because it is the most liquid asset used to satisfy the firm's obligations but it is a sterile asset as it does not yield anything.
- A replacement project is an undertaking in which the company eliminates a project at the end of its life and substitutes another investment. The possibility of replacement projects must be taken into account during the process of capital budgeting and subsequent project management.
- Sunk costs are retrospective costs that cannot be recovered, and are therefore irrelevant to future investment decisions in the project which incurs them. Sunk costs are retrospective costs that have already been incurred and cannot be recovered.
- An externality is an effect of an economic action, the cost or benefit of which is shouldered by someone outside the transaction. In economics, an externality is a cost or benefit that is not transmitted through prices and is incurred by a party who was not involved as either a buyer or seller of the goods or services.
- A statutory tax rate is the legally imposed rate. An income tax could have multiple statutory rates for different income levels, whereas a sales tax may have a flat statutory rate.
- A cash flow analysis is a method for checking up on your firm's financial health. It is the study of the movement of cash through your business, also called a cash budget, to determine patterns of how you take in and pay out money.

REVIEW QUESTIONS

1. What is cash management, and why is it important for businesses?
2. Describe the overall cash flow through the firm in terms of cash flow from operating activities, cash flow from investment activities, and cash flow from financing activities.
3. Why do we exclude interest expense and taxes from operating cash flow?
4. How do businesses analyze their cash flow and liquidity positions?
5. What are some best practices for developing and implementing robust cash management policies and procedures?

MULTIPLE CHOICE QUESTIONS

1. **Which of the following is NOT a primary objective of cash management?**
   a. Maximizing cash flows
   b. Minimizing idle cash balances
   c. Maximizing interest income
   d. Maximizing shareholder dividends
2. **What is the primary purpose of cash budgeting?**
   a. To forecast future cash inflows and outflows
   b. To analyze historical cash flows
   c. To determine the optimal cash reserve
   d. To assess investment opportunities
3. **Which of the following is an example of a cash management technique for reducing cash outflows?**
   a. Increasing credit sales
   b. Accelerating accounts receivable collections
   c. Extending accounts payable payment terms
   d. Investing excess cash in short-term securities
4. **Which of the following ratios measures a company's ability to meet short-term obligations using its cash and cash equivalents?**
   a. Current ratio
   b. Quick ratio
   c. Cash ratio
   d. Debt-to-equity ratio
5. **Which of the following statements about the cash conversion cycle (CCC) is true?**
   a. A shorter CCC indicates better cash management efficiency
   b. CCC measures the time it takes for a company to collect accounts receivable
   c. CCC is calculated by subtracting accounts payable turnover from inventory turnover
   d. CCC is not influenced by inventory management practices
6. **Which of the following is a cash inflow for a company?**
   a. Payment for inventory purchases
   b. Payment of salaries to employees
   c. Collection of accounts receivable
   d. Payment of interest on loans
7. **What is the purpose of a cash flow statement?**
   a. To report the profitability of a company

b. To provide information about changes in equity
c. To show how cash balances have changed over a period
d. To disclose related party transactions

8. Which of the following factors would NOT affect a company's optimal cash balance?

a. Seasonal variations in sales
b. Interest rates on short-term investments
c. Credit policy of suppliers
d. Long-term debt obligations

9. Which of the following cash management techniques involves investing excess cash for short periods to earn interest?

a. Cash pooling
b. Float management
c. Sweeping
d. Cash concentration

10. Which of the following liquidity ratios considers cash and cash equivalents in addition to current assets?

a. Quick ratio
b. Cash ratio
c. Current ratio
d. Working capital ratio

Answer to Multiple Choice Questions

1. (d); 2. (a); 3. (c); 4. (c); 5. (a); 6. (c); 7. (c); 8. (d); 9. (c); 10. (a)

REFERENCES

1. Abbasov, S. "Improving Cash Flow Management." *Economic Herald of the Donbas*, no. 4 (66) (2021): 33–38. http://dx.doi.org/10.12958/1817-3772-2021-4(66)-33-38.
2. Almeida, Heitor, Murillo Campello, and Michael S. Weisbach. "The Cash Flow Sensitivity of Cash." *Journal of Finance* 59, no. 4 (August 2004): 1777–804. http://dx.doi.org/10.1111/j.1540-6261.2004.00679.x.
3. Bitz, Michael, and Udo Terstege. "Cash-Flow-Analyse und Cash-Flow-Management." *WiSt - Wirtschaftswissenschaftliches Studium* 32, no. 1 (2003): 2–7. http://dx.doi.org/10.15358/0340-1650-2003-1-2.
4. Dandekar, Pushkar V., and Ketki M. Ranade. "ATM Cash Flow Management." *International Journal of Innovation, Management and Technology* 6, no. 5 (October 2015): 343–47. http://dx.doi.org/10.18178/ijimt.2015.6.5.627.
5. Dang Ngoc, Hung, Van Vu Thi Thuy, and Hung Nguyen Duy. "The sensitivity of cash flows to cash holdings: case studies at Vietnamese enterprises." *Investment*

Management and Financial Innovations 17, no. 1 (March 30, 2020): 266–76. http://dx.doi.org/10.21511/imfi.17(1).2020.23.

6. Ericsson, Sebastian, and Gabriel Enelund. "Cash Management : Hur arbetar små företag med cash management?" Thesis, Högskolan i Halmstad, Sektionen för ekonomi och teknik (SET), 2014. http://urn.kb.se/resolve?urn=urn:nbn:se:hh:diva-26216.
7. Goldberg, Stephen R., and Joseph H. Godwin. "Cash is king: Cash management and risks." *Journal of Corporate Accounting & Finance* 15, no. 1 (October 22, 2003): 75–76. http://dx.doi.org/10.1002/jcaf.10220.
8. Jooste, Leonie. "An evaluation of the usefulness of the cash flow statement within South African companies by means of cash flow ratios." Thesis, Pretoria : [s.n.], 2004. http://upetd.up.ac.za/thesis/available/etd-04182005-092836.
9. Lienert, Ian. "Modernizing Cash Management." *Technical Notes and Manuals* 2009, no. 03 (2009): 1. http://dx.doi.org/10.5089/9781462304127.005.
10. Oriekhova, K. V., and O. Hr Golovko. "CASH FLOW MANAGEMENT STRATEGY." *Economics and Law*, no. 1 (May 10, 2022): 89–97. http://dx.doi.org/10.15407/econlaw.2022.01.089.

CHAPTER 5

Operations Budgeting

LEARNING OBJECTIVES

After studying this chapter, you will be able to:

- Understand the budgeting
- Define the budget cycle
- Discuss on operating budgets
- Identify the roles of operational budgets

INTRODUCTORY EXAMPLE

The Monte Carlo Method: The Forecast Is for Less Uncertainty

Most capital budgeting decisions involve some degree of uncertainty. For example, a company faces some degree of uncertainty associated with the demand for a new product. One method of accounting for this uncertainty is to average the highest and the lowest prediction of sales. However, such a method is flawed. Producing the average of the expected possible demand can lead to gross overproduction or gross underproduction, neither of which is as profitable as having the right volume of production.

To combat uncertainty in the decision-making process, some companies use a Monte Carlo simulation program to model possible outcomes. Developed by mathematicians in World War II while working on the atomic bomb, the Monte Carlo method was not widely used until the advent of the personal computer. A Monte Carlo simulation program randomly generates values for uncertain variables over and over to simulate a model. The simulation then requires project practitioners to develop low, high, and most likely cost estimates along with correlation coefficients. Once these inputs are derived, the Monte Carlo program can be run through just a few simulations, or thousands, in just a few seconds.

A Monte Carlo program usually builds a histogram of the results, referred to as a frequency chart, for each forecast or output cell that the user wants to analyze. The program then delivers a percentage likelihood that a particular forecast will fall within a specified range, much like a weather forecast. The program also has an optimization feature that allows a project manager with budget constraints to figure out which combination of possible projects will result in the highest profit.

One of the problems with using a Monte Carlo program is the difficulty of establishing the correct input ranges for the variables and determining the correlation coefficients for those variables. However, the work put into developing the input for the program can often clarify some uncertainty in a proposed project. Although Monte Carlo simulation is not the perfect answer to capital budgeting problems, it is another tool that corporations, including ALCOA, Motorola, Intel, Procter & Gamble, and Walt Disney, use to manage risk and make more informed business and strategic decisions.

UNIT INTRODUCTION

A budget is a forecast of income and outlays for a given future period of time that is typically created and reviewed on a regular basis. A person, a group of people, a company, the government, or pretty much anything else that earns and spends money can all create budgets. A budget illustrates the trade-off made when one good is substituted for another in microeconomic terms. Concerning the final outcome of this trade-off, or the bottom line, a surplus budget indicates that profits are projected, a balanced budget indicates that revenues and expenses are expected to be equal, and a deficit budget indicates that expenses will exceed revenues. An operating budget, which is typically presented in the form of an income statement, displays the company's anticipated revenue and related expenses for a future period, usually the following year. Typically, management creates the budget prior to the beginning of the year and then updates it monthly after that. An operating budget could include a high-level summary schedule with supporting details for each budget line item.

5.1. BUDGETING

→Learning Objectives

- To describe types of budgets
- To discuss the budget forecasting and planning
- To define the benefits of budgeting
- To explain the budget control

A budget is essentially a business plan that is stated in monetary terms. A manager needs to plan ahead in order to make important decisions regarding the future. Making forecasts or budgets is one way to plan ahead. There are very basic forecasts. For a proprietor or operator of a restaurant, the budget may consist solely of projecting how many patrons the establishment will see tomorrow and making the necessary purchases of food and supplies to meet this demand. On the other hand, in a large organization, a budget may need to account for both daily expenses (like staff scheduling) and forecasts up to five years in the future (like furniture and equipment purchases). Budgets that aren't stated in monetary terms may specify the quantity of clients to be served, the number of rooms to be occupied, the number of workers needed, or some other quantity instead of dollars.

The three main purposes of budgeting can be summarized as follows:

1. To provide organized estimates of future unit sales, sales revenues, expenses, net income, staffing requirements, or equipment needs, broken down by operating period and department.
2. To provide management with long-term and short-term goals. These goals can be used to plan future activities.
3. To provide a method of control so that actual results can be evaluated against budget plans and adjustments, if necessary, can be made.

5.1.1. Types of Budgets

There are a number of different kinds of budgets.

5.1.1.1. Long-Term Versus Short-Term Budgets

Long-term and short-term budgets are two common classifications for them. One year to five years ahead of time is the range for a long-term budget. These kinds of budgets, which are also known as strategic budgets, address the organization's main goals (such as financing, market expansion, and other related issues). Such long-term plans are the starting point for developing short-term budgets as well as policies pertaining to the day-to-day operations of the company. Budgets for the short term can cover one day, one week, one quarter, or one year. These budgets require middle management to use its resources in order to achieve the long-term plans' goals.

5.1.1.2. Fixed Versus Flexiblc Budgets

A fixed budget is predicated on a particular volume of sales or activity. This level of sales is the basis for expense estimates. There is no attempt to alter the budget's expense amounts to reflect higher or lower levels of sales revenue. The drawback of this type of budget is that, should the actual sales level deviate from the projected sales level, there is no plan in place to account for this possibility, and short-term adjustments to expenses can only be made based on educated guesswork. Let's say, for instance, that the hotel room department budget is based on a 70% average year-round room occupancy. Running expenses (e.g., payroll, supplies, laundry, and linen) are determined by this occupancy level. Should unanticipated economic circumstances cause actual occupancy to fall to 60%, the department manager in charge of the room may find it challenging to determine the appropriate payroll level in the near future. This also applies to all other costs.

Keyword

Long-term budget, is a financial plan that outlines a company's projected income and expenses over an extended period of time, typically between three to five years, though it can extend to ten years or more in some cases.

A budget that is flexible or variable is created by taking into account multiple activity levels. Sales revenue could be predicted for occupancy levels of 60%, 70%, and 80% in our example room department (or as many levels as are appropriate). The level at which the operation will fit in best can be ascertained as the year goes on, and the relevant expense levels will have already been established for this level. To put it another way, adjustment is simpler. Using the rooms department as an example, one could question whether the budgeting is actually flexible (variable) or if it is actually three fixed budgets at three different occupancy levels (or more, if additional occupancy levels are used). The practical outcome is that management is ready to adapt to the real situation when necessary, despite the validity of the question.

Fixed expenses stay the same while variable expenses fluctuate based on sales volume when using flexible budgeting. For instance, a restaurant's budget may be created depending on various sales revenue thresholds. Each distinct revenue level is taken into account when calculating expenses. Variable costs can be stated as a dollar amount per unit sold or as a percentage of sales revenue. On the other hand, advertising costs may be fixed, meaning they won't change based on actual sales revenue. Put differently, a specific, fixed amount is budgeted for this expense, independent of sales volume. A truly flexible budget would display both fixed costs expressed in dollars and truly variable expenses expressed as a percentage of sales revenue.

5.1.1.3. Capital Budgets

A capital budget is a plan that is used to replace or purchase new fixed assets. A capital budget is a schedule for replacing hotel room furnishings every five years.

5.1.1.4. Operating Budgets

An operating budget is concerned with the continuous estimates of expenses and revenue that have an impact on the income statement. An operating budget, for instance, contains a projection of a restaurant's monthly sales income. Similarly, the operating budget in a multi-department hotel is the projected total payroll expense for the year.

Keyword

Budget monitoring is crucial for an organization to be able to enforce accountability related to spending.

5.1.1.5. Department Budgets

Department budgets represent the financial plans and allocations specific to individual departments within an organization. These budgets outline anticipated revenues, expenses, and resource needs to facilitate departmental objectives and responsibilities effectively. They often include revenue estimates, expense categories covering personnel costs, supplies, equipment, utilities, and maintenance, alongside provisions for capital expenditures and initiatives aimed at achieving departmental goals. Department budgets may also incorporate performance metrics to evaluate effectiveness and allocate funds accordingly. Department managers typically oversee budget monitoring, ensuring compliance and reporting on financial performance to higher management or governing bodies. Such budgets play a critical role in aligning resources with departmental goals, optimizing operational efficiency, and supporting the organization's overall mission and objectives.

5.1.1.6. Master Budgets

The most extensive budget out there is called a master budget. The balance sheet for the previous year and all of the departmental income and expense statements for the following year are typically included in a master budget, which is typically prepared for a year.

5.1.2. Budget Forecasting and Planning

You might want to plan your spending or budget for the next six months to a year after you've created your first one, started using it, and gained some experience with how it can help you keep your finances in check. By doing this, you can predict with ease which months you will have extra money and which ones you might be struggling financially. After that, you can try to find ways to balance out your financial highs and lows to make things more bearable and enjoyable. You can estimate how much money you will be able to save for significant purchases like a new car, a vacation, your first house or renovations, an emergency savings account, or retirement by projecting your budget further into the future. You can truly benefit from using a realistic budget to estimate your annual spending when it comes to long-term financial planning. After that, you can project your annual income and expenses and plan for long-term financial objectives like launching your own company, purchasing a home for investment or recreation, or retiring.

5.1.3. Benefits of Budgeting

1. **Gives You Control Over Your Money**: Making deliberate decisions about how you spend and save your money is possible with a budget. Budgeting is supposed to give you control over your finances rather than letting them rule you. Budgeting spares you the headache of having to make last-minute adjustments to your spending because you did not plan how you were going to use your money. It also assists you in determining whether you would prefer to forgo daily coffee purchases in favor of a long-term benefit like a cruise or a new HDTV.
2. **Keeps You Focused on Your Money Goals**: You refrain from spending money needlessly on goods and services that don't help you reach your budgetary objectives. Budgeting helps you make ends meet when you are operating on a tight budget.
3. **Makes You Aware What Is Going on with Your Money**: When you create a budget, you can see exactly how much money comes in, how quickly it leaves, and where it will go. By creating a budget, you can avoid wondering where your money went at the end of each month. You can take advantage of buying and investing opportunities, know what you can afford, and plan how to pay off debt when you have a budget. It also lets you know what matters to you based on how you spend your money, how well it works for you, and how close you are to achieving your financial objectives.
4. **Helps You Organize Your Spending and Savings**: A budget informs you of which category of expenses uses what percentage of your income by separating it into savings and expenditure categories. In this manner, you can easily make changes. Your budget can be used as a guide to arrange your financial statements, receipts, and bills. You save time and effort when all of your financial transactions are arranged for tax season or inquiries from creditors.
5. **Enables You to Save for Expected and Unexpected Costs**: Budgeting

allows you to plan to set aside money for emergency costs.

6. **Enables You to Communicate with Your Significant Others About Money**: A budget can help you communicate how you use money as a group if you share your finances with your spouse, family, or anyone else. This reduces conflict over financial decisions and encourages cooperation in achieving shared financial objectives. Together, you and your partner can create a budget that will prevent arguments and settle individual disagreements about how to spend your money. Family members learn spending accountability and responsibility through budgeting.
7. **Provides You with an Early Warning for Potential Problems**: When you budget and take a "big picture" view, you will see potential money problems in advance, and be able to make adjustments before the problem appears.
8. **Helps You Determine If You Can Take Debt and How Much**: Acquiring debt, provided it is affordable or necessary, does not always imply bad behavior. Using a budget helps you determine whether taking on debt is worthwhile or how much debt you can actually handle without feeling overwhelmed.
9. **Enables You to Produce Extra Money**: By creating a budget, you can find and cut out wasteful expenses like interest, late fees, and penalties. Over time, these seemingly insignificant savings can mount up.

5.1.4. Budget Control

The process of managing individual line items within a household or business budget to prevent expenditures over and beyond the allotted amounts is known as budget control. This kind of control is required to ensure that operating costs don't surpass the period's anticipated revenue, which would result in a net loss. Budget control involves a number of activities, such as creating a reasonable spending plan, keeping an eye on income, and doing comparison shopping prior to making any purchases.

The first stage in efficient budget control is to create a budget based on accurate data about the amount of money required to run the family or business. This entails making use of data on prices for various goods and services that will be consumed on a monthly basis that is gathered from consumer markets. As part of the process, budget control entails ensuring that the budget accurately reflects fixed costs and that any items deemed flexible or floating are covered by a budget amount that corresponds to the operation's typical and standard usage.

Budget control is the process of ensuring that expenses for any given line item stay within the applicable budgetary amount after a workable budget has been established. This can occasionally entail cutting back on spending to avoid going over budget on a specific line item. Budget control demands that a household find ways to spend no more than $200 USD on food for the remainder of the month, for instance, if it has a $500 US dollar (USD) monthly budget for food and has consumed $300 USD by the second week of that monthly period. This could entail switching up the foods that are consumed or replacing more expensive purchases with less expensive ones.

It is significant to remember that budget control typically entails making an effort to save money whenever and wherever possible in addition to staying within the allocated amount. Here, the objective is to spend as little money as possible on the things that are covered by the budget while still producing a little monthly surplus. Managers will do this by comparing the costs of comparable goods and services, ultimately selecting the one that offers the best value while maintaining a respectable standard of quality and service. For example, if a household only uses a certain amount of minutes per month, it might decide to switch to a prepaid cellular provider that is half as expensive as its current provider. This budget control strategy lowers the monthly cost for that budget line item, assuming the prepaid provider provides the same level of service as the previous carrier. The savings can then be applied to another line item, transferred to an interest-bearing account, or used for a treat that falls outside the monthly budget.

Keyword

Budget control refers to the process of managing, monitoring, and adjusting a company's budget and cash flow to ensure that the business remains on track to meet its financial goals and deliver on the organization's objectives.

5.1.4.1. Way to Make a Budget

Budgeting is essential to personal finance because it allows you to manage your income, savings, and investments. Making a list of your expenses is the best way to begin creating a budget. You should distinguish between your fixed and flexible expenses during this process. Fixed expenses are predetermined amounts that include loan payments, rent, and mortgage payments. Food and utility bills are examples of flexible expenses that can vary from month to month.

Making a comprehensive record of all your expenses might require multiple list-making sessions. Without accounting for all of your expenses, you will not be able to create a budget that works for you. Think about transportation, groceries, clothes, pet care, gifts, insurance, and any other expenses you may have, in addition to all the costs involved in maintaining your house. Subtracting your expenses from your total after-tax income, or net income, is the next step in creating a realistic budget. In the event that the difference is negative, it indicates that you do not make enough money to save or invest, let alone pay for necessities. In that scenario, in order to better cover the fixed costs, you'll need to reduce your flexible spending and, ideally, generate extra money. Finding a part-time job on top of your regular work might help you not only bridge the income gap but also provide you with a backup source of income in the event that your primary source of income is lost. In addition to taking your income and expenses into account when creating your budget, you should try to account for the worst-case financial situation. If the gap between your income and expenses is positive, the first item you should add to your budget is an emergency savings fund. Ideally, your emergency fund should consist of six months to a year's worth of living expenses. It is possible to progressively accumulate the emergency fund by setting aside savings from each paycheck. You should only think about investing money once you've established a solid savings base.

A spending budget should be created in addition to tracking costs, saving money, and, if available, making wise investments. Setting aside money for savings can be made easier if you allow yourself a reasonable amount to spend on whatever you choose. It's crucial to consistently set aside funds for savings before giving yourself your allotted amount. Making a budget without giving yourself any money to spend isn't practical and could encourage you to spend money that should be saved for emergencies.

5.1.4.2. Evaluate the Effects of Fiscal Policy

Government spending and taxation constitute fiscal policy, one of the main tools of macroeconomic management. It is referred to as an expansionary or reflationary stance when government spending on goods and services rises while tax revenue collection falls. Contractionary policy refers to tax increases or spending cuts by the government. Fiscal policy effects can be revenue neutral, meaning that every adjustment to spending is counterbalanced by an equivalent adjustment to revenue collection. However, the government still has a strong tool to influence people and businesses through changes to tax laws and spending patterns, even in the case of revenue neutral fiscal policy.

Keyword

Corporate tax is a type of direct tax levied on the income or capital of corporations and other similar legal entities.

A government budget deficit is not always the outcome of expansionary policies. Any budget surplus will be decreased, but not necessarily eliminated, if the economy is reasonably healthy at the time spending increases. Particularly if the budget is already balanced, a contractionary policy position may produce budget surpluses. But in both scenarios, the impact on the budget deficit is contingent upon the initial budget as well as the extent and course of the fiscal policy adjustment.

Aggregate demand rises when the government expands spending without altering tax laws. Because of this expansionary policy, the GDP, employment, and output in the economic sectors where government spending is concentrated will all rise. Typically, the defense sector and its suppliers are the primary beneficiaries. Fiscal policy also has additional knock-on effects since workers in these industries spend more, which increases hiring and sales across the board.

Depending on what kind of taxes are lowered, there will be a change in either aggregate demand or supply if the government cuts taxes while maintaining spending at the same level. Reduced payroll taxes and individual income tax rates will increase consumers' disposable income, which they can use to purchase a wider range of goods and services. This will increase aggregate demand. Businesses are likely to grow and hire more people if corporate tax rates are lowered, which will increase aggregate supply as more goods are produced. Prices and GDP rise as a result of these workers' increased personal consumption of goods and services, which also raises aggregate demand.

Fiscal policy's expansionary effects can help the unemployed find new jobs during a recession, with little to no impact on inflation or interest rates. However, increased government spending can overheat the economy in a strong economy with low unemployment. This can strain production capacity or lead to wage increases to fill job vacancies, which can result in inflation and higher interest rates. Crowding out is the process by which higher prices and interest rates caused by government spending drive out private investment and spending. When there is inflation, the government will frequently try to lower prices through fiscal policy, such as reducing its own spending or raising taxes.

Fiscal policy can be fine-tuned by focusing on particular businesses, people, or habits. For instance, the government might decide to offer significant tax breaks to those who buy homes in order to boost the housing market. Tax rates on farmers and agricultural enterprises should be lowered in order to stimulate investment in the sector. On the other hand, governments may impose taxes on undesirable behavior, like levying higher taxes on particular industries or products, like alcohol or cigarettes. A further way that fiscal policy has an impact is on aggregate demand. Spending by the government, businesses, individuals, and net exports make up GDP. Increased government spending could lead to a higher share of government spending in GDP. Modified tax policies will cause a shift in the share of output attributable to individual or business expenditures.

5.1.4.3. Carryout the Budget Variance

A strategic financial plan is the basic definition of a budget. Income and expenses are typically taken into account. A lot of other things might need to be taken into account in the process, like labor and raw material availability. A budget variance arises when there is a difference between the plan and the outcome. It can be crucial to distinguish between factors that influence the budget that are under your control and those that are outside of your control when analyzing budget variance. Budget variances can happen for a variety of reasons. The poorly planned budget is one of the causes. One illustration of a controllable factor is this. It is possible to control some budget variance causes. Another illustration is labor expenses. A business can manage its expenditure in this area by making choices like forbidding overtime and contracting out tasks that would typically call for highly compensated employees.

A variance in the budget can have uncontrollable causes. This category's factors are frequently external. This indicates that organizations other than the business that created the budget determine these factors. An uncontrollable factor could be an increase in utility costs. Another uncontrollable factor is if a natural disaster results in a shortage of certain raw materials. It is not necessary to automatically assume that a budget variance relates to losses. A variance in the budget may be favorable or unfavorable. It is often referred to as a favorable variance when it is positive. It is regarded as an unfavorable variance when it is negative. Budget variances fall into a number of categories. Profit variance is a frequently encountered concept. This is the difference between expected and realized profits, regardless of whether the latter were greater or lower than anticipated. Several budgets are typical for large organizations. Departments, branches, and sectors are a few possible divisions for these. It is possible that there will be multiple budget variances in this scenario. One can approach this in a variety of ways.

Did you get it?

1. **Define the long-term versus short-term budgets**
2. **Describe the fixed versus flexible budgets**
3. **Focus on capital budgets**
4. **Explain the department budgets**

5.2. THE BUDGET CYCLE

The budget cycle refers to the process by which governments, organizations, or individuals plan, execute, monitor, and evaluate their financial activities over a specified period, usually a fiscal year. The budget cycle typically involves several key stages:

5.2.1. Budget Formulation

Budget formulation is the initial stage of the budget cycle, wherein financial goals and priorities are identified, and budget estimates are prepared. Departments or units within an organization submit their funding requests, which are then consolidated and reviewed by budget officials. This phase involves assessing the financial needs of various programs and projects, aligning them with organizational goals, and prioritizing resource allocation accordingly. Budget formulation often requires careful analysis of past spending patterns, economic forecasts, and stakeholder input to develop a comprehensive budget proposal. The goal of this stage is to create a realistic and balanced budget that addresses the needs of the organization while ensuring fiscal sustainability. It sets the foundation for the subsequent stages of the budget cycle, guiding the allocation of resources and decision-making processes throughout the fiscal year.

5.2.2. Budget Approval

Budget approval is a critical stage in the budget cycle where the proposed budget undergoes review and scrutiny by relevant authorities, such as legislative bodies, executive committees, or governing boards. During this phase, the budget proposal is evaluated based on its alignment with organizational priorities, financial feasibility, and compliance with regulatory requirements. Decision-makers assess the proposed allocations of funds and may make adjustments or amendments before granting final approval. The approval process often involves negotiation and compromise to reconcile competing interests and ensure consensus among stakeholders. Once approved, the budget serves as the authoritative financial plan for the organization, guiding resource allocation and expenditure decisions throughout the fiscal period. Effective budget approval mechanisms promote transparency, accountability, and prudent fiscal management, laying the groundwork for responsible governance and organizational success.

5.2.3. Budget Execution

Budget execution represents the phase in the budget cycle where the approved budget is implemented and operationalized. During this stage, funds are allocated to various departments, programs, and projects according to the approved spending plan. Financial transactions are initiated, including payments for goods, services, salaries, and other operational expenses. Budget managers and administrators oversee the disbursement of funds, ensuring that expenditures remain within allocated limits and comply with financial regulations. Effective execution requires efficient coordination among stakeholders, timely processing of financial transactions, and diligent monitoring of spending activities. Any deviations from the approved budget may necessitate adjustments or reallocations to ensure fiscal discipline and maintain organizational priorities. The successful execution of the budget is essential for achieving organizational objectives, delivering services to constituents, and demonstrating accountability in the management of public or institutional resources.

5.2.4. Budget Monitoring and Control

Budget monitoring and control are integral components of the budget cycle, focused on overseeing and managing financial activities to ensure adherence to the approved budget and achievement of organizational goals. This stage involves systematic tracking of actual expenditures and revenues against the budgeted amounts, enabling timely identification of variances and corrective action when necessary.

Keyword

Financial transaction is an agreement, or communication, between a buyer and seller to exchange goods, services, or assets for payment.

Monitoring involves regular review and analysis of financial reports, including income statements, cash flow statements, and balance sheets, to assess the organization's financial performance. Budget managers and financial analysts compare actual spending and revenue generation with the budgeted figures, identifying areas of overspending or underspending, as well as potential revenue shortfalls or surpluses.

Control mechanisms are implemented to manage financial resources effectively, mitigate risks, and maintain fiscal discipline. These controls may include expenditure controls, such as authorization limits and procurement procedures, revenue controls, such as revenue collection processes and fee structures, and compliance controls, ensuring adherence to regulatory requirements and organizational policies.

Continuous monitoring enables proactive management of budget variances, allowing for adjustments in spending priorities, reallocation of resources, or implementation of cost-saving measures to align expenditures with available funding and organizational priorities. Effective budget monitoring and control mechanisms enhance transparency, accountability, and financial stewardship, enabling organizations to optimize resource utilization and achieve their strategic objectives.

5.2.5. Budget Reporting

Budget reporting is a crucial aspect of the budget cycle, facilitating transparency, accountability, and informed decision-making regarding financial activities and performance. This stage involves the generation and dissemination of comprehensive financial reports that provide stakeholders with insights into the organization's budgetary status, spending patterns, and financial health.

Financial reports typically include detailed information on budgeted versus actual expenditures, revenue generation, variances, and performance indicators. These reports may be presented in various formats, such as balance sheets, income statements, cash flow statements, and budget-to-actual comparisons, depending on the needs of stakeholders and the complexity of the organization's financial structure.

The frequency and scope of budget reporting may vary depending on organizational requirements and stakeholder expectations. Regular reporting intervals, such as monthly, quarterly, or annually, allow stakeholders to monitor budgetary performance over time, identify trends, and assess the effectiveness of financial management strategies.

Budget reports serve as valuable tools for decision-makers, enabling them to evaluate the impact of budgetary decisions, identify areas for improvement, and allocate resources strategically to support organizational goals and priorities. Additionally, transparent, and timely reporting fosters trust and confidence among stakeholders, including government officials, investors, donors, employees, and the public, by providing insights into how financial resources are managed and utilized.

Effective budget reporting practices adhere to established accounting standards and regulatory requirements, ensuring accuracy, consistency, and reliability of financial information. By promoting transparency and accountability, budget reporting enhances organizational governance, supports informed decision-making, and contributes to overall financial sustainability and success.

5.2.6. Budget Evaluation and Audit

Budget evaluation and audit represent critical stages in the budget cycle, focused on assessing the effectiveness, efficiency, and compliance of financial activities and expenditures.

Evaluation involves a systematic review of budget performance, comparing actual outcomes against planned objectives and targets. This stage aims to identify strengths, weaknesses, and areas for improvement in budget formulation, execution, and impact. Evaluation criteria may include the achievement of programmatic goals, cost-effectiveness of expenditures, alignment with organizational priorities, and responsiveness to changing circumstances or stakeholder needs.

Auditing is a formal examination of financial records, transactions, and internal controls to ensure accuracy, integrity, and regulatory compliance. External auditors, independent of the organization, conduct audits to provide assurance regarding the reliability of financial information and the effectiveness of internal control systems. Audits may encompass various aspects of budget management, including revenue collection, expenditure authorization, procurement practices, and adherence to legal and regulatory requirements.

The findings and recommendations from budget evaluation and audits inform decision-makers and stakeholders about the organization's financial performance, risks, and opportunities for improvement. By identifying areas of inefficiency, waste, or non-compliance, evaluation and audit reports enable corrective actions to enhance financial management practices, strengthen internal controls, and mitigate risks.

Furthermore, evaluation and audit processes contribute to accountability and transparency by demonstrating the organization's commitment to responsible stewardship of resources and adherence to ethical standards. Compliance with audit recommendations and implementation of corrective measures help build trust and confidence among stakeholders, including government agencies, investors, donors, and the public. Overall, budget evaluation and audit play essential roles in promoting financial integrity, accountability, and sustainability, thereby supporting the organization's mission, goals, and long-term viability.

Did you get it?

1. **Write the budget monitoring and control**
2. **Define the budget reporting**
3. **Describe the budget evaluation and audit**

5.3. OPERATING BUDGETS

→Learning Objectives

- Discuss on diagram of a master budget
- Define sales budget
- Describe the production budget
- Write the direct materials budget
- Explain the direct labor budget
- Identify the manufacturing overhead budget
- Focus on selling expenses budget
- Evaluate the general and administration expenses budget

The operating budgets cover the following: sales, selling expenses, general and administrative costs, manufacturing costs (materials, labor, and overhead), or merchandise purchases. The operating budget is made up of the costs and earnings from the company's regular business activities. Operating expenses, such as cost of goods sold (COGS) and revenue, are the main focus of the operating budget. COGS is the total cost of directly related labor and materials used in a production. The overhead and administrative expenses directly related to providing the goods and services are also included in the operating budget. However, things like long-term debt and capital expenditures are not included in the operating budget. Budgeting and financial planning are essential to keeping a business thriving. A master budget is used by businesses to forecast their future sales and expenses, as well as to manage their cash and other assets. Financial budgets and operating budgets are the two components that make up master budgets, and they function together. Cash and capital expenditures are the main topics of financial budgets. They serve to guarantee that the company has the resources necessary to finance its operations, as well as to maintain and/or modernize its facilities and machinery.

5.3.1. Diagram of a Master Budget

Businesses can use budgets to manage operations, assess their performance in relation to their spending and earnings, and plan for upcoming business cycles once they are established.

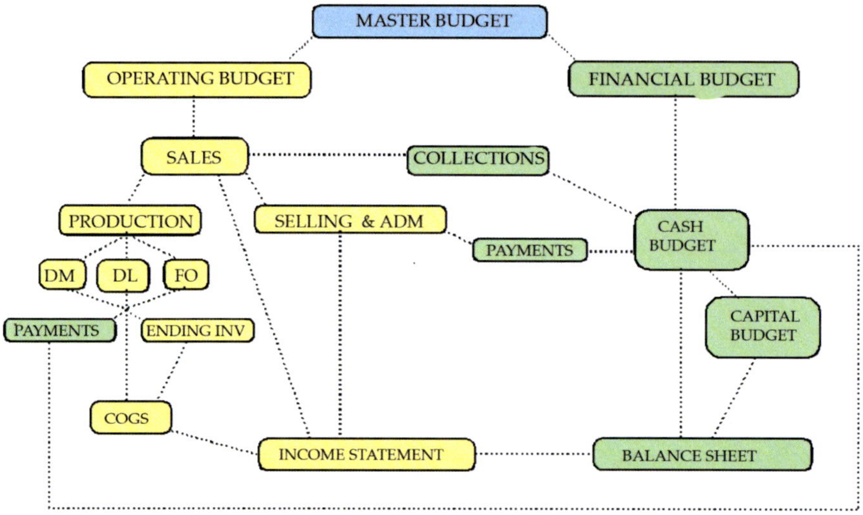

5.3.1.1. Budget Classification Code Systems

The budget classification coding system used by most corporate and organization accounting departments typically dictates how the budget is tracked, displayed, and reported. Particularly in government organizations, budget classification code systems are widely used. Efficient systems categorize income and expenses based on functional, administrative, and economic classifications. Codes for administrative and economic classification, along with the associated income and expenses, are separate and unrelated to one another.

The budget classification is a decision-making, as well as an accountability, tool. It classifies expenditures and revenues, which are important for:

- overall performance analysis
- efficient and uniform resource allocation, and
- daily budget administration

The primary elements of a budget classification system are intended to show:

- a comprehensive overview of all operations for a given period (a consolidated report of all operations)
- overview and breakdown of individual department, divisions, sector, etc., operations' revenues and expenditures (ensuring efficient allocation of resources), and
- consistency between components of the budget (ensuring current expenditures and past investment maintenance are included in the budget)

5.3.2. Sales Budget

The Sales Budget is the first budget in the comprehensive Operational Budget. Also, a lot of other budgets rely on the information in the sales budget. The estimated number of units to be sold or service(s) to be provided, as well as the asking price per unit, are included in the sales budget. Quarterly sales budgets are created along with an extensive annual sales report. To track sales and compare them to anticipated sales projections, monthly sales budgets are frequently created.

Sales Budget = Expected Sales in Units x $ Sales Price

5.3.3. Production Budget

The production budget is a critical component of financial planning for manufacturing companies, outlining the estimated costs and resources required to produce goods within a specific period. It encompasses various elements such as raw materials, labor, overhead costs, and other expenses directly associated with the production process. The production budget typically begins with sales forecasts, which serve as the basis for determining the quantity of goods to be manufactured. From there, factors like inventory levels, production capacity, and lead times are considered to determine the production schedule. By estimating the quantities of raw materials needed, labor hours required, and overhead expenses associated with production, the production budget helps companies manage resources efficiently, minimize waste, and meet customer demand effectively. It serves as a guideline for production managers and finance teams to plan and allocate resources strategically, ensuring that production activities support the organization's overall objectives while maintaining cost-effectiveness and quality standards.

Remember

A production budget is a document that calculates that number of units of a product will be manufactured to meet the estimated sales demand. Manufacturers make a production budget quarterly, though sometimes they will also be produced on a monthly basis.

To effectively budget for annual production, the budget preparer must know:

- the projected quantity of units that must be sold
- the end-of-period level of inventory, and
- the quantity of widgets (if any) in the inventory at the beginning of the year

The same information is required for quarterly budgets.

Production Budget (Needs) = Budgeted Sales + Desired End Inventory in Units or Dollars

5.3.4. Direct Materials Budget

The direct materials budget is a fundamental component of the overall budgeting process for manufacturing companies, detailing the anticipated costs and quantities of raw materials needed for production during a specific period. It serves as a critical planning tool for procurement and inventory management, enabling organizations to ensure an adequate supply of materials while minimizing excess inventory and associated carrying costs. The direct materials budget typically begins with sales forecasts and production plans, which provide the basis for estimating the quantity of finished goods to be produced. From there, factors such as material requirements per unit of production, desired inventory levels, lead times, and supplier capabilities are considered to determine the quantity and timing of raw material purchases. By aligning material procurement with production schedules and customer demand, the direct materials budget helps companies optimize their supply chain operations, mitigate the risk of stockouts or production delays, and control costs associated with inventory holding and ordering. It serves as a valuable tool for production managers, purchasing departments, and finance teams to coordinate activities, manage cash flow, and support the organization's overall strategic objectives.

The budgeted amount needed for the purchase of raw materials is quantitatively determined by multiplying the quantity of units to be purchased by the cost per unit.

DIRECT MATERIALS = Units of Raw Materials x Cost per Unit

All budgeted raw material components used in production operations should be determined by repeating the above process.

5.3.5. Direct Labor Budget

The direct labor budget is a key component of the overall budgeting process for manufacturing companies, outlining the anticipated costs and labor hours required to produce goods during a specific period. It helps organizations plan and manage their workforce efficiently, ensuring that adequate staffing levels are maintained to meet production targets while controlling labor costs.

The direct labor budget typically begins with production plans and sales forecasts, which provide insights into the volume of goods to be manufactured. Based on production requirements, factors such as standard labor hours per unit of production, anticipated overtime, and hiring needs are considered to estimate the total labor hours needed.

Additionally, wage rates, employee benefits, and labor-related expenses are factored into the budget to determine the total labor costs associated with production activities.

The direct labor budget serves as a guideline for human resource managers and production supervisors to schedule shifts, assign tasks, and allocate resources effectively. It helps organizations optimize labor utilization, minimize idle time, and ensure that production schedules are met in a cost-effective manner. By aligning labor resources with production requirements, the direct labor budget enables organizations to maintain competitiveness, enhance productivity, and achieve their operational objectives while controlling labor expenses and supporting overall financial performance.

The Direct Labor Budget shows the total direct labor hours calculated using the cost of the direct labor (number of units produced multiplied by how many hours spent to produce them), multiplied by the cost per labor hour.

Total Direct Labor = (Units x Direct Labor Hours) x Cost Per Labor Hour

5.3.6. Manufacturing Overhead Budget

The anticipated fixed and variable overhead costs for the budget reporting period are shown in the manufacturing overhead budget. Costs that are fixed and variable are distinct. Cost behavior should guide the analysis of costs. Usually, an overhead rate that has been predetermined is used. Every overhead expense that involves paying out cash is settled in the quarter that it is incurred. When calculating expected cash payments, depreciation—a non-cash expense—should be subtracted from the total if it is part of manufacturing overhead.

5.3.7. Selling Expenses Budget

Expenses for both fixed and variable selling during the budget reporting period are included in the selling expenses budget. They are divided into fixed and variable costs. Sales commissions and delivery costs are examples of variable expenses that are commonly based on sales dollars. Sales compensation is one type of fixed selling expense.

Did you know?

The first budget of India was submitted on 18 February 1860 by James Wilson. P C Mahalanobis is known as the father of Indian budget.

5.3.8. General and Administration Expenses Budget

The anticipated fixed and variable overhead costs for the budget reporting period are shown in the general and administrative expenses budget. The general and administrative areas of the company have different fixed and variable costs. Examples of fixed expenses include salaries, rent, and office supplies.

5.3.8.1. Preparing the Operating Budget

The designated department/division manager creates separate operating budgets for every operation. Real expense reports for both the current and previous periods are provided by a budget coordinator. The manager uses historical data from the prior period combined with the most recent activity data to create the new budget. The operating reports from all departments and divisions are gathered by the budget coordinator, who then compiles them into a final, comprehensive operating budget.

The following is a basic process for creating a comprehensive operations budget:

- **Expenditures:** Determine the current period's expenses. Analyze every expense related to every aspect of the business. Costs for marketing, storage, transportation, rent, and administration should all be considered and included. Add to the total of expenditures any money allotted and used to maintain the business's operations.
- **Inventory Turnover:** Determine the current period's production. Ascertain the quantity of units manufactured and sold in the current time frame. Inventory turnover is measured by subtracting sold units from units produced. Trend analysis requires an understanding of inventory turnover.
- **Value of Goods/Services:** The value of goods or services expressed in cost per unit measure may be calculated by dividing expenses by production.

Produced Value of Goods/Services = Units Produced

- **Gross Income:** This is the calculated revenue from the units sold, before expenses.
- **Profit Margin:** Profit margin is a financial metric that measures the profitability of a business by calculating the percentage of revenue that translates into profit after accounting for all expenses. It is a key indicator of a company's financial health and operational efficiency, providing insights into its ability to generate earnings from its core business activities.

Remember

An operating profit is the total income earned from the operations of a company before calculating items like taxes, interest charges and other expenses. This number typically appears on the income statement as a subtotal.

To calculate profit margin, you subtract the total expenses from the total revenue and then divide the resulting profit by the total revenue. The formula for profit margin is:

$$\text{Profit Margin} = \left(\frac{\text{Revenue} - \text{Expenses}}{\text{Revenue}}\right) \times 100$$

Profit margin is typically expressed as a percentage, representing the proportion of revenue that remains as profit. A higher profit margin indicates that a company is more efficient at generating profit from its revenue, while a lower profit margin suggests that a larger portion of revenue is consumed by expenses.

- **Analysis:** An overview of each operation sector's performance for the time period covered by the budget report is provided by the operating budget. Any discrepancy between operating budget and actual performance must be justified, and any necessary accommodations or adjustments must be made.

5.3.8.2. Earnings and Operating Income

"Earnings" and "operating income" are two important financial metrics used to assess the profitability and financial performance of a company, but they represent different aspects of a company's income statement.

1. **Earnings:** Earnings typically refer to the net income or profit earned by a company over a specific period, such as a quarter or a fiscal year. Net income is calculated by subtracting all expenses, including operating expenses, interest, taxes, and other non-operating expenses, from the total revenue generated by the company. Earnings are a comprehensive measure of a company's profitability and financial health, reflecting its ability to generate profits from its core business operations after accounting for all expenses and taxes.

2. **Operating Income:** Operating income, also known as operating profit or operating earnings, specifically measures the profitability of a company's core business operations. It is calculated by subtracting operating expenses, such as cost of goods sold (COGS), salaries, rent, utilities, depreciation, and other overhead costs, from the company's total revenue. Operating income excludes non-operating income and expenses, such as interest income, interest expenses, gains or losses from asset sales, and income taxes. Operating income provides insights into the profitability and efficiency of a company's core business activities, excluding the impact of financial and non-operational factors.
3. **Operational Planning:** Plans for future growth and expansion are created using budgets. Operational planning maps specific goals and objectives strategically with the aim of increasing profit using the Operation Budget. Requests for operating budgets are frequently supported by an operational plan. A five-year plan is a common form of strategic operational planning. Normally, "five operational plans funded by five operating budgets" would be needed for this. Setting up benchmarks and requirements for goal accomplishment is a key component of operational planning.

The strategic plan must include details on

- how the plan will be implemented;
- what plan components will be put into operation; and
- when the plan components will be put into operation.

The strategic plan's commercial applications could be launched at any time during a prearranged operating window, usually the fiscal year. Expenses could be reduced appropriately. For instance, the strategic plan might call for the creation of alternative products that can be produced for less and sold for more in order to pay production fees if too much has been spent on production in comparison to sales. Many budget variations do not appear as negatives, even though they can help provide a financial road map for future business operations. It is possible to establish reserve accounts in order to deposit money saved for ongoing business expenses toward specific new ventures. Future-focused budgeting guarantees that funds will be accessible when opportunities arise and prompt decisions about operations expansion are needed. During times of weak economic growth, the reserve account also acts as a safeguard for operations.

Did you get it?

1. **How does a master budget assist in overall financial planning and control?**
2. **How does the production budget interact with other functional budgets?**
3. **What are the challenges organizations may face in preparing and using the direct labor budget effectively?**

5.4. ROLES OF OPERATIONAL BUDGETS

→Learning Objectives

- To deal with conflicts between major roles
- To explain the planning versus motivation in operational budgeting
- To discuss the motivation versus evaluation in operational budgeting
- To explain the planning versus evaluation in operational budgeting
- To define the reducing role conflict
- To deal with planning versus motivation conflict
- Identify the motivation versus evaluation conflict
- To describe the multiple role conflicts
- To define general recommendations in operational budgeting

Budgets can be called upon to play a variety of roles. We shall discuss five of these. Three are major roles: planning, motivation, and evaluation; two are minor: coordination and education.

1. **Planning**: Operational budgets are plans that outline the specific goals and methods that management hopes to achieve. Their importance in the planning process stems from the fact that budgeting compels management to carefully consider the overall economic environment of which the business operates as well as the economic relationships between all of the company's different operations. Through budgeting, managers can investigate the behavior of costs and revenues under various operating assumptions. The procedure frequently highlights inconsistencies between the goals of top management and the actual capabilities of the business. Budgeting allows management to determine what resources are needed to meet goals and how those resources should be used. If current resources are insufficient to achieve goals, the operational budgeting process may lead to a review of the costs associated with purchasing additional assets (capital budgeting).
2. **Motivation:** Operational budgets are a useful tool for management to inspire employees to follow a predetermined plan of action in order to help the organization accomplish its overall goals. Two components can be identified with

motivation: strength and direction. Since a budget is a quantification of management's goals, it offers guidance. Following the completion of the budgeting process, every manager has a clear goal to strive towards. However, a goal by itself is rarely sufficient. A manager needs to be dedicated to working toward goals in order to achieve them. There are numerous ways for managers to acquire commitment, which is the strength component of motivation. One often employed method is to connect the manager's performance review with the organization's reward scheme. Managers may be more committed to budgeted goals when they understand that their pay and opportunities for advancement are largely dependent on their performance.

3. **Evaluation:** An operational budget's data is used as a benchmark to assess how well a manager or business unit performed in real terms. Senior management wouldn't have anything to compare the outcomes of the present with if there wasn't a standard in place. Comparisons between the present and the past can be fascinating from a historical standpoint, but they frequently offer little insight into how well a manager or company performed. The assumption behind comparing current performance to historical performance is that the business's operating environment and current state are unchanged from the past. Seldom is this the case. Removing the effects of uncontrollable or unexpected environmental changes that have happened during the budget period may also be desirable if the evaluation's goal is to assess managers' operational abilities rather than their forecasting abilities. Unpredictable increases in raw material costs or shortages, labor unrest, and regulatory changes are a few examples of uncontrollable environmental variables. Budgets are supported by other components of the management control system in their evaluation role. Although the budget is a helpful benchmark, the reporting system is responsible for supplying information on the actual outcomes that must be compared to the benchmark. The budget's role in evaluation is further supported by formal evaluation procedures, management review meetings, and predetermined measurement criteria (return on investment, return on assets, etc.).

4. **Coordination:** Operational budgets play a coordinating function as well. Operational budgets provide a consolidated plan of action that, when paired with financial budgets to create an overall master budget, aids in coordinating the activities of the different departments within the organization. Two methods exist for budget coordination. First, there needs to be some decentralization in the way a large organization budgets for its operations. Budgets for the upcoming year are typically created by managers of the various organizational components in most businesses. These budgets are reviewed and consolidated as they move up the organizational ladder, eliminating any inconsistencies between the planned operations of the different organizational components. Production plans and material procurement schedules are

synchronized, distribution across product lines is coordinated, and redundancies in the marketing or sales operations are reviewed, among other things. Output is matched to projected sales. To ensure that resources are not over or underutilized, the operational budget, once it is fully consolidated, acts as a tool for coordinating the actions of the entire organization. After operations have started, the operational budget serves a second coordinating purpose. The coordination that was included in the budget during the planning phase will remain intact if every organizational component is managed to achieve its allocated goals. Revisions to plans and budgets can benefit from the prior understanding of the economic relationships between the company's various activities, should conditions change as is more often the case and all units fail to meet the budget.

5. **Education:** The role of coordination in education is linked to that of the budget. Managers at all organizational levels need to be aware of the behavior of costs and revenues in their units and conduct a methodical, in-depth analysis of how their portion of the business operates in order to properly prepare their budgets. Budgets are also helpful analytical instruments for figuring out how to raise performance. The process of consolidating the budgets of different organizational components may also compel managers to gain a deeper comprehension of the organizational dynamics of the company in its entirety. A manager must first look at how the various activities in his area of the business are related to one another and dependent on one another in order to be able to defend and justify his share of the overall budget. As the budget gets to the more senior line managers, awareness of interdependencies may become more apparent due to the ongoing consolidation that takes place during the process. In actuality, though, managers at all levels need to be more conscious of how their decisions and the operations of their units impact other departments within the organization. Although this isn't always the case in reality, budgeting should be seen as a way to provide managers with a clearer understanding of how the entire company functions.

5.4.1. Conflicts between Major Roles

Because of its primary functions, an operational budgeting system has requirements that are difficult for a single system to satisfy. And role conflicts occur precisely because of these differences in requirements. There can be at least three major role conflicts resulting from the three major roles that any budgeting system has: planning versus motivation, motivation versus evaluation, and planning versus evaluation. In reality, there are just two main conflicts—one between the planning and motivation roles, and the other between motivation and evaluation—when one examines the differences in the requirements of each role in more detail. The third assumed conflict is less serious and is between the planning and evaluation processes.

5.4.2. Planning versus Motivation

A budget should be founded on a realistic evaluation of the business's operational capabilities and management's assessment of the most likely result of the business's interactions with its surroundings in order for it to serve as a planning tool with the greatest effectiveness. The operational budget should represent management's best estimates of revenues and expenses since the company's capital and financial budgets are partially dependent on the data in it. Should the operating budget be excessively optimistic, the business might not utilize all of its resources. Should it be excessively negative, there might not be enough resources available to fully take advantage of market opportunities. The most likely scenario should be the basis for the planning budget.

However, an operational budget that is predicated on what is most likely faces the risk of establishing goals that are so low as to negatively impact motivation. A budget should present challenging but attainable goals and set higher goals than those set for planning in order to effectively motivate. It should be uncommon for all managers in an organization to stick to their budgets on average.

However, challenging goals are likely to result in an overly optimistic budget. If the budget is set at a level that is possible but not likely, there is a chance that the goal will not be met and that company resources will be underutilized. It is obvious that a single budget is unlikely to serve as a perfect tool for both planning and motivation.

The tension between motivation and planning becomes more apparent when we consider the budgeting process from the managers' point of view. They might be aware that the business requires their best projections of the likely volume of activity for the upcoming year in order to make plans. They may also be aware from past experience that their supervisors will probably increase the likely activity levels required for planning in order to reflect goals they believe are challenging but doable. Managers are also aware that they might face unforeseen challenges in achieving the allocated goals. Managers frequently feel compelled to inflate their budget proposals or introduce "budget slack" to increase the likelihood of positive comparisons between projected and actual results. In balancing their ambition and the need for stability, some managers purposely set lower objectives than what they consider attainable.

Budget slack may affect the budget's efficacy in the planning and motivational roles if the budget review and approval process does not eliminate it. Firstly, the fact that a padded budget represents objectives that satisfy the realistic, most probable outcome criterion is purely coincidental. Second, since the padded budget is unlikely to present challenging yet achievable objectives, a manager's motivation to maximize his own performance may be compromised. The possibility of conflict persists even though, in reality, budget slack is probably going to be eliminated as budgets are pushed upward. For motivational purposes, something that works well for planning may not be the best choice.

5.4.3. Motivation versus Evaluation

The widely held notion that the manager should regard the budgetary objectives as fixed benchmarks by which to evaluate performance is crucial to comprehending this role conflict. Supporters of this viewpoint think that after the goals are established, they should be more or less fixed to prevent the person working toward them from getting lost. Furthermore, if a manager is aware that failing to meet budgeted objectives could be interpreted as subpar performance, it is believed that the manager will be more dedicated to meeting those targets.

However, it is frequently preferable to exclude the effects of expenses or events that the manager had no control over from the budgeted standards when evaluating specific managers. Some expenses that a manager may consider "uncontrollable" include gains or losses resulting from fluctuations in foreign exchange rates, corporate overhead, and corporate research and development expenses.

It may also be preferable to eliminate the effects of unpredictable and uncontrollable environmental changes that have happened during the budget period if the evaluation's goal is to assess managers' operational abilities rather than their forecasting abilities. Changes in government regulations, labor unrest, shortages, and unanticipated increases in raw material costs are a few examples of uncontrollable environmental variables. The budget that serves the evaluation role best in many circumstances is sometimes referred to as an ex post facto budget. It is one that is created or modified after the fact and takes into account the effects of unpredictable or uncontrollable events. The impact of applying an ex post facto standard during the evaluation process on motivation is the potential source of role conflict between the evaluation and motivation roles. If managers are aware that the performance criteria they will be evaluated by could alter, they are not likely to be fully dedicated to meeting the budget's goals. However, the strict application of a "fixed standard" philosophy can just as easily undermine motivation. If a manager encounters persistently high negative variances brought on by uncontrollable factors, she may become disillusioned with the system because she will be held strictly responsible for meeting budgeted targets regardless of what occurs during the period. Once a person reaches a certain level of annoyance, all chance of fulfilling the budget may vanish. It is easy for hopelessness to turn into a lack of effort.

5.4.4. Planning Versus Evaluation

On the surface, it might seem that the need to isolate or remove the effects of unpredictable or uncontrollable environmental variables from the budget used for evaluation purposes would conflict with the planning role's requirement to provide a realistic assessment of future prospects. Actually, though, there is less of a conflict between these requirements because of their temporal separation. Management should create a reasonable budget at the start of the budgeting period that reflects their estimation of the most likely course of events involving the company and its surroundings. However, since the budget will not be used for evaluation until the end of the budgeting period (or subdivisions thereof), the impact on the evaluation role can be mitigated.

For changing environmental conditions that happened during the budgeting period, adjustments or modifications can be made at the end of the budget period. This can be accomplished without negatively impacting the budget's previous function in planning. It appears feasible to have two budgets: one for planning and the other for evaluation, if we temporarily disregard the budget's influence on motivation and concentrate solely on the planning and evaluation responsibilities. Therefore, there is no reason for these roles to conflict. The motivational role of the operating budget may make it impossible to use two very different versions. But take note that this fact alone does not put the demands of the planning and evaluation roles at odds with one another.

5.4.5. Reducing Role Conflict

The conflicts that arise from the main roles of an operational budget have been lessened through the application of various managerial strategies. Some of these strategies are the outcome of senior management's deliberate efforts to minimize role conflicts in the budgeting system's design. In other situations, the budgeting system's design may have an unintentional, undetectable benefit of reducing role conflict.

5.4.6. Planning versus Motivation Conflict

The belief that an operational budget should include challenging but attainable goals is the most prevalent way in which the conflict between planning and motivation manifests itself. The goals of such a budget are obviously unlikely to be achieved, on average, by all managers and business units within the organization, as we have already seen. In order for the senior manager to meet his budget, his subordinates would also need to (on average) meet theirs if the goals in each of their budgets are challenging but attainable, and the senior manager's budget is the sum of all of the subordinates' goals. This might not happen very often if the senior manager has five or six managers reporting to him. One company approaches this issue by utilizing what it refers to as general manager's judgment (GMJ). Although GMJ is a type of budget slack, it is not utilized in the same manner as the budget slack that was previously covered. Budgeted targets are set high enough in this company to effectively motivate managers at lower organizational levels. Then, as the budget is consolidated upward, the goals are lowered to levels that are better suited for coordination and planning.

The company's general managers request that their staff members commit to goals that they think will be challenging to accomplish. When the general manager combines the budgets of his staff members, he lowers the overall consolidated budget's goals to levels that are, in his opinion, more practical for financial planning. This lessens the apparent conflict between the roles of the budget.

This company is taking a risk by using GMJ. There may appear to be two budgets to subordinates: one for planning and a less optimistic one for evaluating the performance of senior managers. This is because the budget for motivation is used for one purpose. They might also feel that the senior managers are held to a standard that isn't really applied to them. This could have a negative impact on their motivation to meet the initial budget.

Another strategy for lessening the tension between motivation and planning is embodied in a tight ship policy, which is a management control philosophy. Here, the budgeted goals are the foundation for planning, and the objectives are set high enough to inspire. There are no unfair practices or inflated budgets like there were with GMJ. Every manager is supposed to meet their financial goals.

Knowing that the budgeted objectives won't be met and keeping top management in the dark about it is the only sin worse than not meeting the budget according to the tight ship philosophy. Senior managers at such a company feel that by anticipating a business unit's failure to perform within budget, they can lessen the potential impact of the shortfall on other operational units within the organization. They also think that by taking prompt and efficient corrective action, the budget's benefits for coordination and planning can frequently be maintained.

Contingency planning is another way to lessen the potential negative effects of planning with budgets whose goals are high enough to inspire. At the start of every budgetary period, one company's operating units create backup plans using a tight ship policy-based budgeting system. These plans are designed with sales levels that are 20% and 40% lower than those specified in the operating budget.

While the main goal of this kind of contingency planning is to enable managers to respond to deviations from scheduled activity levels faster, it may also lessen role conflict. Top management is able to anticipate how various outcomes could impact the organization as a whole because they have multiple contingency plans.

5.4.7. Motivation versus Evaluation Conflict

Differentiating between organizational levels regarding the use of revised or ex post facto budgets for manager evaluations is one way to lessen the conflict between the role of evaluation and motivation. At the lower levels of an organization, there are undoubtedly fewer opportunities to anticipate, control, or influence random, external variables. Therefore, managers at these levels may not be held accountable for exceeding budgeted goals if the reason for the shortfall stems from external factors beyond their control or influence.

The ability of the production manager, for instance, to adhere to budgeted requirements for variable costs, fixed costs, delivery schedules, and (product) quality standards may be taken into consideration when evaluating him. The effects of any significant emergency shipment that he had to make during that time may be seen separately from the outcomes of the rest of his operations.

The number of external variables that can be anticipated, managed, or influenced increases with one's level of position within an organization. Furthermore, a major factor in senior managers' seniority is their aptitude for handling a more difficult and complex environment. As a result, the bonuses and other financial incentives provided to these managers may be much more directly linked to meeting the goals specified in the initial budget. Such a division of the foundation for performance evaluation and reward supports the motivation of those lower in the organization whose goals are not achieved due to circumstances they may believe are out of their control, as well as the dedication of those at the top to budgeted targets.

Another way to lessen the conflict between the roles of motivation and evaluation is to use "adjustable budgets." These are operational budgets, meaning that, in certain predefined scenarios, the goals may change. As a result, changes to the performance standard are possible during the operating period. One company that employs this type of budgeting system has managers commit to a budget, but they also understand that top management will revise it and set new performance criteria if any of the five major economic or environmental variables change significantly. Every time any one of these five factors significantly changes, this company automatically updates the budget. Naturally, the relative importance of each variable will determine the threshold at which a new budget is initiated. Managers using this system are aware that they must stick to their spending plans. Because it contains attainable goals, the budget continues to have its inspiring quality. Budgeted objectives cannot be impacted by uncontrollable events in a way that makes them unlikely to be achieved. However, changes don't always have to have a negative impact.

5.4.8. Multiple Role Conflicts

To lessen multiple role conflicts, some businesses implement rolling budgets. A rolling budget means that each budgetary period will probably be much shorter than the standard twelve months, maybe as short as four months or even just a quarter. The process of creating a budget becomes almost constant. Budgets for the upcoming periods are created or updated as each budget period comes to an end. A rolling budget could operate, for instance, as follows. When Period 3 (an arbitrary starting point for this example) ends, top management evaluates performance by contrasting the period's actual results with the planned goals. It also makes the final revision to the Period 5 budget at this time. It also creates the first draft budget for Period 7 and makes the first revision to the budget for Period 6. By the end of the previous period, the budget for the upcoming one, Period 4, was finished. Bonus payments will not be made until a manager's performance during the current period meets the budgeted objectives.

A rolling budget helps managers stay committed because they are aware that once the budget is finalized, it cannot be changed for assessment purposes. If budgeted goals are not met, incentive compensation is forfeited. Nonetheless, the individual manager finds it easier to accept the financial fallout from such a failure because the budgeting period has been drastically shortened. The final version of the budget is subject to two revisions. Therefore, in a more traditional budgeting system, it could be modified for events that could be considered unanticipated. This somewhat lessens the negative effects of not revising budgets. A second strategy employed by some businesses to lessen conflicts between multiple roles is to mandate the regular submission of updated forecasts throughout the year. For reporting purposes, these companies, along with the majority of others, split the budgetary period into quarters or months. Managers are expected to provide a forecast of the operating results for the remaining portion of the overall budget period at the end of each reporting period, in addition to ensuring that the actual results of operations are reported.

The planning process uses these updated forecasts as inputs to update plans that were created using the previous budget or the most recent forecast. These forecasts, which are updated continuously, bring back some of the realism required for thoughtful planning. The manager's aptitude for projecting future operating conditions can also be seen by tracking changes over time between the initial budgets and the updated forecasts.

In an organization that employs a methodology akin to the one just outlined, performance evaluation is predicated on comparisons between the initial budget and actual outcomes as well as the most recent forecast and actual results. Because performance evaluation is based in part on a comparison between actual results and the most recent forecast, this company's role conflict between motivation and evaluation is thereby lessened. The manager's performance is compared against a fixed standard as well as one that has probably been modified to account for unforeseen or uncontrollable changes in the environment.

5.4.9. General Recommendations

It can be challenging to resolve conflicts between the different budgeting system roles. This is partly because, although motivation and assessment are concepts within a complex field of the behavioral sciences, planning is essentially a simple business activity. Therefore, generalizations about how management should proceed to reduce such conflicts should be avoided. Nonetheless, the following points might help senior managers when they are considering how to resolve or alleviate such problems:

- Recognize that role conflicts exist. While the negative consequences of conflicts can frequently be mitigated, they cannot be completely eradicated. Acknowledging the existence of role conflicts is a significant first step in solving the issue. An excessive amount of dissatisfaction with modern budgeting methods arises from attempts to use a single budget for several purposes.
- Remember that the relative importance of each of the budget's roles may vary with the level of the organization. Based on the idea that the level of the organization involved determines the relative importance of the various roles a budget serves, the GMJ technique was previously discussed. Depending on what level of the organization the budget is being used at, different planning and motivational factors are important. At lower levels, incentive is derived from the budget. Its importance to intraorganizational coordination and financial planning increases at higher levels. Setting priorities for each role at the different organizational levels helps lessen the effects of role conflicts, even though GMJ does not completely eliminate them.

Similarly, the technique of differentiating among the levels of the organization as to where the performance of managers will be evaluated on the basis of revised or ex post facto budgets is based on the principle that particular roles of the budget do not have the same importance at all levels of the organization.

- Remember that reliance on other elements of the management control system can be helpful in reducing role conflicts. Businesses that implement the tight ship policy could be said to place a high value on motivation. For motivational purposes, budget objectives are set at challenging but attainable levels. Any negative consequences on financial planning are addressed by putting in place efficient reporting systems, backup plans, and other management coordinating tools in a timely and hopefully effective manner.
- Recognize that role conflicts may be reduced by restructuring the budgeting system itself. Role conflict is lessened in rolling and adjustable budget scenarios by repeating the budgeting process multiple times a year. This recycling makes it possible to provide the planning process with continuously updated data. Additionally, it enables the explicit consideration of unanticipated or uncontrollable factors that would not be included

in a more traditional budgeting system's process of setting the budgeted objectives. The application of fixed standards—or, in the case of adjustable budgets, variable standards based on predetermined parameters—maintains motivation.

Where regular revised forecasts are submitted, role conflicts can be reduced both by providing continually updated information for the planning process and by partially basing the evaluation of performance on a comparison of actual results with latest forecast.

Did you get it?

1. **What role do operational budgets play in performance evaluation and goal setting?**
2. **How do operational budgets assist in planning and controlling business activities?**
3. **What impact do operational budgets have on decision-making processes within organizations?**

ROLE MODEL

MILTON FRIEDMAN: AMERICAN ECONOMIST AND STATISTICIAN

Milton Friedman was American economist and educator, one of the leading proponents of monetarism in the second half of the 20th century. He was awarded the Nobel Prize for Economics in 1976. With George Stigler and others, Friedman was among the intellectual leaders of the Chicago school of economics, a neoclassical school of economic thought associated with the work of the faculty at the University of Chicago that rejected Keynesianism in favor of monetarism until the mid-1970s, when it turned to new classical macroeconomics heavily based on the concept of rational expectations. Several students, young professors and academics who were recruited or mentored by Friedman at Chicago went on to become leading economists, including Gary Becker, Robert Fogel, Thomas Sowell and Robert Lucas Jr.

1. **Education and Career:** Friedman was one year old when his family moved from Brooklyn, New York, to Rahway, New Jersey, where he grew up. He won a scholarship to Rutgers University, studied mathematics and economics, and earned a bachelor's degree there in 1932. While at Rutgers he encountered Arthur Burns, then a new assistant professor of economics, whom Friedman ultimately regarded as his mentor and most important influence. Burns introduced him to Alfred Marshall's Principles of Economics, and Friedman later would approvingly quote Marshall's description of economics as "an engine for the discovery of concrete truth." Friedman always insisted that the study of economics was not merely a mathematical game and that it should enable one to understand how the real world works. Friedman continued his economics studies at the University of Chicago (A.M., 1933) and Columbia University (Ph.D., 1946). While at Chicago he took Jacob Viner's price theory course and met his future wife, Rose Director. In 1935 he moved to Washington, D.C., to assist with a consumer budget study for the Natural Resources Committee. Two years later Friedman took a job with the National Bureau of Economic Research in New York City so that he could join Simon Kuznets in studies of income and wealth distribution, in particular the distribution of professional incomes. His finding—that barriers to entry maintained by the American Medical Association helped to explain the much higher incomes of physicians relative to other comparable professional groups—was the source of some controversy when it was finally published. In the early years of World War II, Friedman worked at the Department of the Treasury in the Division of Tax Research and later for the Statistical Research Group at Columbia University, where he was a member of a team that applied statistical analysis to war research. He also taught for one year each at the Universities of Wisconsin and Minnesota. In 1946 he accepted a position in the

economics department at the University of Chicago, which, except for occasional sabbaticals or visiting appointments, would be his academic home for the next 30 years. He became a full professor in 1948, was named the Paul Snowden Russell Distinguished Service Professor of Economics in 1962, and became an emeritus professor in 1983.

At Chicago Friedman taught courses in price theory and monetary economics, and in 1953 he established the Money and Banking Workshop—an important forum for faculty members, graduate students working on dissertations in the field, and occasional outside visitors. The workshop became renowned for the presentation and critical appraisal of papers in monetary economics. In 1947 Friedman attended the opening meeting of the Mont Pèlerin Society, an organization founded by F.A. Hayek and dedicated to the study and preservation of free societies. Friedman would later say that his participation at the meeting "marked the beginning of my active involvement in the political process." His multifold involvement included advising Presidents Richard M. Nixon and Ronald W. Reagan on economic policy, participating in various institutes and societies, and writing a regular column from 1966 to 1984 for Newsweek magazine, in which his articles would alternate with those presenting more liberal views on economic matters, by scholars such as Paul Samuelson and Lester Thurow. Friedman's public policy positions included support of flexible exchange rates and a monetary growth rule, school vouchers, a balanced budget amendment, and the decriminalization of recreational drugs (see also drug use); he opposed conscription and various forms of price controls—from the minimum wage to rent controls.

2. **Contributions to Economic Theory:** Friedman's contributions to economic theory are numerous. One of his earliest, described in A Theory of the Consumption Function, was the articulation of the permanent income hypothesis, the idea that a household's consumption and savings decisions are more affected by changes in its permanent income than by income changes that household members perceive as temporary or transitory. The permanent income hypothesis provided an explanation for some puzzles that had emerged in the empirical data concerning the relationship between the average and marginal propensities to consume. It also helped to explain why, for example, fiscal policy in the form of a tax increase, if perceived as temporary, might not lead to the intended reductions in consumption; instead, the increased tax might be financed out of savings, leaving consumption levels unchanged. That was Friedman's novel finding: if households do not perceive permanent income as changing, they will maintain their established spending patterns.

Friedman's best-known contributions are in the realm of monetary economics, where he is regarded as the founder of monetarism and as one of the successors of the "Chicago school" tradition of economics. In the 1950s macroeconomics was dominated by scholars who adhered to theories promoted by John Maynard Keynes. Keynesians believed in using government-sponsored policy to counteract the business cycle, and they held that fiscal policy was more effective than monetary policy in neutralizing, for example, the effects of a recession. Friedman opposed the Keynesian view that "money does not matter," instead promoting the theory that changes in the money supply affect real economic activity in the short run and the price level in the long run. He stated his case in his introduction to Studies in the Quantity of Money, a collection of articles that had been contributed by participants in the Money and Banking Workshop. That work was followed by an article, "The Relative Stability of Monetary Velocity and the Investment Multiplier in the United States, 1897–1958", coauthored with David Meiselman, in which the stability and importance of the Keynesian multiplier was questioned. The multiplier, forming a link between changes in autonomous expenditure and subsequent changes in national income, is a key element in the Keynesian case for effective and predictable fiscal policy.

In 1963 Friedman published the first of three books he would coauthor with Anna J. Schwartz, A Monetary History of the United States, 1867–1960. Combining theoretical and empirical analysis with institutional insights, that volume provided an intricately detailed account of the role of money in the U.S. economy since the Civil War. Especially influential was the authors' claim that the Great Depression would have been a typical downturn had it not been for policy errors made by the Federal Reserve.

In 1967 Friedman made another seminal contribution to Keynesian-monetarist debates in his presidential address before the American Economic Association. In it he questioned the validity of another key Keynesian construct, the Phillips curve, which asserted that a stable trade-off exists between the rate of wage inflation and the unemployment rate. Friedman argued that the trade-off was temporary and depended on workers' being "fooled" by unanticipated wage inflation into thinking that a rise in their nominal wage was a rise in their real wage, thus inducing them to produce more output. According to Friedman, reducing unemployment below what he dubbed the "natural rate" required not a one-time wage increase but accelerating wage inflation. The "stagflation" of the 1970s (literally, a combination of economic stagnation and inflation), impossible in a simplified Keynesian framework, was seen by many as confirmation of Friedman's hypothesis. In any event, it marked the end of the dominance of the Keynesian model in macroeconomics.

In 1975 Friedman traveled to Chile, where he delivered a series of lectures and public talks and met with the country's then military dictator, Augusto Pinochet. Friedman advised Pinochet in a subsequent letter to administer a "shock treatment" to the Chilean economy to cure it of runaway inflation. His prescriptions, eventually implemented under the direction of a group of Chilean economists who had trained at the University of Chicago in the 1950s and '60s (the "Chicago boys"), included drastic cuts in public spending, the privatization of state-operated enterprises, the elimination of wage and price controls, and the deregulation of financial markets and foreign trade. The consequences of those measures have been intensely debated in numerous studies. Friedman was widely criticized for apparently lending support to the dictatorship, a charge that he and his supporters regarded as unfair. In 1976, the year he retired from the University of Chicago, Friedman was awarded the Nobel Prize for Economics. In 1977 he became a member of the Hoover Institution on War, Revolution and Peace, a conservative think tank. About the same time, he began work with his wife, Rose, on the Public Broadcasting Service (PBS) television series Free to Choose, a counterpoint to John Kenneth Galbraith's Age of Uncertainty. Their popular series extolling the virtues of a free market system eventually led to a book and a set of educational videos of the same title. In 1998 the Friedmans published their memoirs, Two Lucky People. Over the course of his career, Friedman became an articulate spokesman for free markets and free societies in an era when many social scientists disparaged market solutions to social problems. Friedman's collaborative work with Anna J. Schwartz has remained a vital resource for those interested in the monetary history of the United States. Other legacies include Friedman's revival of a monetary approach to macroeconomics and his persistent critique of Keynesian economics.

SUMMARY

- A budget is an estimation of revenue and expenses over a specified future period of time and is usually compiled and re-evaluated on a periodic basis. Budgets can be made for a person, a group of people, a business, a government, or just about anything else that makes and spends money.
- An operating budget concerns the ongoing projections of revenue and expense items that affect the income statement.
- A master budget is the most comprehensive of all budgets. Generally, a master budget is prepared for a year and includes a balance sheet for a year hence and all the departmental income and expense statements for the next year.
- Budget control is a term that is used to describe the process of managing individual line items within a household or business budget so that expenditures over and above the allocated amounts do not take place.
- Fiscal policy is a key tool of macroeconomic policy, and consists of government spending and tax policy.
- The operating budgets include the budgets for sales, manufacturing costs (materials, labor, and overhead) or merchandise purchases, selling expenses, and general and administrative expenses.
- The Direct Labor Budget shows the total direct labor hours calculated using the cost of the direct labor (number of units produced multiplied by how many hours spent to produce them), multiplied by the cost per labor hour.
- The selling expenses budget includes the variable and fixed selling expenses for the budget reporting period.
- The production manager, for example, might be evaluated on the basis of his ability to meet budgeted standards for variable costs, fixed costs, delivery dates, and (product) quality standards. If a sizable emergency shipment was required of him during the period, the effects of this shipment on his reported results might be shown apart from the results of the remainder of his operations.

REVIEW QUESTIONS

1. Discuss the importance of forecasting in operations budgeting.
2. Explore the challenges and obstacles that businesses commonly encounter during the operations budgeting process.
3. What is the primary objective of operations budgeting in businesses?
4. How does operations budgeting contribute to effective resource allocation?
5. How does operations budgeting facilitate goal setting and performance evaluation within organizations?

MULTIPLE CHOICE QUESTIONS

1. **What is the primary purpose of operations budgeting?**
   a. To track historical expenses
   b. To project future revenues
   c. To allocate resources effectively
   d. To calculate return on investment
2. **Which of the following is NOT a typical component of an operations budget?**
   a. Sales forecast
   b. Marketing expenses
   c. Capital investments
   d. Human resource costs
3. **Which budget is focused on predicting the costs associated with producing goods or delivering services?**
   a. Sales budget
   b. Production budget
   c. Marketing budget
   d. Capital budget
4. **Which method of budgeting involves preparing budgets based on the expected level of activity?**
   a. Zero-based budgeting
   b. Incremental budgeting
   c. Activity-based budgeting
   d. Flexible budgeting
5. **What does a variance analysis in operations budgeting involve?**
   a. Comparing actual performance with budgeted figures
   b. Comparing actual performance with industry benchmarks
   c. Analyzing trends in historical data
   d. Forecasting future performance based on past results
6. **Which type of budgeting starts with a blank slate and requires justifying every expense?**
   a. Zero-based budgeting
   b. Incremental budgeting
   c. Activity-based budgeting
   d. Flexible budgeting
7. **In operations budgeting, what does the term "rolling budget" refer to?**
   a. A budget that is continually adjusted throughout the year

b. A budget that is fixed for a specific period
c. A budget that only considers variable costs
d. A budget that is prepared once and never revised

8. Which budget focuses on the expected sales revenue for a specific period?
a. Sales budget
b. Production budget
c. Cash budget
d. Capital budget

9. What is the primary benefit of activity-based budgeting?
a. It encourages cost control
b. It simplifies the budgeting process
c. It identifies cost drivers and allocates resources more accurately
d. It allows for easy comparison with historical data

10. What is the purpose of a cash budget in operations budgeting?
a. To track sales revenue
b. To monitor expenses related to production
c. To forecast cash inflows and outflows
d. To evaluate return on investment

Answer to Multiple Choice Questions

1. (c); 2. (c); 3. (b); 4. (d); 5. (a); 6. (a); 7. (a); 8. (a); 9. (c); 10. (c)

REFERENCES

1. Baker, W. M., & Powell, G. E., (2009). *Understanding Financial Management: A Practical Guide*. John Wiley & Sons.
2. Blocher, E., Stout, D., Juras, P., & Cokins, G., (2019). *Cost Management: A Strategic Emphasis*. McGraw-Hill Education.
3. Bragg, S. M., (2013). *Budgeting: A Comprehensive Guide*. John Wiley & Sons.
4. Collier, P. M., (2012). *Accounting for Managers: Interpreting Accounting Information for Decision Making*. John Wiley & Sons.
5. Debarshi, B., (2018). *Financial Statement Analysis: Theory, Application, and Interpretation*. CRC Press.
6. Drury, C., (2018). *Management and Cost Accounting*. Cengage Learning EMEA.
7. Emblemsvåg, J., (2010). *Managerial Economics*. Routledge.
8. Garrison, R. H., Noreen, E. W., & Brewer, P. C., (2017). *Managerial Accounting*. McGraw-Hill Education.

9. Hansen, D. R., & Mowen, M. M., (2018). *Cost Management: Accounting & Control*. Cengage Learning.
10. Helfert, E. A., (2001). *Financial Analysis Tools and Techniques: A Guide for Managers*. McGraw-Hill Professional.
11. Hilton, R. W., (2017). *Managerial Accounting: Creating Value in a Dynamic Business Environment*. McGraw-Hill Education.
12. Horngren, C. T., Datar, S. M., & Rajan, M. V., (2018). *Cost Accounting: A Managerial Emphasis*. Pearson.
13. Jiambalvo, J., (2017). *Managerial Accounting*. John Wiley & Sons.
14. Kaplan, R. S., & Atkinson, A. A., (2015). *Advanced Management Accounting*. PHI Learning.
15. Rappaport, A., (2015). *Expectations Investing: Reading Stock Prices for Better Returns*. Harvard Business Press.

CHAPTER 6

Financial Decisions and Risk

LEARNING OBJECTIVES

After studying this chapter, you will be able to:

- Understand the financial decisions
- Describe the financial risk
- Discuss on financial risk management
- Define the overdue financial obligations

INTRODUCTORY EXAMPLE

Asset Management

In finance, asset management refers to the overseeing of investment portfolios. Investment banks or individual asset managers will oversee the assets contained within this portfolio, mitigating risk while finding ways to increase their value. Investment services include a variety of products to achieve these goals, including equity, real estate, commodities, and mutual funds. Asset managers conduct research at both the macro and micro level, analyzing market trends to grow the portfolio successfully. As a company grows, its assets will increase accordingly. It's important to know the current value of each asset at any given time, to be sure that they're being used efficiently. It's also important to check the value of assets on a regular basis to ensure that all financial statements are accurate.

Asset management also helps a business identify and manage any associated risks. Additional benefits of asset management include:

- Improved efficiency – by tracking the company's assets from the beginning to end of their life cycles, asset managers can uncover wasteful purchases and inefficient uses.
- Reduced expenditure – assets like tools, equipment, and vehicles can be managed from a central system, which reduces new expenditures.
- Improved compliance – companies and government agencies are required to provide detailed reports regarding the acquisition and disposal of assets. Using a central asset management system keeps this information close at hand for compiling reports.

1. **High-End Asset Management Institutions:** Clients open an asset management account that comes with a personal financial advisor. You'll have access to a range of investment options to make the most existing assets. Asset managers at institutions like BlackRock or Fidelity Investments will look at the client's tax situation, liquidity needs, and income requirements.
2. **Mid-Range Asset Management Firms:** Mid-range asset management companies like Vanguard specialize in serving smaller investors, with options like mutual funds that pool together resources. Mid-range clients don't need to worry quite as much about tax structures or asset placement, but assets can still be put to work in a central investment portfolio.
3. **Digital Asset Management Tools:** If you'd prefer to put an internal asset management plan in place, look for digital platforms and software that use algorithms to manage portfolios. Tracking software can also be used as a central database of your existing assets.
4. **Individual As**set Managers: Asset management tools also include registered investment advisors, who outsource the management to a third party but can provide bespoke advice.

UNIT INTRODUCTION

The financial manager must make a critical decision regarding the financing mix of an organization, known as the financing decision. The main focus of financing decisions is the borrowing and distribution of capital needed for the company's investment choices. There are two possible funding sources from which the financing decision is made. The first is the company's own funds, which include retained earnings and share capital. The second method involves taking out loans, bonds, debentures, or other external funding sources. A balanced optimal capital structure is the goal of the financial decision. Financial risk is the possibility that a company won't be able to pay back its debts, which could result in potential investors losing their money invested in the business. The potential financial risk of a company increases with its debt load. Anyone considering investing will be made aware of various financial risks, including currency risk, and strategies to reduce them, like hedging. Businesses are subject to financial risk, and shareholders and prospective shareholders need to be aware of this.

6.1. FINANCIAL DECISIONS

→Learning Objectives

- To describe the types of financial decisions
- To define the factor influencing financial decisions
- To explain the working capital management decision
- In what ways managers can use finance to make better decisions
- To discuss the importance of financial decision

Managerial choices pertaining to a company's finances are referred to as financial decisions. These choices have a significant impact on the company's financial health. These choices may relate to purchasing assets, obtaining financing, and raising capital, managing daily capital expenditures, etc. Thus, a company's assets and liabilities are impacted by its financial decisions. They can result in revenue generation, profits, and the acquisition of assets and money for the business. They may also pertain to costs incurred, liabilities created, or money leaving the company.

Naturally, all of these financial choices may be made with both the long and short terms in mind. Financial decisions classified as long-term are those that are made with a year or longer in mind. These could include capital budgeting, investment choices, and the acquisition of long-term funding and loans with terms ranging from five to ten years. Financial decisions that are made for a brief duration—typically less than a year—are referred to as short-term decisions. These choices have to do with managing working capital, setting up short-term credits and funds, paying dividends, etc., (Figure 6.1).

Figure 6.1. *Financial decisions.*

Source: https://www.etmoney.com/blog/top-tips-for-better-financial-decisions/.

6.1.1. Types of Financial Decisions

Everything you need to know about the different kinds of financial decisions that businesses make. Financing, investments, dividends, and working capital management are the main focuses of financial decision-making. A business enterprise cannot survive over time if minimum financial performance levels are not met, and decision-making aids in utilizing available resources to help achieve organizational objectives.

Therefore, financial management basically provides a conceptual and analytical framework for financial decision making. Every company is required to take three main financial decisions, they are:

- Investment Decision
- Financing Decision
- Dividend Decision

1. **Investment Decision:** An investment decision is a financial choice that affects how the company's money is allocated among various assets. One may make short-term or long-term investment decisions. Capital budgeting decisions are long-term investment choices that entail significant long-term investments and are non-reversible unless they come at a high cost. Working capital decisions are short-term investment choices that have an impact on a company's daily operations. It involves choosing how much cash, inventory, and receivables to have on hand. The financial success of a business can typically be seriously harmed by a poor capital budgeting decision. A poor choice regarding working capital has an impact on a company's liquidity and profitability.

Keyword

Business enterprise is any endeavor where the primary motive is profit and not mere employment for oneself and others. It is the activity of providing goods and services involving industrial, financial, and commercial aspects.

Factors Affecting Investment Decisions / Capital Budgeting Decisions:

- **Cash flows of the project:** The series of cash receipts and payments over the life of an investment proposal should be considered and analyzed for selecting the best proposal.
- **Rate of return:** The expected returns from each proposal and risk involved in them should be taken into account to select the best proposal.
- **Investment criteria involved:** The various investment proposals are evaluated on the basis of capital budgeting techniques. Which involve calculation regarding investment amount, interest rate, cash flows, rate of return etc. It is to be considered which technique to use for evaluation of projects.

2. **Financing Decision:** A financial decision that includes determining how much money needs to be raised over the long term from different sources, such as bank loans, debentures, equity shares, and preference shares. Defined as a financial choice. Stated differently, it refers to a choice regarding the organization's "capital structure."

Capital Structure Owner's Fund + Borrowed Fund

Factors Affecting Financing Decision:

- **Cost:** The cost of raising funds from different sources is different. The cost of equity is more than the cost of debts. The cheapest source should be selected prudently.
- **Flotation Cost:** The price associated with issuing securities, including prospectus costs, underwriter fees, and broker commissions is known as the flotation cost. The source of financing is less appealing the higher the flotation cost.
- **Cash Flow Position of the Business:** In case the cash flow position of a company is good enough then it can easily use borrowed funds.
- **Control Considerations:** When current shareholders are prepared to cede control of the company, they can raise capital through the sale of equity shares. However, borrowing money is still an option if current shareholders wish to maintain total control over the company.
- **State of Capital Markets:** It is easy to raise money during a boom by issuing shares, but it is also easy to raise money during a depression by taking on debt.

3. **Dividend Decision:** Dividend decisions are financial decisions that address how much of the company's profits should be paid to shareholders as dividends and how much should be set aside for potential future needs as retained earnings. The portion of the profit that is given to shareholders is referred to as the dividend. The ultimate goal of increasing shareholder wealth should be considered when making a dividend decision.

Factors affecting Dividend Decision:

- **Earnings:** A company with strong and consistent earnings can declare a high dividend rate because dividends are paid from both current and historical earnings.
- **Stability of Dividends:** Businesses typically adhere to a steady dividend policy. In the event that earnings fluctuate slightly or grow temporarily, the dividend per share remains unchanged.
- **Growth Prospects:** If the company has room to grow in the near future, it will keep its earnings and not declare a dividend, or only a small amount of one.
- **Cash Flow Positions:** Since paying dividends requires a cash outflow, having enough cash on hand is a prerequisite for declaring dividends.
- **Preference of Shareholders:** The preferences of shareholders are also considered when determining

dividends. If shareholders want a dividend, the company can decide to declare one. In this scenario, the dividend amount is determined by the level of shareholder expectations.

- **Taxation Policy:** A business that declares a dividend must pay tax on it. A company that faces higher dividend taxes will likely choose to pay out fewer dividends; conversely, a company that faces lower tax rates will be able to declare more dividends.

6.1.2. Factor Influencing Financial Decisions

Making financial decisions requires a great deal of skill and caution because they have a long-term impact on an organization's financial health. Therefore, considering both internal and external factors when making decisions would be appropriate. Now, we'll quickly go over how these factors affect financial decisions (Figure 6.2).

Figure 6.2. *Factor influencing financial decisions.*

Source: https://mylibrary24.com/wp-content/uploads/2019/01/factors-influencing-financial-decisions-1.jpg.

6.1.2.1. External Factors

The environment that a business enterprise must function in is referred to as an external factor. These are external factors that are out of management's control and influence. A prudent management team implements policies that are best suited to the nation's current and future political, socioeconomic, and social environments.

The following external factors enter into decision making process:

1. **State of Economy:** A finance manager would be wise to refrain from taking on new investment activities or expanding existing expansion programs during a period when the economy as a whole is engulfed in a state of uncertainty, there is little chance of recovery in the coming years, and investing carries a significant amount of risk. Alternatively, should it be determined that the economy is poised to bounce back from its current precarious situation, the finance manager should seize the opportunity to make profitable investments. In addition, he ought to decide on the most lucrative project beforehand after assessing the current project's economic viability so that it can be seized when the chance arises. Decisions about financing are also influenced by the nation's economy. When the economy is doing well and investors are eager to invest more and more of their savings, the company can raise the required amount of money from the market by floating securities. However, keep in mind that when demand increases, interest rates tend to harden, forcing the company to offer a higher interest rate (dividend rate). The company's cost of capital would rise as a result. Debenture financing should be prioritized

by finance managers in order to reduce financing costs, as it offers advantages over equity trading in terms of cost reduction. Raising outside capital presents serious challenges during recessions. In such a situation, internal financing should be prioritized more, necessitating a strengthening of the company's reserve position. A company's dividend policy ought to be responsive to shifting market circumstances as well.

Conservatism should be practiced if there are signs that the company is about to enter a period of decline. This is because the company might require all of its cash resources to safely navigate the period of decline until its sales soar. Businesses typically offer higher dividend rates during boom times in order to attract capital from the market. As a result, the management is forced to declare a higher dividend rate. Since the company's earnings increase significantly during prosperous times, the management shouldn't have any financial difficulties as a result. During boom times, there's also a good chance that management will implement a cautious dividend policy in order to ensure the company has enough cash on hand to support its expansion needs.

2. **Structure of Capital and Money Markets:** Business owners will not have many difficulties obtaining even a sizable amount of capital in environments where the institutional structure of capital and money markets is well developed and organized, with a multitude of financial institutions offering both short- and long-term financial assistance and investors who are risk-takers displaying a keen interest in security dealings in the stock market. Businesspeople are free to choose the best financing combination to lower cost of capital, and a variety of alternative sources are at their disposal. Additionally, the organization is better equipped to modify its funding sources in reaction to significant shifts in its financial requirements. It gives business owners more negotiating leverage when interacting with potential fund suppliers in addition to allowing them to use the kind of funding that is most easily accessible at any given time. Entrepreneurs find it challenging to obtain significant amounts of resources from the market when there is no organized capital market. They have to raise capital from closely held circles. In such a state of affairs, policy of internal financing is pursued so as to enable the firm to draw upon its resources in times of need for funds.

3. **State Regulations:** A finance manager is required to make investment decisions within the state-provided legal framework. It is not free for entrepreneurs to start any business they want in a socialist nation like India. Industrial Policy Resolution 1956, spells out clearly the industrial fields in which the Govt. will enter and those where private sector will have freedom to operate. Through industrial licensing system the Government seeks to ensure that the private sector business entrepreneurs do not intrude into prohibited areas. Under such circumstances a finance

manager has to consider the viability of only those projects which are permissible by the Government.

4. **Taxation Policy:** Taxation is the most predominant factor influencing business decisions since it takes away bigger slice of business income. While deciding to invest in projects, a finance manager has to keep in view the existence of tax incentives.

5. **Requirements of Investors:** A finance manager should carefully evaluate the needs of possible investors when making financing decisions. Investor types may differ in terms of their perceptions of safety, liquidity, and profitability. Prudent and liquidity-conscious investors prefer to hold securities that can guarantee a return of capital and a guarantee of return after a predetermined period of time. On the other hand, there might be investors who prioritize profitability over liquidity and who are less risk-taking. Investors of this kind would rather put their savings into stocks. To accommodate as many investors as possible, the management must therefore issue a variety of securities in order to raise a sizable amount of capital for this project. Additionally, the shifting business and economic environments have an impact on the psychology of investors. When there is economic turmoil or a business depression, even risk-taking investors would prefer to hold senior securities. Conversely, when there is economic prosperity, shares are valued higher even by less risk-taking investors. Therefore, , finance managers need to be well-aware of the current sentiment within the investing community. Dividend policy must be geared to investors in general and existing stockholders and potential stockholders in particular. This helps in maximization of the market value of the firm.

6. **Lending Policy of Financial Institutions:** Financial institutions' lending policies may also have an impact on a company's investment choices. If financial institutions decide to grant loans to non-priority projects on extremely strict terms and conditions while adhering to the policy of concessional financing to priority projects, the finance manager would logically give the former group of projects more weight when making investment decisions than the later ones, assuming all else stays the same. Furthermore, the lending practices of the financial institutions should be closely considered when determining which sources of funding must be used to raise capital. Financial institutions occasionally provide loans on terms and conditions that the management may find unacceptable. For instance, financial corporations in India usually insist on maintenance of debt-equity ratio for medium and large scale project as 1.5:1 and promoter's contribution of 20–25% of the project cost while considering loan application of a firm. Under such a condition, a firm seeking loan from the financial institutions must maintain the ratio of debt to equity at a level desired by them. As a result, the finance manager must appropriately alter the company's financing mix

to make it follow the intended pattern. Therefore, the finance manager will need to investigate whether it would be practical to obtain loans from the institutions in the previously mentioned circumstances.

Keyword

Economic environment refers to all the external economic factors that influence buying habits of consumers and businesses and therefore affect the performance of a company.

6.1.2.2. Internal Factors

Internal factors are those that are associated with the internal workings of the company, including its size, nature, expected return, cost, and risk; asset structure; ownership structure; expectations of consistent and predictable earnings; age of the company; liquidity of company funds and working capital requirements; limitations in debt agreements; control factor; and management attitude. A finance manager must make financial decisions within the nation's economic and legal framework while taking the company's many attributes into consideration. Impact of each of these factors upon financial decisions will now be discussed in the following lines.

1. **Nature of Business:** Business nature can have an impact on a company's dividend policy, capitalization structure, and investment pattern. A significant portion of funds in trading concerns are invested in current assets, with fixed assets claiming a nominal proportion. In manufacturing and public utility concerns, on the other hand, the majority of funds must be utilized for the acquisition of fixed assets. The requirements for fixed assets in capital goods industries are always greater than those in consumer goods industries, similar to other manufacturing sectors. It is also important to carefully consider how the nature of business operations affects the composition of capitalization. Because the demand for their products is likely to remain constant throughout business booms and downturns, companies that produce staple goods typically see stability in their earnings levels. Because of this, they might rely more heavily on debt to raise money for the company. In contrast, the level of business earnings varies for industrial enterprises that produce non-essential products because the demand for those products varies in line with fluctuations in the economy. Such businesses' management would not decide to impose fixed fees on themselves. Similarly, companies in the public utility and industrial sectors that produce necessities may adopt a liberal dividend policy in order to declare a higher dividend rate due to their consistent and gradual earnings growth.
2. **Size of Business:** Businesses in the same industry may invest differently from one another, mostly due

to differences in operational scale. Larger companies require comparatively larger sums of money to purchase fixed assets because they automate their production processes, something that smaller businesses cannot afford. Larger companies typically build their own buildings to house the factory and acquire plant and machinery to carry out production work, but small businesses with limited capital can operate by renting or leasing plant and equipment and buildings. Compared to their larger counterparts, smaller businesses have less access to capital and the money market due to their poor credit standing. Generally speaking, investors are wary of purchasing stock and debentures in smaller companies. These smaller businesses also lack the necessary number of fixed assets to be able to guarantee a loan. For this reason, management in smaller companies must arrange funding from tightly knit groups. Smaller businesses' owners may be reluctant to list their companies for public offering if they want to keep control over the company, even if they are well-positioned to raise equity share capital. Larger companies, on the other hand, have an easier time obtaining the money they need from various capital sources and money markets. As a result, management in these companies believes it is beneficial to use increasing amounts of debt to satisfy business needs because doing so would typically lower the cost of capital. A company's size has an impact on its dividend decision as well. Smaller businesses are forced to rely on internal funding sources due to the difficulty of accessing external funding sources, and as a result, management may choose to implement a conservative dividend policy in order to keep a higher share of company profits.

3. **Expected Return, Cost and Risk:** The project's estimated return on investment, cost, and associated risk are important considerations when making an investment. When the distribution of results is known and the risk of each project is the same, a finance manager will naturally choose the investment proposal that yields the highest returns relative to its cost. Where different projects have varying degrees of riskiness, allowance will have to be made for the absorption of risk. This is usually done by adjusting the discount rate, i.e., rate of interest which is employed to discount future net cash flows of the project to present values.

   As a result, a higher discount rate is used in relation to a wider range of outcomes, which implies that returns will be decreased more quickly due to the increased allowance for the risk associated with their realization. The risk-free discount rate is used for investments that carry no risk. Higher and higher discount rates are used as risk rises. In this manner, the ultimate course of action is selected after the necessary adjustments for the risk factor. A finance manager making a dividend decision should consider the earning potential of the current investment projects. If a company has many investment projects with enormous earning potential that could exhaust its earnings and the company's shareholders strongly prefer current dividends, the finance manager in this scenario needs to make a strong case to the shareholders for the necessity of retaining an increasing amount of earnings and enforcing a strict dividend policy. To satisfy shareholder preferences, management should adopt a liberal dividend policy in cases where the projects at hand only offer a normal return.

4. **Asset Structure of Firm:** Businesses that have a sufficient amount of fixed assets are forced to use debt in order to benefit from less expensive sources of funding. For instance, because they can mortgage their assets to secure loans, steel and public utility companies can rely significantly on debentures to raise capital. However, trading companies should rely more on short-term debt and less on long-term debt for their financial needs, as their assets, which are primarily receivables and inventory values, are reliant on the company's continued profitability.

5. **Structure of Ownership:** In private companies with concentrated ownership, the management may have an easier time convincing the owners to adopt a strict dividend policy that is in the best interests of the company. However, the finance manager must insist on the continuation of the generous dividend policy in public limited companies with a large number of shareholders with different preferences.

6. **Probabilities of Regular and Steady Earnings:** The finance manager needs to see the company's past few years' worth of earnings trends in order to plan the capitalization and determine how debt and equity are related. Reliance on debt may be preferable in situations where the company's earnings have historically been fairly stable and this trend is likely to continue in the future. The management may issue preferred shares in order to raise money if the company's earnings have historically been erratic but, when averaged over a number of years, provide a fair margin over the preferred stock dividend. When a company's earnings have historically fluctuated significantly and it is impossible to predict its future earnings with any degree of confidence, it runs the risk of taking on debt. There must be common stock issued. When a company's earnings have historically fluctuated significantly and its future earnings are not predictable, it runs the risk of taking on debt. Common stock must therefore be issued. The degree of earnings stability is a significant factor affecting dividend policy. However, a policy like this will put businesses at risk, especially those whose earnings are highly variable. Even with relatively high business earnings, it would be wise for such companies to declare a lower dividend rate in order to use those earnings to maintain the dividend rate during difficult times.

7. **Age of the Firm:** Because there are comparatively more risks associated with investing in new ventures, most investors are reluctant to do so. Because of their weak capital foundation, lenders also hesitate to make loans. As such,

new businesses face significant challenges when trying to raise capital from the market. They go after stock brokers and underwriters, offering them greater commissions and brokerage for the sale of their securities. Therefore, the amount of debt in a new company's total capitalization will be minimal. Even though new businesses are well-positioned to raise capital through the issuance of debentures, a finance manager should try to avoid taking on a lot of debt because, in that scenario, interest on loans could consume a significant portion of business revenue, leaving only a small amount for dividend distribution and retention for additional funding.

8. **Liquidity Position of the Firm and Its Working Capital Requirements:** When making decisions about dividends, a finance manager must take into account the company's cash position, its need for funds to pay off maturing obligations, and its requirements for working and fixed capital. Typically, dividend payments are made in cash. Therefore, the finance manager needs to take care to ensure that there is enough cash on hand to pay dividends. Large surpluses do not always indicate that the company has cash on hand, especially when a sizable portion of sales are made on credit. When sale proceeds associated with receivables are collected, the company might require money to purchase supplies for production processing. Therefore, even in the event of profit and cash availability, the company's working capital needs might be so pressing as to justify the implementation of a conservative dividend policy. Once more, when a company's past-due loans are coming due and it has enough cash on hand, the finance manager should preserve cash to cover those obligations and modify the dividend schedule appropriately. Businesses frequently use their earnings to finance the purchase of fixed assets. Even though a sizable profit has been made, the management in such cases must also exercise restraint in dividend distribution, at least for a few years.

> **Keyword**
>
> **Fixed assets** are items that a company plans to use over the long term to help generate income. Fixed assets are most commonly referred to as property, plant, and equipment.

9. **Restrictions in Debt Agreements:** When choosing how to raise capital and set a dividend policy, it is important to carefully review the terms of debt contracts as most of them have clauses that forbid using new debt or issuing debentures of the previous kind. Additionally, they limit and occasionally completely prohibit dividend payments until a set of requirements is met. It goes without saying that the finance manager should provide the board of directors with a summary of all contractual clauses that have any bearing whatsoever on dividends and capital structure.

6.1.3. Working Capital Management Decision

The financial manager can determine the proportion of funds that need to be raised from investors and potential sources of short-term funding by making decisions about working capital management. Understanding the right amount of cash and inventory is also beneficial. Essentially, managing a company's short-term funds is the main focus of working capital management. A high degree of working capital management is imperative for the finance manager. Working capital affects the company's profitability and liquidity. More current assets equate to high liquidity. A reduction in earnings. This will lower the possibility of the organization's short-term obligations being missed. This financial decision's interdependency is what makes it beautiful. We use the present value of cost and benefit calculations, which heavily rely on the discount rate, to make capital budgeting decisions. Whereas, the result of capital structure i.e., cost of capital has its usage as the discount rate in capital budgeting decision. Hence, we can say that there is interdependency in both investment and financial decisions. Similarly, due to huge investment in the capital budget the operating risk increases which leads to lower debt capital and reduces the financial risk. Hence it is very important for an organization to have a sound financial decision in order to reduce risks.

6.1.4. Ways Managers Can Use Finance to Make Better Decisions

Making decisions is a crucial managerial ability that has the power to both promote and inhibit financial performance. Businesses with quick and effective decision-making procedures are twice as likely to report recent decisions that resulted in financial returns of at least 20%. Developing your financial literacy and knowledge to comprehend and overcome business challenges is essential to helping position your organization for success and avoiding these pitfalls. These are five ways using finance can help you make better decisions and develop into a more capable manager.

1. **Perform Financial Statement Analysis:** When it comes to making decisions, financial statements are some of the most crucial tools at your disposal. You ought to be able to decipher and evaluate the information they offer in addition to reading them. Knowing the numbers on your balance sheet can help you determine the current state of your company's finances and whether it is headed toward success or failure. You can learn more about how cash is created and utilized by looking at its cash flow statement. You can assess how your company is performing in comparison to its anticipated performance by looking over its income statement. These statements, when examined in the context of an annual report, can provide important details about your business, including its annual profits and losses as well as the elements that have helped or hindered its expansion. With this knowledge at your disposal, you can decide more intelligently how to divide up the resources of your business and pursue its objectives.
2. **Estimate the Financial Impact of Projects and Initiatives:** You must make decisions about which projects and initiatives are worthwhile to pursue in order to lead your

team and department effectively. The projected return on investment (ROI) of a project can be calculated to provide numerical evidence for your proposal, demonstrating the potential profit margin and resources required to see the project through to completion.

The return on investment (ROI) of finished projects can also provide important information about how your company spent money and completed projects, giving you insightful knowledge for next time. Making better decisions with finance also involves doing a cost-benefit analysis. This data-driven decision-making approach offers a framework for conducting an evidence-based assessment of an initiative, enabling you to determine how the initiative's estimated benefits stack up against its costs. By using this method, you can choose which projects are likely to produce the best results and deconstruct complicated business decisions.

3. **Learn How to Budget:** An essential financial skill for managers and other decision-makers is budgeting. Your team's budget, at its core, is an essential tool for making sure your company has the resources it needs to accomplish its objectives. During the budgeting process, your team's work is broken down into a comprehensive set of deliverables. This allows you to track your spending against estimated expenses and adjust your project management strategy as needed to ensure tasks are finished on schedule and within budget. The planning and execution of company-wide initiatives can be influenced by your ability to effectively communicate performance and progress to stakeholders within your organization through effective budget management.

4. **Involve Your Team in Decision-Making:** In the process of making decisions, gathering, and evaluating a variety of options is crucial. Incorporating your team into significant business decisions can encourage more innovative problem-solving and enable a thorough assessment of the current problems. You can rely on the knowledge of your team members to provide important clarifications and to map out a course of action when dealing with financial decisions. It's possible that one of your staff members knows more about financial jargon than the other, or that they're better informed about the distinctions between IFRS and GAAP accounting rules. You can fill in your knowledge gaps and come up with a variety of viable solutions to business problems by asking your coworkers for their opinions and promoting dialog.

Keyword

Return on investment (ROI) is an approximate measure of an investment's profitability. ROI is calculated by subtracting the initial cost of the investment from its final value, then dividing this new number by the cost of the investment, and finally, multiplying it by 100.

5. **Track Financial Performance:** Making wise decisions requires having a thorough understanding of your company's financial performance in the past and present. By keeping an eye on financial KPIs, or key performance indicators, like working capital, return on equity, and gross profit margin, you can gain insight into the state of your company's finances and how your team is contributing to its strategic goals. Metrics such as profit and cash flow are also helpful in monitoring the financial health of your business, which can help you make decisions about allocating resources and personnel to meet your objectives. Developing an intuitive grasp of finance to support your decision-making can help you succeed in your position and improve team and organizational performance. Gaining knowledge of financial concepts and principles can help you succeed professionally even if you don't have a background in finance. It can also help you improve your management abilities. A company's ability to make sound financial decisions is essential to its success. Maximizing the financial worth/value of the business and its stakeholders is the primary goal and critical efficiency of professional managers. They need to boost profits while keeping the business's liquidity adequate additionally to reduce the company's level of risk. It is their responsibility to set objectives, work toward achieving them, weigh options and select the best course of action, carry out financial plans efficiently, update and review those plans on a regular basis, and, when needed, take corrective action.

6.1.5. Importance of Financial Decision

Among the various financial choices, capital budgeting or fixed asset investments are particularly important. The financial manager needs to exercise extra caution while making this choice. These decisions are relatively more important because of the following reasons (Figure 6.3):

1. **Long-term Growth and Effect:** Long-term assets are at stake in these choices. These resources are beneficial for production. Selling the products made in this way generates profit. Thus, it can be concluded that the longer these decisions are made, the more the business will grow. Furthermore, these impact the business's potential in the future.
2. **Large Amount of Funds Involved:** The capital budgeting preview includes decisions about fixed assets. These assets have significant capital invested in them. Should these choices prove to be incorrect, a significant loss of capital—a finite resource—occurs.
3. **Risk Involved:** Risk is inherent in capital budgeting decisions. There are two explanations for this. First of all, these choices are meant to last for a long time, so it is reasonable to expect profits for a number of years. It's possible that these estimations are off. Second, it is extremely difficult to reverse a decision once it has been made due to the significant investment involved.

4. **Irreversible Decisions:** These choices have a nature that makes them difficult to reverse quickly. The old machinery and other fixed assets, for example, would have to be sold at a throwaway price if a cotton mill was to be changed soon after it was established. There will be significant loss involved in doing this. Thus, it is exceedingly difficult to change these choices.

Figure 6.3. *Financial management: importance, functions, risk, and strategy.*

Source: https://navi.com/blog/wp-content/uploads/2022/06/financial-management.jpg.

Did you get it?

1. **How do changes in economic conditions, interest rates, and regulatory environments impact financial decision-making processes?**
2. **How do financial decisions impact shareholder value and overall corporate performance?**
3. **What are the ethical considerations that businesses should take into account when making financial decisions?**

6.2. FINANCIAL RISK

→Learning Objectives

- Define the financial risks for businesses
- Write the credit risks
- Describe the liquidity risks
- Focus on income risk

The risk of losing money on an investment or business endeavor is known as financial risk. Credit risk, liquidity risk, and operational risk are a few more prevalent and unique types of financial risks. One kind of risk that can cause interested parties to lose money is financial risk. This may indicate to governments that they are unable to manage monetary policy and may experience bond or other debt default. Corporations may fail in an endeavor that results in financial hardship for the company, but they also run the risk of defaulting on debt they take on.

Financial markets are exposed to risk because of a number of macroeconomic factors, shifts in the market interest rate, and the potential for sector or large corporation default. When people make choices that could endanger their income or their capacity to repay debts they have taken on, they put themselves at risk financially. Risks associated with money are ubiquitous, multifaceted, and impact almost everyone. There are financial risks, which you should be aware of. While being aware of the risks and taking precautions to keep yourself safe won't make them go away, they can lessen damage and the likelihood of a bad consequence.

6.2.1. Financial Risks for Businesses

Starting a business from the ground up is costly. Every company must at some point seek outside funding in order to expand. The business and any investors or stakeholders that have a stake in the company are exposed to financial risk as a result of this funding requirement. The risk involved in taking out a loan is called credit risk, sometimes referred to as default risk. In the event that the borrower is unable to make loan payments, they will default. Investors exposed to credit risk experience principal and interest losses in addition to a reduction in income from loan repayments. Additionally, the cost of collecting the debt may increase for creditors. A specific risk exists when one or a small number of businesses are having difficulty. This risk pertains to a business or small group of businesses and involves concerns about exposure to default, financial transactions, and capital structure. The phrase is usually employed to express an investor's doubts about receiving returns and the resulting risk of suffering a financial loss. When a company has inadequate management or faulty financial analysis, operational risk may arise. This is the risk of not succeeding in its endeavors due to internal factors.

6.2.2. Credit Risks

6.2.2.1. Lending Policies

Credit risk is the possibility of suffering losses on outstanding credit as a result of member nations' unwillingness or incapacity to make repurchases, or return credit that has been extended to them. Given that the International Monetary Fund (IMF) typically provides financing when other sources are unavailable to a member and has limited ability to diversify its loan portfolio, credit risk is inherent in the IMF's special role in the global monetary system. Furthermore, because of the nature of its lending, the IMF has a generally high credit concentration. The IMF uses a wide range of strategies to reduce credit risk. The main instruments for mitigating credit risk are the effectiveness of IMF lending policies regarding access, including phasing, program design, and conditionality. These factors are crucial in guaranteeing that IMF financial assistance aids members in resolving their balance of payments challenges. These regulations include evaluations of members' ability to carry out IMF repayment plans and adjustment plans, as well as the special access policy for significant commitments. With regard to potential users of Fund resources, this policy imposes more stringent scrutiny. It also reviews adherence to substantive criteria and involves the Executive Board early on, discussing potential risks to the IMF in the event that access surpasses 200% of their quota per year or 600% cumulatively, net of scheduled repurchases. The way charges and maturities are structured, as well as having sufficient junior co-financing from other official lenders, all help to reduce credit risks. In order to help borrowers adjust, the IMF passes along its low funding costs to them. However, when access to market financing is restored, a level- and time-based surcharge premium is added to help moderate large and/or prolonged resource use and to encourage timely repayment.

Keyword

Credit risk is the probability of a financial loss resulting from a borrower's failure to repay a loan.

6.2.2.2. Precautionary Balances

Precautionary balances support the IMF's financing mechanism, bolster its balance sheet, and help to guarantee the value of members' reserve positions. The provision of financial assistance by the IMF may lead to significant exposures, and the organization's duty to address members' balance of payments needs is likely to result in high credit concentration. Precautionary balances shield the IMF's balance sheet from losses resulting from credit or other financial risks by addressing residual risks after other multilayered risk management framework components have been applied. This role is essential to maintaining the value of members' reserve assets and fostering trust in the safety and liquidity of members' reserve positions as seen from the perspective of the balance sheet. Additionally, precautionary balances aid in ensuring that International Financial Reporting Standards are met by the IMF. The balance in the Special Contingent Account as well as the reserves kept in the General and Special Reserves make up the IMF's precautionary balances. Reserves are increased through three methods: contributions from IMF debtors and creditors under the burden-sharing mechanism, which may be refundable, and net income allocations decided upon annually by the Executive Board (including from surcharges). Regular reviews of the sufficiency of precautionary balances are carried out by the IMF.

6.2.2.3. Review of the Adequacy of Precautionary Balances

The Executive Board decided that the IMF's reserve accumulation should be formalized under two guidelines: (1) Reserves should cover credit outstanding to members in protracted arrears. (2) Reserves should include a margin for potential exposure to risk associated with credit in good standing. An indicative target of 3 to 5% was established for the latter. The Executive Directors requested that the IMF staff create a framework for reserve accumulation that is more open, regulated, and includes elements that look ahead to account for the variability in IMF lending. They stated that the mechanisms for building up reserves, the handling of reserves that exceed the target, and the setting and modification of the reserves target over time should all be covered by this framework. The Directors stressed that since the new income model is anticipated to greatly reduce the IMF's overall income risk, credit risk ought to be the main factor taken into account when evaluating reserve adequacy. They also backed the continued development of scenario analyzes and stress tests, as well as the use of a range of forward-looking indicators. The framework calls for broadly maintaining the precautionary balance target within a range that is correlated with changes in the total amount of credit outstanding. The framework consists of four main elements:

- **Reserve coverage ratio**: The reserve coverage ratio would be determined, subject to a minimum floor, between 20 and 30% of a forward-looking measure of credit outstanding. Although it tries to modify them for the unique conditions of the IMF, this proposal borrows strategies from other international financial organizations.
- **Forward-looking credit measure to anchor the range**: The credit measure that was used to calculate the range would aim to reduce some of the year-to-year volatility of credit movement while also having a significant forward-looking component. It would specifically consist of projections for the next two years, accounting for scheduled disbursements and repayments under all approved non-precautionary arrangements, and a three-year average of credit outstanding covering the preceding twelve months.
- **Treatment of precautionary arrangements**: Although the framework does not currently specifically include commitments made under precautionary measures when determining the range, it does permit the Executive Board to consider these commitments

when determining where to set the target.

- **A minimum floor for the target**: The framework includes a minimum floor for precautionary balances to protect against an unexpected increase in credit risk and ensure a sustainable income position.

6.2.3. Liquidity Risks

The possibility that the IMF won't have enough cash on hand to cover both its own responsibilities and members' financing needs is known as liquidity risk. The IMF needs to have enough readily available resources to fulfill member demand for IMF funding. Although the majority of the IMF's resources are revolving, the organization is nevertheless subject to liquidity risk due to unforeseen changes in the quantity and timing of credit extended to members during economic downturns. Moreover, the IMF must also stand ready to (1) meet, upon a member's representation of need, demands for a drawing of a member's reserve tranche position, which is part of the member's reserves, and (2) make drawings under borrowing agreements to fund encashment requests from lenders under bilateral borrowing agreements or the New Arrangements to Borrow in case of balance of payments need of the relevant creditor member.

Liquidity risk is lessened by the IMF's financial structure, but proper management of this risk is still necessary due to fluctuation and uncertainty in the size and timing of members' financing needs as well as possible member demands to utilize their reserve tranche positions. The IMF does not use market financing to cover unanticipated liquidity needs, but rather takes a multifaceted approach to ensure sufficient financial resources to cover its members' financing needs:

- The Executive Board, management, and staff keep a careful eye on the Forward Commitment Capacity (FCC), the IMF's primary indicator of its ability to provide new GRA resources to its members. The prudential balance is subtracted from the uncommitted usable resources from quota and IMF borrowing, plus repurchases one year ahead of schedule, less repayment on borrowing one year ahead of schedule, and the FCC. The basis for IMF lending is an asset exchange. The Executive Board reviews and approves members whose currencies are used in GRA lending operations in the Financial Transactions Plan (FTP) on a quarterly basis. The amount of SDRs and certain member currencies to be used in transfers and receipts anticipated to be made through the GRA during that time is specified by the IMF staff in the FTP. Exchange rate trends, the size and duration of external debt obligations, and recent and projected developments in the balance of payments and reserves are all taken into consideration when choosing which members to involve in financing IMF lending transactions. FTP members receive a liquid claim on the IMF (reserve tranche position) that earns interest based on the SDR interest rate in exchange for using the IMF's holdings of these currencies in lending operations. The Resource Mobilization Plan (RMP), a quarterly liquidity review conducted by the NAB, is comparable.
- The evaluation of longer-term resource requirements occurs at least every five years during

General Quota Reviews, which determine whether members' quotas are sufficient to meet the demand for IMF funding. The Articles of Agreement do not specify the methodology, but historically, the IMF's quota size has been evaluated in relation to estimates of member needs as well as trade and capital flows, GDP, and other global economic indicators.

- To increase its quota resources, the IMF may take on debt. It has two standing borrowing agreements: the General Arrangements to Borrow, which is only applicable in certain situations, and the New Arrangements to Borrow, which serves as the primary safeguard for quota resources. The IMF may borrow from the private markets, though it has never done so. It has also used ad hoc bilateral borrowing with official lenders.
- The prudential balance is meant to protect the claims of creditors' liquidity and account for the possibility of the IMF's resource base eroding. The IMF's Executive Board established a prudential ratio of 20%, which is based on past experience and assessments of the indicative level of uncommitted usable resources that the IMF would typically not use to make financial commitments.
- Level- and time-based surcharges encourage the repurchase of IMF credit when market access is restored, thereby mitigating the large and prolonged use of IMF credit and supporting the revolving nature of IMF resources.
- Risks to the Fund's liquidity are also mitigated by commitment fees. In 2009, the GRA lending toolkit underwent broader reforms that included the introduction of the current upward sloping fee structure. The purpose of this structure is to discourage excessively risky access.
- To further protect Fund liquidity and the revolving nature of Fund resources, access limits are another component of the Fund's risk management framework.

6.2.4. Income Risk

The risk of an annual income shortfall in relation to expenses is another issue the IMF has to deal with. This risk has happened in the past on occasion, such as in the lead-up to the global financial crisis when lending dropped to extremely low levels. The IMF creates revenue to pay for its administrative costs, demonstrating how it has modified the financial structure to increase the variety of revenue streams available to it. The new income model is based on more diversified revenue sources that are suitable to support the IMF's mandated broad range of activities and aims to reduce income risk associated with reduced lending. Furthermore, precautionary balances provide additional income from investments, further safeguarding the Fund's income. Changes to the margin on the basic rate of charge and surcharges, as well as adjustments to the burden sharing mechanism, are additional strategies to reduce income risk.

6.2.4.1. Interest Rate Risk

Interest rate risk is the chance that shifts in market interest rates will have an impact on future cash flows. The primary method by which the IMF reduces interest rate risk is by tying the rate of charge to the rate of compensation. The IMF directly links the rate of charge to the SDR interest rate (and thus to the rate of remuneration, which is frequently set at 100% of the SDR interest rate prior to burden-sharing adjustments) in order to reduce the impact of interest rate fluctuations on income.

The current SDR interest rate is used to compensate claims from drawings, so there is less interest rate risk associated with bilateral borrowings, issued notes, and borrowings under the enlarged and amended NAB. The borrowing proceeds are utilized for two purposes: either to repay borrowings under bilateral borrowing agreements and the enlarged and amended NAB, or to extend credit to member countries at the rate of charge, which is based on the SDR interest rate plus a margin.

Prudent duration limits help to reduce interest rate risk on investments. Interest rate risk is controlled for investments made through the Investment Account Fixed-Income Subaccount and for resources kept in the trust accounts by keeping the investment portfolio's duration to a weighted average effective duration of no more than three years. The Endowment Subaccount's investments are subject to a wider range of risks, including interest rate risk, because of its return objective.

These risks are kept to a minimum and are balanced by the Endowment Subaccount asset allocation, which is cautious and diversified. Additionally, because of its relatively small size, the IMF's overall balance sheet is less vulnerable to negative market movements. There are established protocols for routinely evaluating the Investment Account's performance, including the suitability of its risk limitations. By adopting the IA Rules and Regulations, the Executive Board, acting within the purview of its investment authority under the Articles, approves the investment objective, strategic benchmark, and primary risk control procedures for each and every IA investment. Managers and custodians are required to follow the IMF's risk approach by formal agreements.

6.2.4.2. Exchange Rate Risk

Exchange rate risk is the possibility that changes in foreign exchange rates will have an impact on the cash flows and financial position of an organization. The IMF is not exposed to exchange rate risk on its currency holdings of members in the GRA because members are obligated by the Articles of Agreement to maintain the value of their holdings in terms of SDR. A currency valuation adjustment receivable or payable results from any depreciation or appreciation of a member's currency relative to the SDR. This adjustment must be settled by the member as soon as possible following the conclusion of the fiscal year, or at other times upon request from the IMF or the member. Other than SDRs, the IMF's assets and liabilities include trade receivables and payables, and it mostly makes administrative payments in U.S. dollars, but these other assets and liabilities have minimal exposure to exchange rate risk. The trusts' and the Fixed-Income Subaccount's investments are subject to extremely little exchange rate risk. The securities in the portfolios are government bonds and Bank for International Settlements (BIS) Medium-Term Instruments, each of which is valued according to its weight in the SDR basket. However, the weight of each currency in the portfolio varies slightly from the weights in the SDR basket due to the securities included in the portfolio changing in value over time and producing cash flows. This results in some residual exchange rate risk. This risk is mitigated by regular (at least monthly) rebalancing of the portfolio. Regarding the Endowment Subaccount, the impact of foreign exchange volatility is controlled through mandatory hedging of part of the assets back to the base currency, the U.S. dollar.

Did you get it?

1. **What are the main types of financial risks that businesses encounter, and how do they differ?**
2. **What are the implications of credit risk for financial institutions and how do they manage it?**
3. **How does market risk affect investment portfolios and how can investors diversify to manage this risk?**

6.3. FINANCIAL RISK MANAGEMENT

→Learning Objectives

- Explain the pros and cons of financial risk
- Define the tools to control financial risk

Managing financial risks is a high priority for businesses, irrespective of their size or industry. In order to take control of the financial risks, you need to:

- identify and measure the risks
- decide on the level of risk you are willing to accept
- consider insurance to protect against business risk
- identify potential issues with cash flow
- review your financial arrangements with creditors
- be careful if extending credit to customers
- diversify your income sources
- regularly reassess your risks

Make sure to consider the various factors affecting financial risk. Broadly, these fall under two categories:

- **External Factors:** including economic downturns, market rates, industry changes, law changes, etc.
- **Internal Factors:** including underperformance, poor cash flow management, bad investments, new competition, staff issues, etc.

Financial risk is managed differently by different organizations. This procedure is contingent upon the nature of the business, the market it serves, and the amount of risk it is willing to take. In this way, the business owner and the company's directors are responsible for determining the risks, evaluating them, and determining how best to manage them.

1. **Identifying the Risk Exposures:** The first step in risk management is to identify the financial risks as well as their origins or causes. The balance sheet of the business is an excellent place to start. This gives an overview of the company's debt, liquidity, exposure to foreign exchange, interest rate risk, and vulnerability

to changes in commodity prices. In order to understand how income and cash flows change over time and how this affects the organization's risk profile, you should also look over the income statement and the cash flow statement.

Questions to ask here include:

- What are the main sources of revenue of the business?
- Which customers does the company extend credit to?
- What are the credit terms for those customers?
- What type of debt does the company have? Short-term or long-term?
- What would happen if interests rates were to rise?

Remember

The financial risk most commonly referred to is the possibility that a company's cash flow will prove inadequate to meet its obligations.

2. **Quantifying the Exposure:** Quantifying or assigning a numerical value to the hazards you have identified is the second step. Naturally, risk is unpredictable, so it is impossible to precisely quantify risk exposure. The standard deviation and regression method are two common statistical models used by analysts to assess a company's exposure to different risk factors. These tools calculate the deviation of your data points from the mean or average. Excel and other computer software can be used by small businesses to perform basic analysis in an accurate and efficient manner. Generally speaking, the riskier the data point or cash flow you're quantifying, the higher the standard deviation.
3. **Making a "Hedging" Decision:** You need to make a decision about your course of action based on your analysis of the risk sources. Based on a number of variables, including the company's objectives, its business environment, its appetite for risk, and whether the expense of mitigation outweighs the reduction in risk, you must decide whether to live with the risk exposure or take steps to mitigate it or hedge against it.

Generally, you might consider the following action steps:

- Reducing cash-flow volatility.
- Fixing interest rates on loans so you have more certainty in your financing costs.
- Managing operating costs.
- Managing your payment terms.
- Putting rigorous billing and credit control procedures in place.
- Saying farewell to customers who regularly abuse your credit terms.

- Understanding your commodity price exposure, that is, your susceptibility to variations in the price of raw materials. If you work in the haulage industry, for example, a rise in oil prices can increase costs and reduce profits.
- Making sure the right people are given the right jobs with the right degree of supervision, to reduce the risk of fraud.
- Performing due diligence on projects, for example, considering the uncertainties associated with a partnership or joint venture.

Remember

In a small business, the business owner and senior managers are responsible for risk management. It's only when the business grows to include multiple departments and activities that you may wish to bring in a dedicated Financial Risk Manager to manage risk — and make recommendations for action — on behalf of the company.

6.3.1. Pros and Cons of Financial Risk

Financial risk is merely present to varying degrees and is not intrinsically good or bad. Naturally, the word "risk" carries a bad connotation by definition, and financial risk is no different. A risk can emanate from a single enterprise and impact an entire industry, market, or global community. Uncontrollable external forces or sources can give rise to risk, which is frequently challenging to manage. Even though it's not exactly a good thing, being aware of the possibility of financial risk can help you make wiser business or investment decisions. The degree of financial risk connected to a security or asset is evaluated in order to help establish or determine the investment's value. The opposite of reward is risk. It could be argued that without taking some risk, neither growth nor progress can happen in a business or portfolio. Ultimately, even though financial risk is typically uncontrollable, it can be limited or managed.

Pros:

- Encourages more informed decisions
- Helps assess value (risk-reward ratio)
- Can be identified using analysis tools

Cons:

- Can arise from uncontrollable or unpredictable outside forces
- Risks can be difficult to overcome
- Ability to spread and affect entire sectors or markets

6.3.2. Tools to Control Financial Risk

Fortunately, there are a variety of tools that enable people, organizations, and governments to determine the level of financial risk they are assuming. The following are the most popular techniques used by financial experts to assess the risks connected to long-term investments or the stock market overall.

- The process of calculating a security's intrinsic value through a thorough assessment of the underlying business, including the company's earnings and assets, is known as fundamental analysis.
- Technical analysis, the process of evaluating securities through statistics and looks at historical returns, trade volume, share prices, and other performance data.
- Quantitative analysis, the evaluation of the historical performance of a company using specific financial ratio calculations.

For instance, the debt-to-capital ratio calculates the percentage of debt utilized in relation to the total capital structure of the business when assessing businesses. An investment that is riskier is indicated by a high debt ratio. A different ratio, the capital expenditure ratio, calculates how much money a company will have left over after paying off its debt by dividing its cash flow from operations by its capital expenditures. To lessen their exposure to different risks, professional money managers, traders, individual investors, and corporate investment officers employ hedging strategies. Hedging against investment risk is the deliberate use of tools, like options contracts, to reduce the likelihood of any unfavorable changes in price. To put it another way, you hedging your bet by making another.

Did you get it?

1. **What are some common challenges businesses encounter in implementing and maintaining robust financial risk management practices?**
2. **How do businesses use financial instruments such as derivatives and insurance to hedge against financial risks?**

6.4. OVERDUE FINANCIAL OBLIGATIONS

→Learning Objectives

- Describe the cooperative strategy on overdue financial obligations
- Understand the arrears clearance modalities for finance
- To deal with special charges

Past-due bills necessitate a calculated approach. Determine the extent of your financial obligations first, then rank them in order of urgency. Be honest in your communication with creditors, outlining your circumstances and looking into possible payback arrangements or extensions. If necessary, take assistance programs or debt consolidation options into consideration. Negotiate terms that are reasonable for your financial situation. Seek guidance from financial experts to establish a reasonable plan that you can stick with, paying your bills on time, and reviewing your spending plan on a regular basis. By being proactive and communicating well, you can gradually get back on track financially and lessen the weight of unpaid bills.

6.4.1. Cooperative Strategy on Overdue Financial Obligations

Three components make up the Strengthened Cooperative Strategy: (1) preventive actions to stop new arrears from arising, (2) increased cooperation with members who are behind on their payments, and (3) remedial actions of increasing severity to motivate members to work with the IMF to find a resolution to their arrears.

1. **Prevention:** The caliber of programs funded by the IMF is the best defense against the emergence of arrears. The IMF prioritizes the following in this situation: (1) helping members create robust and all-encompassing economic plans; (2) closely monitoring members' access to and the phasing of IMF financial support; (3) carrying out a clear evaluation of a member's ability and willingness to repay the IMF; and (4) guaranteeing sufficient balance of payments financing during the IMF arrangement. In order to get a reasonable assurance that member countries' central banks using IMF resources have the proper control systems in place to manage the resources appropriately and to provide accurate information, the IMF also introduced the safeguards policy in 2000. Furthermore, the IMF keeps stressing how important it is to stay up to date with the IMF. Certain financial or administrative arrangements, such as the upfront purchase of SDRs to cover

future obligations, may be utilized in some circumstances to guarantee on-time repayments to the IMF.

2. **Collaboration:** The collaborative component of the arrears strategy offers a framework for cooperating members in arrears to build a solid record of policy performance and payments to the IMF in order to normalize relations with the organization. As a result, in order to pay off their debt to the IMF and reclaim their right to financial support from the organization, members rely on their own funds or assistance from creditors. To assist members who are behind on their payments in establishing the necessary record, the IMF created the Staff-Monitored Program (SMP) and Rights Accumulation Program (RAP) in this regard.

i. **The Rights Accumulation Program:** The rights approach was created in 1990, and the 11 members who were in long-term arrears to the IMF at the end of 1989 were the only ones who could apply. A member who is behind on their payments may be eligible to receive a "right" under the RAP, which is a claim to a future payment from the IMF under a future agreement. This upcoming payment is contingent upon the member fulfilling their past due obligations, clearing their record on policies and payments to the IMF within the framework of an adjustment program under IMF supervision, and receiving IMF approval of a replacement arrangement.

Modified financing assurances are required for all RAPs, and upper credit tranche conditionality is present. Members of these programs are expected to adopt and carry out robust adjustment plans that demonstrate a reliable track record of enforcing policies, as well as contribute to the establishment of favorable conditions for long-term growth and significant advancements toward external viability. Programs in this category ought to follow the macroeconomic and structural policy guidelines linked to the PRGT and programs in the higher credit tranches. Adequate external financing, including debt rescheduling and relief from bilateral and private creditors as well as new financing from various sources, is necessary for the program in order to support the member's adjustment efforts. In order to participate in the RAPs, members must, at the very least, keep up with their obligations to the World Bank and the IMF that fall due during the program's duration. RAPs typically last three years, but they can be customized to a member's unique situation by extending the track record period.

ii. **Staff-Monitored Programs:** If capacity limitations and/or inadequate financing assurances make it difficult for a member with prolonged arrears to adopt and implement programs that satisfy the requirements of upper credit tranche conditionality, Staff-Monitored Programs (SMPs) may be used in arrears cases. In these situations, informal staff monitoring has made it possible for IMF staff members to have in-depth policy discussions, assisting in the establishment or restoration of a track record on policies and IMF payments that can also serve as a source of information for creditors and donors regarding the member's dedication to sound and credible policies. It is expected that the member will pay the IMF at least the amount that newly matured obligations would requirc.

3. **Remedial Measures:** Member nations with past-due IMF obligations that do not actively collaborate with the IMF to find a solution to their arrears issue are subject to corrective measures. Under an increasing timetable, corrective actions are implemented. The schedule directs the Executive Board's deliberation of corrective actions ranging in severity; however, the implementation of each specific action is evaluated in the context of the member in question. Periodically, a member's cooperation with the IMF is assessed. Every six months, the Board reviews the circumstances surrounding a member who has been declared ineligible to use the IMF's general resources or, in the case of the PRGT, after the Executive Board has restricted the member's use of such resources. The application of these measures is postponed or suspended until the IMF can make a decision about a member's cooperation on policies and payments in situations where a civil conflict, the collapse of a functioning government, or international sanctions prohibit the IMF from doing so.

6.4.2. Arrears Clearance Modalities

Members who owe the IMF money can pay off their arrears through a variety of channels, such as using their own funds, grants from donors, or a bridge loan from significant creditors. If the latter is the situation, the IMF can help the member set up an interest-free intraday bridge loan from major creditors. After clearing its arrears with the IMF and having a new IMF financial arrangement approved by the Executive Board, the member uses the funds from the first disbursement—which is made available on the same day as the arrears clearance—to pay off the outstanding bridge loan. Most arrears clearances in the past have been accomplished through the use of bridge loans.

6.4.3. Special Charges

There are a number of reasons why financial accounts may incur special charges, such as overdraft fees, late payment penalties, or unforeseen costs. It's critical to carefully examine these charges in order to comprehend their causes and ramifications. Examine your account statements first to find any unusual charges that have been made. After these charges have been located, evaluate the causes to see if they were due to preventable mistakes, unanticipated events, or poor financial management. Proactively address and correct these charges by contacting your financial institution to arrange waivers or by setting up alerts to ensure that they don't happen again. Furthermore, make an effort to develop better financial practices and put plans in place to reduce the possibility of paying extra fees down the road. You can lessen the negative effects of special charges on your financial health and well-being by being vigilant and managing your finances proactively.

A CLOSER LOOK

If these sentiments sound familiar, rest assured you are not alone. While marketing is often one of the larger components of a company's overall budget, it is also sometimes the least understood outside of the marketing function. As a member of your company's finance leadership team responsible for major financial decisions across the company, you possess a good understanding of other functions such as operations, supply chain, manufacturing or procurement. You also have proven and well-established techniques such as Discounted Cash Flow Analysis (DCF), Net Present Value (NPV) and Internal Rate of Return (IRR) to analyze the returns and profitability of projected investments in these functions. However, with marketing, this is not always the case.

Source: https://analytic-edge.com/blog/why-finance-decision-makers-should-take-a-closer-look-at-marketing-mix-modeling/.

While most non-marketing professionals believe that marketing works and is necessary, they don't always have a good understanding of how it works. They often view marketing as a function where decisions are driven more by intuition and gut feel, rather than by the hard data, numbers, and empirical evidence they are used to. While other functions have ways to estimate or measure the effectiveness of investments, such measures for marketing are not well known or widely known. The metrics that marketers quote – click thru rates, conversion rates, engagement, brand awareness etc. – don't help either. These, again, are completely foreign to most outside the marketing function. This is especially true for finance professionals, used to the specificity of measures like Return on Investment (ROI).

And therein lies the problem. CMOs and marketers on the one hand, and finance decision-makers on the other, just do not speak a common language. Consequently, finance professionals don't have the tools and methodologies to scrutinize marketing expenditure and measure accountability, the way they would with every other spend they oversee in a company. And that's not an ideal situation for either function.

Marketing Mix Modeling (MMM) is an analytical technique that looks at the historical relationship between marketing spending and sales to determine how each marketing activity has impacted performance. The learnings are then adopted to adjust marketing tactics and strategies to drive maximum growth. As such, MMM is the perfect solution to help "translate" marketing expenditures to a language that both you and your CMO can understand.

MMM defines the effectiveness of each marketing activity like TV, print or out-of-home advertising, digital marketing, promotions etc., in terms of its contribution to sales or revenue and provides planning and simulation tools to decide on the optimal allocation of future budgets. In other words, it not only helps in measuring the ROI of every marketing expenditure, but also assists in maximizing ROI – enabling exactly the kind of data-driven investment decisions that you, as a financial decision-maker, are familiar and comfortable with. Simply put, a robust MMM solution gives you the confidence to trust marketing spend decisions.

Unlike traditional MMM solutions that took months to generate insights (often based on outdated data), current MMM solutions continuously measure the effectiveness of marketing activities and campaigns, allowing marketers to tweak spending in near real-time. For you, this means an 'always-on' and proactive approach to managing marketing expenditures and maximizing sales, revenues, and ROI. It allows you or your Marketing Controller to ask specific questions (e.g. is this campaign doing as well as expected? should we reduce spending on advertising and invest more in promotions?) and your marketing team to provide specific, accurate, data-based answers to help maximize growth.

Today, MMM can be deployed in-house and on-demand making it faster, cheaper, and easily scalable. This means it can be run more frequently and for more of your company's brands and markets, rather than limiting it to just the biggest ones, on account of cost and time constraints. This makes ROI-focused decision making and optimization possible for a larger part of your overall budget, contributing to your Key Performance Indicators (KPIs) and growth objectives.

For these reasons, Marketing Mix Modeling can be a useful ally that helps the marketing team and the finance team speak a common language, work more closely together and align both your priorities with business objectives. MMM correctly deployed can add up to 10% top-line growth to the business through more efficient and effective marketing spending. And that's something worth taking a closer look at. If MMM is a technique you are not yet familiar with, get together with your Marketing Controller and CMO and speak to us to find out how it can help you achieve faster, more responsive marketing decision making that maximizes ROI.

ROLE MODEL

HARRY MARKOWITZ: AMERICAN ECONOMIST

Harry Max Markowitz is a Nobel-prizing winning economist. Even though he was raised in Depression-era Chicago, Markowitz and his family lived a relatively comfortable life and avoided the woes that afflicted the nation. As a youth, he became enamored with the philosophical writings of David Hume and went on to receive a B.A. in philosophy from the University of Chicago. Markowitz chose economics as his upper-division concentration. Captivated, he continued his education in the field and remained at Chicago for graduate study.

As a graduate student, Markowitz studied the theory of games and expected utility theory of John von Neumann. Markowitz was a student member of the Cowles Commission when he had his epiphany on portfolio theory. Building upon the idiom "don't put all the eggs in one basket," he developed a method of portfolio analysis that was concerned with finding diversified porfolios with maximum return for a given level of risk and, alternatively, minimum risk for a given level of return. This basic concept, which he officially introduced in his 1954 dissertation, would become the basis of modern financial engineering. At the suggestion of Yale professor James Tobin, Markowitz expanded this work into a book and published Portfolio Selection: Efficient Diversification of Investments in 1962. Prior to the completion of his dissertation, Markowitz accepted a position with the RAND Corporation. It was at RAND when he was first introduced to Linear Programming. He was asked to study George B. Dantzig's paper on the simplex method. Markowitz was tasked with the supervision of computationally applying Dantzig's method on an IBM Card Programming Calculator. This greatly sped up RAND's ability to solve linear programming problems. After working on various other simulation problems, Markowitz received and accepted a job offer from General Electric. Feeling stifled by proprietary issues at GE he returned to RAND and developed SIMSCRIPT, a very powerful computer simulation language. After the continued development and integration of SIMSCRIPT languages at California Analysis Center, Inc. (CACI), Markowitz entered academia as a professor at the University of California, Los Angeles in 1968. He held a series of other academic and consultant positions (including a nine year stint at IBM's T. J. Watson Research Center) before settling down in San Diego. Since 1993, he has been an adjunct professor at the Rady School of Management at the University of California, San Diego.

In 1989, Markowitz was awarded the Jon Von Neumann Theory Prize for his work on portfolio selection, mathematical programming, and simulation. The following year he was jointly awarded the Nobel Prize in Economic Sciences along with Merton H. Miller and William F. Sharpe "for pioneering work in the theory of financial economics." Markowitz was elected as a fellow of the Institute for Operations Research and the Management Sciences in 2002 and remains an active researcher and publisher.

SUMMARY

- Financial decisions are crucial determinants of an organization's success, encompassing choices related to investments, financing, and risk management.
- Investment decisions involve allocating resources to various projects or assets, aiming to maximize returns while considering factors such as profitability, growth potential, and risk tolerance.
- Financing decisions focus on determining the optimal mix of debt and equity financing to fund operations and investments, balancing the need for capital with the associated costs and risks.
- Risk management is integral to financial decision-making, encompassing strategies to identify, assess, and mitigate risks that could impact the achievement of organizational objectives.
- Financial decision-makers must weigh the potential rewards against the inherent risks associated with different investment and financing options, considering factors such as liquidity, solvency, and market conditions.
- Effective financial decision-making requires a thorough understanding of financial principles, analytical tools, and regulatory frameworks, enabling informed choices that align with organizational goals and stakeholder interests.
- Uncertainty and volatility in financial markets necessitate proactive risk management strategies, including diversification, hedging, and insurance, to safeguard against adverse events and market fluctuations.
- Financial decisions involve trade-offs between risk and return, with higher potential returns typically associated with greater levels of risk, requiring careful consideration of risk appetite and tolerance levels.
- Behavioral biases and cognitive limitations can influence financial decision-making, leading to suboptimal outcomes, underscoring the importance of rational analysis and disciplined decision-making processes.
- Continuous evaluation and monitoring of financial decisions are essential to adapt to changing market conditions, regulatory requirements, and business dynamics, ensuring the ongoing alignment of financial strategies with organizational objectives and stakeholder expectations.

REVIEW QUESTIONS

1. What are financial decisions? How does risk affect a company's financial decisions?
2. Why are financial decisions important?
3. Explain the investment criteria factor affecting investment decision.
4. How do businesses evaluate the trade-offs between risk and return when making financial decisions?
5. What role does financial planning and forecasting play in supporting sound financial decision-making and long-term business success?

MULTIPLE CHOICE QUESTIONS

1. **Which of the following best describes financial risk?**
   a. The potential for loss of market share
   b. The potential for loss of capital investment
   c. The potential for changes in interest rates
   d. The potential for changes in consumer preferences
2. **What is the primary objective of financial decision-making?**
   a. Maximizing shareholder wealth
   b. Minimizing operational costs
   c. Maximizing revenue growth
   d. Minimizing tax liabilities
3. **Which financial ratio measures a company's ability to meet short-term debt obligations?**
   a. Debt-to-Equity ratio
   b. Current ratio
   c. Return on Investment (ROI)
   d. Price-Earnings (P/E) ratio
4. **What does the concept of leverage refer to in financial decision-making?**
   a. The use of debt to finance investments
   b. The use of equity to finance investments
   c. The use of retained earnings to finance investments
   d. The use of operating income to finance investments
5. **Which of the following is considered a systematic risk?**
   a. Changes in consumer preferences
   b. Labor strikes within the company
   c. Regulatory changes in the industry
   d. Poor management decisions
6. **What is the role of diversification in managing investment risk?**
   a. Concentrating investments in a single asset class
   b. Spreading investments across different asset classes
   c. Focusing investments in high-risk securities
   d. Ignoring potential risks associated with investments
7. **How does the Capital Asset Pricing Model (CAPM) measure the expected return on an investment?**
   a. By considering the historical performance of the investment

b. By evaluating the market risk premium and the asset's beta

c. By analyzing the company's financial statements

d. By comparing the investment's price-earnings ratio

8. Which financial decision involves determining the optimal mix of debt and equity financing?

a. Capital budgeting

b. Working capital management

c. Capital structure management

d. Dividend policy

9. What is the purpose of financial derivatives in risk management?

a. To eliminate all financial risks

b. To transfer financial risks to other parties

c. To increase the level of financial risk

d. To speculate on future market movements

10. Which financial metric measures the efficiency of a company's operations in generating profits?

a. Debt-to-Asset ratio

b. Earnings per Share (EPS)

c. Price-to-Earnings (P/E) ratio

d. Return on Assets (ROA)

Answer to Multiple Choice Questions

1. (b); 2. (a); 3. (b); 4. (a); 5. (c); 6. (b); 7. (b); 8. (c); 9. (b); 10. (d)

REFERENCES

1. Block, S. B., & Hirt, G. A., (2005). *Foundations of Financial Management*. McGraw-Hill Education.
2. Clive, M., (2009). *Mastering Financial Management*. Financial Times Prentice Hall ISBN 978-0-273-72454-4.
3. Emery, D. R., Finnerty, J. D., & Stowe, J. D., (2019). *Corporate Financial Management*. Pearson Education.
4. Gitman, L. J., & Zutter, C. J., (2019). *Principles of Managerial Finance*. Pearson Education.
5. James, V. H., & John, W., (2009). *Fundamentals of Financial Management* (13th edn.). Pearson Education Limited. ISBN 9705614229.
6. Lawrence, G., & Chad, J. Z., (2019). *Principles of Managerial Finance* (14th edn.). Addison-Wesley Publishing, ISBN 978-0133507690.

7. McNeil, A. J., Frey, R., & Embrechts, P., (2005). *Quantitative Risk Management: Concepts, Techniques and Tools* (pp. 2, 3). Princeton University Press. ISBN 978-0-691-12255-7.
8. Modigliani, F., & Miller, M. H., (2000). The cost of capital, corporation finance, and the theory of investment. *The American Economic Review, 48*(3), 261–297.
9. Myers, S. C., & Majluf, N. S., (2000). Corporate financing and investment decisions when firms have information that investors do not have. *Journal of Financial Economics, 13*(2), 187–221.
10. Oberoi, J., (2018). "Interest rate risk management and the mix of fixed and floating rate debt" (PDF). *Journal of Banking & Finance, 86*, 70–86. doi: 10.1016/j.jbankfin.2017.09.001.
11. Poitras, G., (2013). *Commodity Risk Management Theory and Application*. New York: Routledge. ISBN 978-0-415-87929-3.
12. Weston, J. F., & Brigham, E. F., (2018). *Essentials of Managerial Finance*. Cengage Learning.

CHAPTER

7 Liability

LEARNING OBJECTIVES

After studying this chapter, you will be able to:

- Understand the concept of liability
- Learn about current liabilities
- Identify the non-current liabilities

INTRODUCTORY EXAMPLE

Bonds Payable

Bonds payable is an accounting term that refers to the long-term debt issued by a corporation, government, or other organization that is recorded on the issuer's balance sheet as a liability. These bonds are sold to investors, who lend money to the issuer in exchange for periodic interest payments and the promise of repayment of the principal amount upon maturity.

The key features of bonds payable include:

- **Face Value (Par Value):** This is the principal amount of the bond that the issuer agrees to repay upon maturity. The face value is typically stated in increments of $1,000, although it can vary depending on the specific bond issuance.

- **Coupon Rate:** This is the interest rate that the issuer agrees to pay on the bond's face value. The interest is paid periodically, usually semiannually, to bondholders.
- **Maturity Date:** This is the date on which the bond's principal amount is due to be repaid to the bondholders. Bonds can have various maturities, ranging from short-term (less than three years) to long-term (over ten years).
- **Bond Indenture:** This is a legal document that outlines the terms and conditions of the bond, including the payment schedule, covenants, and any special features such as call provisions or sinking funds.
- On the issuer's balance sheet, bonds payable are reported as a long-term liability, reflecting the issuer's obligation to repay the principal amount and make interest payments over the life of the bond. The bonds payable account is typically adjusted over time to account for amortization of bond premiums or discounts, interest expense accruals, and principal repayments.

Suppose that ABC Corp., a manufacturing company, decides to issue 10-year corporate bonds to finance the construction of a new production facility. The details of the bond issuance are as follows:

- Face value: $1,000 per bond
- Coupon rate: 6% per annum, paid semiannually
- Maturity date: 10 years from the date of issuance
- Total bonds issued: 2,000 bonds

Upon issuing the bonds, ABC Corp. will receive a total of $2,000,000 in funds from investors (2,000 bonds x $1,000 face value). On its balance sheet, ABC Corp. will record this amount as bonds payable under long-term liabilities, reflecting its obligation to repay the borrowed funds in the future.

Throughout the life of the bonds, ABC Corp. will make semiannual interest payments to the bondholders. The interest payment for each bond can be calculated as follows:

Interest payment = Face value x Coupon rate x (Payment frequency)

Interest payment = $1,000 x 6% x (1/2) = $30

For the entire bond issuance, the semiannual interest payment will be:

Total semiannual interest payment = 2,000 bonds x $30 = $60,000

Over the 10-year life of the bonds, ABC Corp. will make regular interest payments totaling $1,200,000 ($60,000 semiannual payment x 20 periods). At the end of the 10-year period, when the bonds reach maturity, ABC Corp. will repay the principal amount of $2,000,000 to the bondholders, and the bonds payable will be removed from its balance sheet. In this example, the bonds payable account reflects ABC Corp.'s long-term debt obligations arising from the issuance of corporate bonds. The company is responsible for making periodic interest payments to bondholders and repaying the principal amount upon maturity.

UNIT INTRODUCTION

A liability is something that an individual or business owes, typically money. Over time, debts are paid off by the transfer of financial gains like cash, products, or services. Liabilities are shown on the right side of the balance sheet and consist of accrued expenses, bonds, accounts payable, mortgages, deferred revenues, and warranties. A liability is an unfulfilled or unpaid obligation that exists between two parties. Within the accounting domain, a financial liability is an obligation that is further characterized by prior business dealings, occurrences, sales, trade of goods or services, or anything that could yield financial gains in the future. Non-current liabilities are typically regarded as long-term (12 months or more), whereas current liabilities are typically regarded as short-term (expected to be concluded in 12 months or less) (Figure 7.1).

Figure 7.1. *Structure of liability.*

Source: https://officetechnologypartners.com/wp-content/uploads/2015/07/liability-and-insurance.jpg.

A liability's temporality determines whether it is considered current or non-current. They may consist of a future service obligation owed to third parties (such as short- or long-term loans from banks, people, or other organizations) or an unresolved obligation resulting from a prior transaction. Larger liabilities, such as bonds payable and accounts payable, are typically the most prevalent. Due to their ongoing current and long-term nature, these two line items will be present on the balance sheet of the majority of businesses.

7.1. CONCEPT OF LIABILITY

→Learning **Objectives**

- Define types of liabilities
- Discuss the liabilities of a corporation
- Write the examples of company liabilities
- Discuss the examples of asset/liability management

Any type of financial obligation that a company has to pay to a person or another business at the conclusion of an accounting period is referred to as a liability in accounting. Transferring economic benefits, such as cash, products, or services, settles liabilities. The balance sheet's right side is devoted to recording liabilities, which comprise various loan categories, creditors, lenders, and suppliers. It covers a wide range, from tortious behavior and statutory duties to contractual agreements. Liability essentially establishes the bounds of accountability in different exchanges, transactions, and situations. In the framework of contracts, parties take on responsibility for keeping their word and carrying out their duties. In tort law, one is obligated to make up for damages suffered when one's own actions or negligence cause harm to others. Furthermore, statutory liabilities are the result of legislative directives that place legal obligations on people or organizations to follow guidelines or rules. Liability is a fundamental idea that promotes responsibility, facilitates the administration of justice, and keeps the balance in legal and economic systems. Its careful application highlights the complex interactions among rights, obligations, and outcomes that define legal relationships and social norms.

7.1.1. Types of Liabilities

Liabilities can be classified into three main categories, which are:

1. Current Liabilities
2. Non-current Liabilities
3. Contingent Liabilities

1. **Current Liabilities**: Liabilities that are due and must be paid within the accounting period—typically a year or 12 months—are referred to as current

liabilities. Because of the comparatively short turnaround time, current liabilities are also referred to as short-term liabilities. A company's management must keep a careful eye on its current liabilities because paying off current liabilities requires a substantial amount of liquidity in the form of current assets. Liquidity and working capital of the company are directly impacted by current liabilities.

2. **Non-Current Liabilities**: Financial obligations that are due more than a year from now are referred to as non-current liabilities, also known as long-term liabilities. Long-term liabilities are crucial to the long-term funding of the company. These liabilities supply the necessary capital, which enables businesses to purchase capital assets. Companies can also use the money they receive from long-term debts or liabilities to invest in new capital projects. Long-term liabilities are a crucial sign of a company's solvency. A corporation that cannot afford to pay its long-term debts when they are due is either experiencing a solvency problem or another type of business crisis. Prior to making an investment, investors always consider the business's long-term liabilities.

> **Keyword**
>
> **Long-term liabilities** are liabilities that are due beyond a year or the normal operation period of the company.

3. **Contingent Liabilities**: Contingent liabilities are a unique kind of liability that can arise in the course of a business, contingent on the outcome of a potential future event. According to accounting standards, contingent liabilities are only recorded as potential or probable liabilities when the amount of the liability can be accurately estimated and there is a 50% likelihood of the liability occurring.

7.1.2. Liabilities of a Corporation

A common reason for small businesses to incorporate is to protect their personal assets from liabilities or obligations resulting from the operations of their businesses. In terms of the law, corporations function as "persons" since they are clearly distinct legal entities with a lengthy legal history in the United States. As such, they are fully independent of their owners in terms of their ability to own assets and incur liabilities. These liabilities may include debt-related commitments, contractual duties, and personnel-related liabilities.

1. **Liabilities Defined:** Liabilities are debts that your business has to pay. Liabilities of your company could be legal, accounting, or finance related. A claim, such as a lien or promissory note, made against the assets of your business is usually associated with financial liabilities. Generally speaking, accounting liabilities are those that show up on the balance sheet. Liabilities come from things your

business or its employees did or said while conducting business. One type of legal liability is product liability (Figure 7.2).

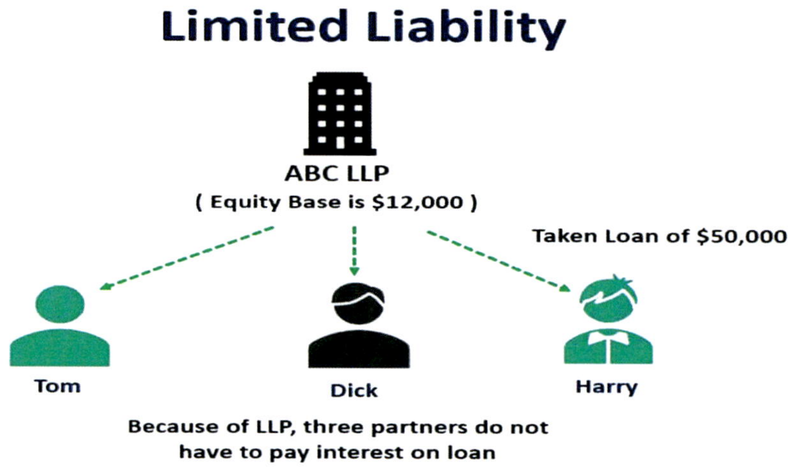

Figure 7.2. *Limited-liability.*

Source: https://cdn.wallstreetmojo.com/wp-content/uploads/2019/11/Limited-Liability.jpg.

2. **Types of Debt:** Your company incurs debt liabilities when it gets a bank loan, a company credit card, or terms of payment from a supplier after an application is approved. Debt obligations with terms of a year or more are classified as long-term debt on the balance sheet of your company. Additional types of long-term debt include mortgages and bank term loans. Debt obligations with a duration of less than a year is also listed on the balance sheet under the category of short-term debt. Short-term debt examples include lines of credit, accounts payable linked to suppliers, and credit cards payable.
3. **Contractual Liabilities:** Contract-related liabilities arise from any explicit or implicit contracts that your company makes with other individuals or organizations. Your business enters into a contract when it accepts an engagement proposal from a consulting firm. Your company enters into a contract when it signs a service agreement. When your business places an order for office supplies, it implicitly agrees to pay for those supplies. Contracts typically go through without any problems. It is possible, though, for a partner, contractor, or vendor to take issue with how your company is carrying out its end of the bargain and take legal action to resolve the default.
4. **Human Resource–Related:** Liabilities pertaining to human resources include unpaid salaries and wages, payroll taxes, unemployment insurance, and compliance with worker's compensation regulations. Businesses that neglect to pay mandatory payroll taxes are aggressively pursued by the IRS and state revenue departments. If your company doesn't make up the lost payroll taxes and penalties on time, one of these organizations may close its doors until your company pays them. Employee lawsuits, such as those involving early termination, can also affect businesses. Additionally, they may be held accountable for the deceptive or sexually harassing behavior of their employees.

Did you know?

In the modern global economy, liability has become increasingly complex, encompassing a wide range of legal, financial, and ethical considerations. Businesses, governments, and individuals navigate liability issues in diverse contexts, including corporate governance, financial reporting, risk management, and insurance.

7.1.3. Examples of Company Liabilities

The difference between your assets and liabilities is the value of your company on any given day. While many assets, like goodwill, patents, and recipes, have intangible benefits, liabilities are frequently simpler to measure. Gaining an understanding of the various liabilities your business faces will help you better control, manage, and take action to minimize or eliminate them.

1. **Debt:** Any amount of money owed is considered debt. For a lot of entrepreneurs, debt mostly consists of loans and credit card balances. In a broader sense, debt could include unpaid taxes, interest that was accrued during the month but hasn't yet been charged to your account, and wages and salaries that have been paid to employees thus far. For accounting purposes, these latter amounts are not regarded as debt because they haven't been offered to you for payment yet. When you purchase machinery or equipment, it turns into an asset, but any outstanding debt—such as credit card debt or remaining loan balances—remains a liability.
2. **Accounts Payable:** The bills you owe are categorized as accounts payable and placed under liabilities on your balance sheet, which lists your assets and liabilities. Invoices you have received for the materials you purchased to make your product, a bill for services like graphic design, or the current balance owed for utilities, phones, Internet, insurance, or other items for which invoices have been presented are examples of payables. Interest and your monthly credit card payment are not regarded as payables; rather, they are regarded as debt service amounts.
3. **Payroll and Taxes:** An additional liability is the money you owe your employees. Payroll taxes, insurance, benefits, and salaries and wages may all be due. Sales and income taxes are among the additional liabilities. Your previous fiscal year's balance sheet shows the amount you owed for taxes, while this year's books show the taxes you incurred but haven't yet paid, like income, sales, or quarterly payroll taxes. You have to include gains in taxes as liabilities if you have an investment portfolio.
4. **Contracts, Leases, Warranties:** You agree to pay for the products or services you receive when you sign a contract. Certain contracts have the option to be terminated early with adjusted fees or partial payments due. Certain contracts require full payment in order to be canceled. For example, if you are unable to terminate your Internet service contract without incurring penalties, then it is deemed a liability. Once your monthly bill is submitted, it will be categorized as an accounts payable liability. If you terminate your service early and are

assessed an early cancellation fee, that sum is immediately owed. Unless the business can precisely estimate the liability's amount, contracts, leases, and warranties aren't usually shown as liabilities on balance sheets. If you offer warranties, guarantees, or service agreements for products you've bought, those need to be listed as liabilities when you sell your company. You have entered into a contract if you have accepted deposits or prepayments; these are obligations until you deliver the goods or services to them.

Keyword

Investment portfolio is a basket of assets that typically include stocks, bonds, cash, real estate and more. Investors generally aim for a return by diversifying these securities in a way that reflects their risk tolerance and financial goals.

7.1.4. Examples of Asset/Liability Management

At its most basic level, asset/liability management is the process of managing assets and cash flows to meet obligations, though it has developed to reflect shifting conditions in the markets and economy. It's a type of risk management where the investor tries to reduce or hedge the possibility of not fulfilling their obligations. Along with risk management, success should boost the organization's profitability. To better convey the idea of maximizing assets to meet increasingly complex liabilities, some practitioners prefer to refer to the process as "surplus optimization." As an alternative, the surplus is sometimes referred to as net worth or the difference between the present value of liabilities and the market value of assets. From a long-term viewpoint, asset and liability management controls risks associated with the accounting of assets vs. obligations. It can therefore be both tactical and strategic (Figure 7.3).

An example of a liability that a consumer typically pays for with current cash inflows is a monthly mortgage. In order to pay their mortgage, the mortgagor needs to have enough assets each month. Similar problems exist in institutions, but they are far more complicated. For instance, a pension plan's contractual obligations to retirees must be met while maintaining an asset base through wise asset allocation and risk management, which will yield future, continuous payments.

Institutions have a wide range and complexity of liabilities. Understanding their traits and structuring assets in a complementary and strategic manner present a challenge. If assets were the only thing taken into consideration, this might lead to an asset allocation that seems less than ideal. Liabilities and assets are typically viewed as two concepts that are deeply entwined. These are a few instances of the asset/liability problems that both individuals and institutions face.

Figure 7.3. *Asset-liability-management.*

Source: *https://cdn.wallstreetmojo.com/wp-content/uploads/2020/02/Asset-Liability-Management-main.jpg.*

1. **The Banking Industry:** Banks act as financial intermediaries, accepting deposits for which they have interest obligations (liabilities) and providing loans with interest payments (assets). Security portfolios make up bank assets in addition to loans. Banks have to control interest rate risk because it can cause an imbalance between their liabilities and assets. A major factor in this issue was the removal of Regulation Q, which set a ceiling on the rate at which banks could pay their depositors, and unstable interest rates.

   Interest rate sensitivity, the volume and composition of assets and liabilities, and the difference between the rate a bank pays on deposits and the rate it receives on its assets (loans and securities) determine its net interest margin. There is frequently a mismatch between a bank's short-term and long-term lending, which the bank must address by structuring its assets and liabilities or by using derivatives to make sure all of its liabilities are satisfied.

2. **Insurance Companies:** The two primary categories of insurance firms are non-life and life. Annuities that are guaranteed rate accounts (GICs), stable value funds, life, or non-life contingent (e.g., property and casualty) are also provided by life insurers.

   Life insurance usually entails a longer-term commitment. The standard for a life insurance policy is to pay out a lump sum to a beneficiary upon the owner's death. The specifics of each type of policy may differ. To calculate the estimated annual obligations that an insurer will probably have each year, actuarial planning must be used, taking into account life expectancy tables and other relevant factors.

   Annuities have liabilities that include paying income during a payout period that starts on a given date. Interest rate risk affects GICs and stable value products, which can reduce surpluses and lead to an imbalance between assets and liabilities. Life insurers typically have longer-term liabilities. As a result, even though product lines and their requirements differ, longer duration and inflation-protected assets are chosen to match those of the liability (longer maturity bonds and real estate, equity, and venture capital).

   Since non-life insurers typically have a three- to five-year underwriting cycle, they must handle liabilities (accident claims) of a much shorter duration. The need for liquidity in a company is often determined by its business cycle. Compared to life insurers, non-life insurers give less thought to interest rate risk. Liabilities frequently have erratic values and timeliness. A company's liability structure is determined by its product line as well as the claims and settlement procedure, which are frequently influenced by the so-called "long tail," or the interval between the time of the event and the reporting of the claim and the actual payment to the policyholder. This is due to the fact that commercial clients make up a far bigger share of the property and casualty market than does the life insurance industry, which primarily serves individual clients.

Keyword

Guaranteed rate accounts (GICs) either come with fixed interest rates or variable rates linked to the prime rate or stock market index. Investors choose a term length, typically spanning from 30 days to 10 years, and deposit their funds knowing they typically won't receive their funds back until the end of the term.

3. **The Benefit Plan:** A traditional defined benefit plan has to live up to its pledge to pay the benefit formula outlined in the sponsor's plan document. As a result, investments have a long-term focus with the goal of preserving or expanding the asset base and funding retirement benefits. Using an estimate of the length of benefit payments and their present value, managers assess the liabilities in a process called liability-driven investing (LDI).

   A benefit plan's funding typically entails matching fixed-rate assets with fixed-rate liabilities (income payments to retirees) and variable-rate assets with variable-rate liabilities (future retirement payments based upon salary growth projections of active workers). Strategies like duration matching and portfolio immunity can be used to shield portfolios from interest rate fluctuations because both liabilities and portfolios are susceptible to them.

4. **Foundations and Non-Profits:** Foundations are organizations that receive funding from gifts and investments and distribute grants. Long-term funds held by nonprofit institutions are known as endowments. Their designs are typically eternal. Their annual spending commitment expressed as a percentage of the assets' market value typically constitutes their liability. Because these agreements are long-term in nature, they frequently result in a more aggressive allocation of investments designed to grow the portfolio, beat inflation, and support and maintain a particular spending policy.

5. **Wealth Management:** Liabilities incurred by people with private wealth may take many different forms, just like the people themselves. These include saving for retirement, financing for education, buying a house, and dealing with particular situations. The asset allocation and risk management process that chooses the right asset allocation to satisfy these liabilities will be framed by taxation and risk preferences. Asset/liability management strategies can

be compared to institutional strategies, specifically fund strategies that aim to target cash flows beyond a given date (Figure 7.4).

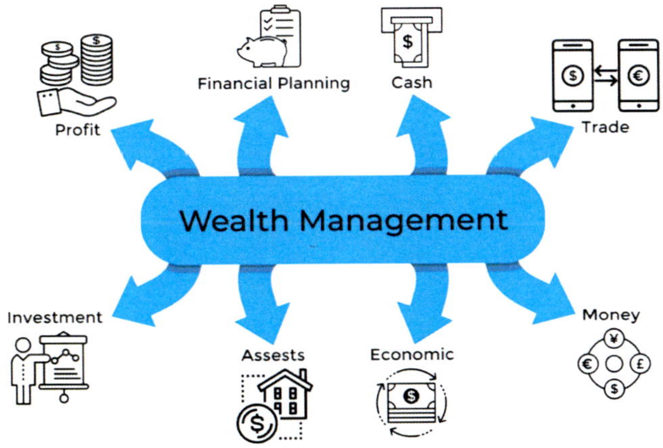

Figure 7.4. *Wealth-management.*

Source: https://igniteoutsourcing.com/wp-content/uploads/2018/09/wealth-management-technology-trends-1024x675.jpg.

Remember

A nonprofit organization (NPO) is one that is not driven by profit but by dedication to a given cause that is the target of all income beyond what it takes to run the organization.

6. **Large Conglomerate, Multi-National Corporations:** Lastly, there are a variety of uses for asset/liability management strategies within corporations. Liquidity, foreign exchange, interest rate, and commodity risks are a few possible reasons. An airline, for instance, might use fuel price hedging to protect itself from volatility and keep asset/liability matching in check. Additionally, multinational corporations may use the foreign exchange market to hedge the risks of currency losses so that they can improve their forecasts for asset management vs. money transfers.

Did you get it?

1. **How do contractual liabilities differ from other types of liabilities, and what role do contracts play in defining them?**
2. **Can you provide examples of contractual liabilities in business and personal finance contexts?**

7.2. CURRENT LIABILITIES

→Learning Objectives

- To know the current liabilities work
- To define the types of current liabilities
- To explain the accounting for current liabilities
- To differentiate between a current liability and a contingent liability
- To deal with current vs. long-term liabilities

A company's current liabilities are its financial obligations that need to be settled within a year or during its regular operational span. The operational span, otherwise known as the cash conversion cycle, is the duration it takes for a company to acquire inventory and convert it into cash through sales. An instance of a current liability is the outstanding payment owed to suppliers, categorized as accounts payable. Current assets are assets that are depleted in less than a year and are usually used to settle current liabilities. Cash and accounts receivable—amounts that customers owe for purchases—are examples of current assets. One key indicator of a company's continued ability to pay its debts as they become due is the ratio of current assets to current liabilities.

Unpaid supplier invoices are represented by the accounts payable account, which is usually one of the biggest current liability accounts on a company's financial statements. In order to collect their accounts receivable before their suppliers' accounts payable are due, businesses attempt to align their payment dates. For example, a company might have 60-day terms for money owed to their supplier, which results in requiring their customers to pay within a 30-day term. Current liabilities can also be settled by creating a new current liability, such as a new short-term debt obligation. Below is a list of the most common current liabilities that are found on the balance sheet:

- Accounts payable
- Short-term debt such as bank loans or commercial paper issued to fund operations
- Dividends payable
- Notes payable—the principal portion of outstanding debt
- Current portion of deferred revenue, such as prepayments by customers for work not completed or earned yet

- Current maturities of long-term debt
- Interest payable on outstanding debts, including long-term obligations
- Income taxes owed within the next year

Businesses occasionally use the "other current liabilities" account on their balance sheets as a catch-all line item for any other obligations that are due within a year and are not otherwise broken down. Government regulations or industry-specific differences may apply to current liability accounts.

The current ratio is frequently used by creditors and analysts. The current ratio evaluates a company's capacity to settle its immediate debts or commitments. The ratio illustrates how well a business manages its balance sheet to settle its short-term debts and payables. It is computed by dividing current assets by current liabilities. It indicates to analysts and investors if a company's balance sheet contains sufficient current assets to cover its current liabilities and other payables (Figure 7.5).

Figure 7.5. *Balance-sheet-current-liabilities.*

Source: https://cdn.wallstreetmojo.com/wp-content/uploads/2017/06/Balance-Sheet-Current-Liabilities.png.

With the exception of deducting the total inventory value upfront, the quick ratio formula is the same as the current ratio formula. Since it only takes into account current assets that can be swiftly turned into cash to settle current liabilities, the quick ratio is a more cautious measure of liquidity. For both the current and quick ratios, a number greater than one is optimum as it indicates that there are more current assets to cover current short-term debts. If the figure is excessively high, though, it might indicate that the business is not making the most of its assets as it could be. For creditors and investors alike, the examination of current liabilities is crucial. Before granting credit, banks, for instance, want to be sure that a business is timely collecting its accounts receivable (or getting paid for them). However, timely payment of the business's payables is equally crucial. The quick and current ratios are useful tools for managing a company's current liabilities and analyzing its financial solvency.

7.2.1. Current Liabilities Work

Depending on the sector or industry, each company may handle current liabilities differently. Analysts, accountants, and investors use current liabilities to determine a company's ability to pay its short-term debts. A business must make enough money in the near future to pay off its current debts. Because of this, a lot of financial ratios use current liabilities in their computations to assess how quickly or effectively a business is paying them down. Any kind of debt or obligation that must be paid off in full within a single calendar year is considered a current liability. These liabilities include things like goods invoices that need to be paid for within thirty days of receipt, short-term loans that need to be repaid in six months to a year, or even urgent debt payments. Most of the time, current liabilities are paid off with cash assets on hand, adhering to a planned schedule that reduces the amount of new debt that accrues in the form of finance charges (Figure 7.6).

Remember

The accounts payable (AP) process is responsible for paying suppliers and vendors for goods and services purchased by the company. AP departments typically handle incoming bills and invoices but may serve additional functions depending on the size and nature of the business.

Figure 7.6. *Current-liabilities-formula.*

Source: https://cdn.educba.com/academy/wp-content/uploads/2019/03/Current-Liabilities-Formula.jpg.

The monthly costs that are recorded as accounts payable in the accounting records are among the most prevalent types of current liabilities. These kinds of liabilities include minimum payments owed on credit cards or loans, utility bills, and basic monthly costs like rent or mortgage payments. Liabilities of this kind are listed on the balance sheet. In certain instances, the line items are organized according to the due date linked with every obligation, facilitating the settlement of each debt on or ahead of that date and preventing the imposition of late fees or extra interest.

It's critical to accurately account for current liabilities because many lenders will take these costs into account before extending credit. The cash assets available to pay off those debt obligations will be compared to the total amount of all liabilities that are due each month. The primary source of cash assets for numerous households and businesses is their monthly income or revenue. The likelihood of getting approved for a loan is significantly increased if the lender determines that the applicant's current liabilities to current assets ratio shows that the loan can be repaid in accordance with the terms of the loan contract.

Every household, business, or other type of entity has an interest in identifying and managing current liability obligations. By doing this, one can preserve a higher credit score, particularly if creditors consistently report that minimum payments are made on schedule and that debts are settled in accordance with terms. If you don't, your credit rating may suffer, which will make it more difficult to get credit and financing when you need or want it. This irresponsible management of current liability over time may cause the entity to completely collapse and possibly enter bankruptcy.

7.2.2. Types of Current Liabilities

Below is a listing of frequently seen current liabilities.

7.2.2.1. Accounts Payable

The short-term debt owed by an organization to its suppliers and creditors is known as accounts payable (AP). Under current liabilities on the balance sheet, it can be found. All of the money owed to vendors or suppliers for unpaid invoices is represented by accounts payable. Vendors usually give customers terms of 15, 30, or 45 days to pay; this allows the buyer to receive the supplies now and pay for them later. These bills function as a short-term vendor loan and are entered into accounts payable. A business can increase revenue from the sale of supplies and better manage its cash needs by giving itself more time to pay off an invoice. Suppliers prefer shorter terms because it helps their cash flow to be paid sooner rather than later. Suppliers will even give businesses discounts if they pay early or on schedule. A supplier may, for instance, offer terms of "3 percent, 30, net 31," which denotes that a business will receive a 3 percent discount if it pays 30 days in advance and will be responsible for the remaining balance 31 days after that. On the other hand, businesses may utilize accounts payable to increase their cash flow. In an effort to improve their short-term cash flow, businesses may attempt to extend the terms or the amount of time needed to settle their payables to suppliers.

7.2.2.2. Accrued Expenses

Costs of expenses that are documented in accounting but have not yet been paid are known as accrued expenses. The accrual method of accounting is used for accrued expenses, which means that costs are recorded as incurred rather than as paid for. Since accumulated expenses are short-term financial obligations, they are shown in the balance sheet's current liabilities section. Usually, businesses will pay them with cash or other short-term or current assets.

- Examples of Accrued Expenses

Some examples of accrued expenses include:

- A supply purchase from a vendor but have yet to receive an invoice to pay it

- Interest payments on loans that are due in the near term
- Warranty on a service or product but has yet to be fully paid
- Real estate and property taxes that have accrued for the period
- Accrued federal, state, and local taxes
- Accumulated employee wages, bonuses, and commissions for a period that might be paid at a later date such as the following period

7.2.2.3. Taxes Payable

There are different types of taxes that companies owe and are recorded as short-term liabilities. Some of the most common taxes owed are:

- Income taxes owed to the government that have yet to be paid
- Payroll taxes that have been held from an employee but haven't been paid
- Taxes collected from their customers and paid to the government, which are recorded as sales taxes payable

7.2.2.4. Short-Term Debt

The total amount of debt payments due within the next year is usually considered short-term debt. The proportion of short-term debt to long-term debt is a crucial factor to consider when assessing the financial standing of a business. For illustration, suppose that the total debt of two businesses in the same sector is equal. If a company has a large amount of short-term debt, it may experience cash flow problems if it does not generate enough revenue to cover its obligations. Additionally, the company may not raise its dividend or may miss paying its dividend entirely if cash flow is predicted to be tight during the course of the next year. Companies pay their shareholders cash dividends in exchange for their stock investments.

- **Types of Short-Term Debt:** Another type of short-term debt instrument that a business may issue is commercial paper. Usually used to finance short-term or current liabilities like accounts payable or inventory purchases, the debt is unsecured. Short-term bank loans taken out to increase the capital of the business can be considered short-term debts. Although they are considered short-term debts, overdraft credit lines for bank accounts and other brief advances from financial institutions may be reported as separate line items. A current liability also includes the current portion of long-term debt that is due within the next year.
    - **Payroll Liabilities:** Payroll liabilities that are due within the year may fall under the purview of an employer. These obligations may include employee Medicare payments that have been withheld. Current liabilities may also include employer benefits like health insurance premiums or contributions to retirement plans.
    - **Dividends Payable or Dividends Declared:** Current liabilities are defined as dividends declared by the board of directors of a company but not yet distributed to shareholders.
    - **Unearned Revenue:** Money

received or paid to a business for a good or service that hasn't yet been rendered or supplied is known as unearned revenue. Since unearned revenue is a form of debt owed to the customer, it is recorded as a current liability. The unearned revenue is shown as revenue on the income statement once the service or product has been rendered.

7.2.3. Accounting for Current Liabilities

A company is required to record a credit entry for a current liability as soon as it discovers it received an economic benefit that needs to be paid back within a year. The company's accountants categorize received benefits as either an expense or an asset, which will be debited based on the type of benefit received. For instance, one of the vendors of a major automaker sends a shipment of exhaust systems, and the manufacturer has 90 days to pay the vendor $10 million. The company's accountants record a debit entry to inventory, an asset account, for $10 million and a credit entry to accounts payable because these materials are not immediately put into production. When the business settles its outstanding balance with suppliers, accounts payable is debited and $10 million is credited to cash (Figure 7.7).

Assume an organization pays $1 million to its external auditor, for whom tax preparation services are provided, in the upcoming sixty days. A $1 million debit entry is made to the audit expense account and a $1 million credit entry is made to the other current liabilities account by the company's accountants. The company's accountant debits $1 million from the other current liabilities account and credits $1 million to the cash account upon receiving a $1 million payment.

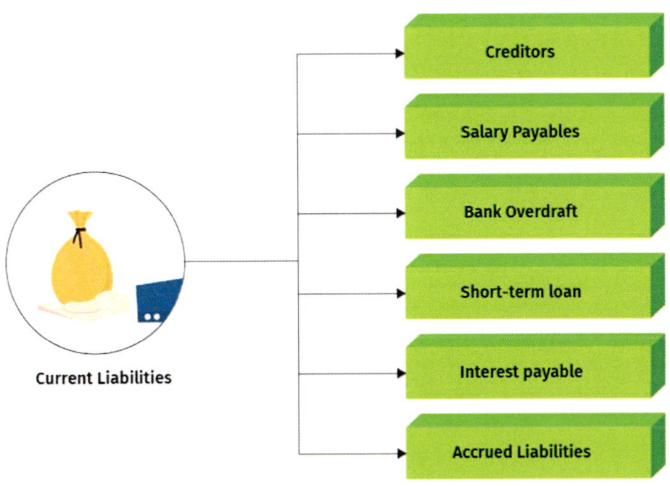

Figure 7.7. *Current-liabilities-examples.*

Source: https://resources.tallysolutions.com/wp-content/uploads/2019/11/current-liabilities-examples.jpg.

7.2.4. Differences between a Current Liability and a Contingent Liability

For a business, both current and contingent liabilities are crucial financial issues. A current liability is an amount that you currently owe, while a contingent liability is an amount that you may owe in the future based on certain events. This is the main distinction between the two. A liability in accounting is the sum of money you owe a creditor. There are two main types of liabilities: current and long-term. Your debts that you anticipate paying off in the upcoming year are included in your current liabilities. Accounts payable to suppliers and short-term loans are typical examples. The amount of current liabilities you have influences how well you can pay off short-term debt and other bills.

Keyword

Contingent liabilities are liabilities that may be incurred by an entity depending on the outcome of an uncertain future event such as the outcome of a pending lawsuit.

1. **Contingent Liability Basics:** A debt that you might or might not accrue is known as a contingent liability. Your approach to a contingent liability will rely on how likely it is that the obligation will materialize as well as how well you can estimate its size. Contingent liabilities include things like lawsuits, fines from the government, and warranty payments. If a customer files a $100,000 lawsuit against you, for example, that sum is considered a contingent liability because, although you do not currently owe it, you might in the future.
2. **Accounting Approaches:** Different methods are used to account for current and contingent liabilities. Accounts for current liabilities are created as soon as the debt is owed. The amount owed is entered into the books in categories such as notes payable or accounts payable. Usually, an increase to an asset account—such as money, real estate, or machinery—offsets the liability. Only when the debt is likely and its amount is estimable is a contingent liability recorded. You could record a $50,000 loan settlement when it seems likely if you are working on one. Typically, you would record the expense in a legal-expenses account or add the sum to a liability account.
3. **Accounting Requirements and Statements:** The regulations governing the recording of contingent liabilities are also significantly different. Liabilities that are truly realized must be recorded. The recording of contingent liabilities, however, is ambiguous. It advises you to only record contingent liabilities in cases where there is a sizable possibility of loss. If not, you can postpone recording the debt until after you truly become obligated to pay it.

7.2.5. Current vs. Long-Term Liabilities

Leaders in business have a fondness for discussing revenues, net profits, and assets. Ultimately, those are all favorable figures on a balance sheet that can enhance a company's image. They also serve as a company's definition of growth and profit. However, corporate executives are missing important clues about the company's financial stability by failing to take the debt into account. Recognize the distinction between current and. long-term obligations, in order to accurately determine the working capital and ratios that are required. Compared to long-term liabilities, current liability obligations have a different function.

1. **Understanding Working Capital:** Working capital is essential for any business. A measure called working capital is obtained by deducting current liabilities from current assets. As it determines whether a company has enough cash or cash-equivalent assets to cover its required liabilities, it serves as a gauge of financial strength. A company is considered to have liquidity issues if its working capital is insufficient. A business is considered to be operating inefficiently when it has an excessive amount of working capital because it isn't effectively reallocating capital into higher revenue growth. A business seeks to maintain a balance between its working capital and its liabilities, or the sum of its financial commitments during a given fiscal year. Company executives need to understand how to maintain operations in the optimal working capital range.
2. **Define Current Liabilities:** Financial responsibilities are known as liabilities. Unless the business has chosen to use a different financial cycle, current liabilities are determined over a 12-month period. Information about current liabilities can be found on the income statement and balance sheet. These responsibilities consist of accrued expenses, notes payable, and accounts payable.
   i. **Notes payable** are any promissory, loan and mortgage note payments. If the note has a term longer than 12 months, only the payments required to pay the next 12 months are considered for current liabilities.
   ii. **Accounts payable** are the monies owed to suppliers who extend the company credit terms, when buying materials or wholesale products. These often have terms of Net 30, Net 60 or Net 90 days, meaning that the net amount is due within 30, 60 or 90 days, respectively.
   iii. **Accrued expenses** are those expenses the company is already obligated to pay but hasn't yet paid. This includes taxes, payroll, and loan interest. Creditors may have a lien on some assets that are associated with liabilities, such as real estate loans, inventory or other secured credit items. Failure to pay not only affects the financial health of the company but also can lead to foreclosure or seizure of assets needed for operations.

3. **Define Long-Term Liabilities:** Long-term liabilities refer to debts and payables that will become due in a future date, specifically at least 12 months from the present. These obligations are recorded in the balance sheet of a company but do not immediately jeopardize its working capital's financial stability. Examples of long-term liabilities encompass mortgage loans, debentures, long-term bonds issued to investors, pension obligations, and any deferred tax liabilities. It is important to note that a portion of all long-term liabilities is considered as part of current liabilities, representing the upcoming 12 months of payments.

   For instance, a frame shop might have bought a structure to use as both a storefront and a framing facility. A $100,000 down payment was used to finance the $500,000 purchase of the building. The $1,500 monthly payment includes interest and property taxes. The building is a valuable asset that is currently worth $500,000. The property has a $400,000 mortgage note that is listed as a long-term liability. The payments that are due over the next twelve months ($1,500 x 12 = $18,000) are the current liabilities. This is a portion of the working capital that is necessary to keep the business running.

4. **Current vs. Long-Term Liabilities:** Because of the urgent need for cash that a business has, current and long-term liabilities are handled differently. Most companies run the risk of going out of business if they don't have enough working capital to last for 12 to 24 months. Businesses that survive must find methods to cut expenses, frequently by forgoing many of the essential revenue-generating tasks like marketing or employing salespeople. Working capital requirements take current liabilities into account. Once more, working capital refers to the funds required to maintain the company's daily operations and keep the lights on. Without it, the business would have to take on more debt in order to survive, reduce staff, or possibly even close.

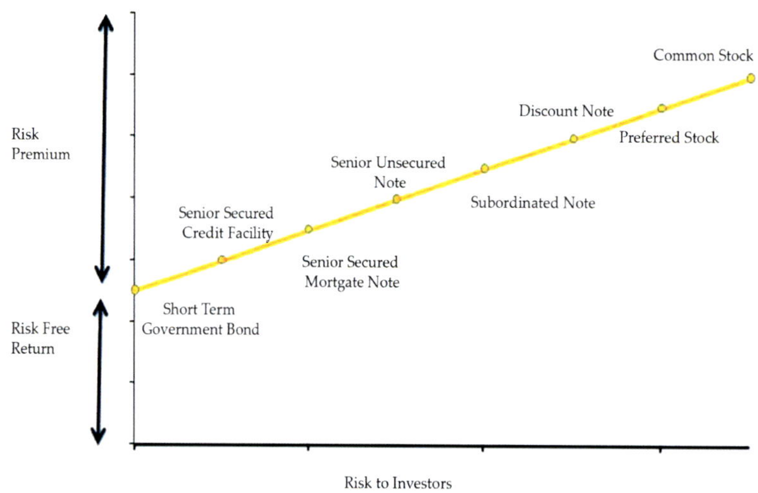

Figure 7.8. *Long-term-liabilities-risk.*

Source: *https://cdn.wallstreetmojo.com/wp-content/uploads/2018/07/Long-Term-Liabilities-risk-profile.png.*

Long-term liabilities are frequently viewed as a capital investment in the company's long-term growth plans. Purchasing a new, large piece of equipment is an investment that may take some time to pay for itself, but it will increase production levels and help the business expand. Even pension plans are seen as investments in the company's employees, fostering loyalty, lowering attrition, and enhancing corporate culture (Figure 7.8).

5. **Reports and Company Financial Health:** A company's ability to continue operating can be determined with certainty by looking at its current liabilities. A company with liabilities greater than its assets, as opposed to current assets, obviously has financial problems that need to be resolved. But, having an excessive amount of current assets sitting around is also bad. A business ought to take into account the working capital ratio in addition to the working capital dollar value.

   The working capital ratio is calculated, using the same current assets and current liabilities.

Working Capital Ratio = Current Assets / Current Liabilities

A ratio can be obtained by simply dividing the assets by the liabilities. A company in good health will have a ratio between 1 and 2 points. If the ratio falls below this range, it indicates that the company does not have enough cash on hand to cover its future liabilities. Operating above that ratio range implies that the business is hoarding cash and not effectively reallocating resources to increase revenue. An organization possessing a greater working capital ratio might have a strategy for managing those resources, like allocating a substantial portion of its earnings to research and development until it can continue doing so without taking on additional debt. However, if the company continues to operate in this manner for long stretches of time, analysts or investors may become concerned about possible business partnerships.

Analysts examine the trends as well. Working capital ratios can be computed on a monthly basis and will display an incline or decline trend. A company that sees a decline in the ratio is undoubtedly heading in the wrong financial direction. The company has negative operating capital if the ratio falls below 1.0, which indicates that it has more debt and current liabilities than cash flow and assets to cover them.

6. **Business Liabilities Example:** Let's examine an example to better understand why creating a plan to keep working capital positive is crucial. A family-run company, Hollis Kitchen Cabinets provides contractors and the general public with kitchen and bathroom cabinetry. The building in which they operate, along with the storefront and warehouse, is owned by the Hollis family. The building is worth $400,000, and the mortgage note still owes $250,000.

   The company gets the cabinets from a wholesaler supplier on credit, with terms being Net 30. The company has $12,000 in these accounts payable.

The current liabilities for the next 12 months look like this:

1. $24,000 mortgage note payments ($2,000 monthly, including interest)
2. $82,000 in accounts payable
3. $75,000 in accrued expenses, including payroll and taxes

This means that the Hollis Kitchen Cabinets company has $181,000 in current liabilities. But what are the current assets? The company generates $16,000 in sales monthly, with $14,000 generally being on credit terms of Net 60, allowing contractors to wait until clients pay them first to complete the invoice order. There is $10,000 in the bank.

If the company is consistent with sales and collecting its payments, it has current assets of $202,000. The working capital ratio is 1.12, meaning that the company is at risk of a bad month, which affects its working capital, so that the company is not able to meet its obligations. Remember that 1.0 is a break-even number with the working capital ratio, and that anything below that number means that the company is operating with more liabilities owed than it has assets to pay.

The company can consider a couple of strategies to alleviate some working capital issues:

1. Leverage the equity in the building to have a safety net of accessible capital;
2. Set a new policy of credit terms.

By obtaining an equity line of credit against its own assets, the company does not inherently increase its debt. It does so if it begins to draw on that credit line to cover a weak revenue month. This is a solution, but it only addresses the immediate issue and doesn't address the larger one. Renegotiating the terms of credit is the alternative tactic. The business may choose to do this with its contractors, suppliers, or both. At least the company will have the same schedule as its customers, which maintains more even cash flow, if it can agree to a Net-60 term schedule with its suppliers. The company gives itself 30 days to recover from a poor month of revenue if it can successfully execute a new policy of Net-30 to its contractors. The company improves its cash flow situation by doing both.

7. **Being Liability Aware:** Businesses can easily become enthused about sales. Revenues are the company's lifeblood. However, a business faces the risk of going bankrupt if working capital and the trends of current assets and current liabilities are not closely monitored. Although it is the last thing that businesses want to do, they may have no choice if they have no assets or cash flow to pay their debts.

   Business executives should monitor working capital ratios on a monthly basis to identify any upward or downward trends. A company may not be heading in the right direction even if its sales figures are high. The business is moving goods without making money if the products are loss leaders or are not priced fairly. Working capital problems eventually arise from this.

On the other hand, if a business experiences cash flow problems, inventory sold during a promotion or sale can quickly generate a large amount of capital.

For businesses, debt can also be a very effective growth tool. Many large conglomerates got their size by using debt as a means of financing a capital investment in the company's long-term growth. Gain control over your debt so that you can use it as leverage. To establish successful strategies and gain a thorough understanding of trends, business leaders should collaborate with essential financial advisors like accountants and bookkeepers. A company can expand to new heights by strategically using long-term debt, but in order to do so, it needs to have enough current assets to cover its current liabilities as well as its new commitments. A company's working capital ratio is a key indicator of the financial management skills of the business leadership, so any company looking to raise investment capital or obtain a small business loan for a capital investment is evaluated closely.

Did you get it?

1. **What do you mean by accounts payable?**
2. **Describe the accrued expenses.**
3. **Write the short-term debt**
4. **Define the dividends payable or dividends declared.**

7.3. NON-CURRENT LIABILITIES

→Learning Objectives

- Define the examples of noncurrent liabilities
- Discuss on types of non-current liabilities
- Write the importance of non-current liabilities in accounting
- Describe the different financial ratios involving non-current liabilities
- Focus on difference between various liabilities

The long-term financial obligations shown on a company's balance sheet are known as noncurrent liabilities, long-term liabilities, or long-term debts. While current liabilities are short-term debts with maturity dates within the next year, these liabilities have obligations that become due more than a year from now.

To determine if a business can sustainably pay its debts, noncurrent liabilities are contrasted with cash flow. Long-term investors use noncurrent liabilities to determine whether a company is using excessive leverage, whereas lenders are primarily concerned with short-term liquidity and the amount of current liabilities. A company's ability to support more debt without raising the risk of default increases with stability in its cash flows. A variety of financial ratios are used by creditors and investors to evaluate leverage and liquidity risk. To get a general idea of how leveraged a company is, the debt ratio compares its total debt to its total assets. A company's equity position is stronger and less leverage is used when the percentage is lower. A company is taking on greater financial risk the higher the ratio. Other variations include dividing noncurrent liabilities by available capital, or the long-term debt to total assets ratio and the long-term debt to capitalization ratio.

A company's financial health can also be evaluated by analysts using coverage ratios, such as the interest coverage ratio and the cash flow-to-debt ratio. The cash flow-to-debt ratio calculates how long a business would need to pay off its debt if all of its cash flow went toward paying it off. The interest coverage ratio measures whether sufficient revenue is being generated to cover interest payments. It is computed by dividing a company's earnings before interest and taxes (EBIT) by its debt interest payments for the same period. Analysts use liquidity ratios such as the current ratio, quick ratio, and acid test ratio to evaluate short-term liquidity risk. The term "non-current liabilities" refers to debts that are typically due for repayment after a year. Non-current liabilities are typically shown as a separate entry on a company's balance sheet. Companies typically assess their long-term financial viability by comparing the cash flow of their venture to the amount of non-current liabilities. Long-term liabilities are thought to be a powerful tool for determining a company's solvency.

Additionally, business entities tend to depend on long-term liabilities to meet their existing capital asset requirements or for investing in more profitable projects.

Some of the non-current liabilities examples include – long-term debt payable, long-term loans payable, deferred tax liabilities, long-term bonds payable, pension benefit obligations, long-term lease obligations, etc.

Keyword

Long-term debt is debt that matures in more than one year and is often treated differently from short-term debt.

The non-current liabilities can be clubbed under five broad categories, namely:

- Bonds payable
- Long term notes payable
- deferred tax liabilities
- mortgage payable
- Capital lease

7.3.1. Examples of Noncurrent Liabilities

The following are examples of noncurrent liabilities: bonds payable, long-term loans, deferred tax liabilities, long-term lease obligations, and pension benefit obligations. A bond liability's portion that won't be paid off in the next year is known as a noncurrent liability. Noncurrent liabilities also include warranties that last longer than a year. Some instances are deferred revenue, deferred compensation, and specific health care obligations.

All debts that are classified as long-term, such as mortgages, auto loans, or other loans for land, machinery, or equipment, are distinguished from current debt by the payments that must be made within the next year. Debt that has a 12-month maturity date may also be reported as a noncurrent liability if the intention is to refinance it and restructure the obligation to be noncurrent through a financial arrangement.

7.3.2. Types of Non-Current Liabilities

The following are the main types of non-current liabilities that are included in the balance sheet:

1. **Credit Lines:** A credit line is an agreement between a lender and a borrower in which the lender provides the business with a predetermined amount of funds as needed. The company does not receive credit in one lump sum; rather, it receives credit as needed in a specified amount up to the lender's maximum credit limit. A credit line is often good for a certain amount of time during which the company is able to access the money. A business credit will be categorized as a non-current liability if it is used to finance the purchase of industrial equipment.
2. **Long-Term Lease:** One of the common expenses that businesses must pay in order to fulfill their purchase commitments is leasing. Businesses can finance the purchase of fixed assets like cars and industrial equipment by using capital leases. Since they lessen the long-term obligations of the lease, lease payments made toward the capital lease are recognized as non-current liabilities if the lease term is longer than a year. On the balance sheet, the property that was acquired through the capital lease is listed as an asset.
3. **Bonds Payable:** A bond is a long-term loan agreement that is used to finance capital projects and is signed by a borrower and a lender. These investment banks are categorized as long-term liabilities if the payment period is longer than a year, and the top banks on the list are Goldman Sachs, Morgan Stanley, BAML, JP Morgan, Blackstone, Rothschild, Scotiabank, RBC, UBS, Wells Fargo, Deutsche Bank, Citi, Macquarie, HSBC, ICBC, Credit Suisse, and Bank of America Merril Lynch. The borrower is required to pay interest at predetermined rates over a predetermined length of time, typically more than a year.
4. **Notes Payable**: A note, also known as a promissory note, is a unique kind of loan agreement in which the borrower unconditionally promises to repay the lender the principal amount plus interest. Promissory notes are used to finance the acquisition of real estate, including buildings and machinery. The note is regarded as a non-current asset if its maturity period is longer than a year.
5. **Deferred Tax Liabilities:** The amount of taxes that a business has not paid in the current period but still needs to pay in the future is referred to as deferred tax liabilities. The difference between the taxes payable and the taxes that have accrued is used to compute the liability. Consequently, because of a transaction that happened during the current period for which tax has not been remitted, the company will have to pay more tax in the future.

7.3.3. The Importance of Non-Current Liabilities in Accounting

Non-current liabilities are crucial in determining the viability of a business endeavor, even though most lenders place a higher priority on current liabilities and short-term liquidity. These liabilities, for example, are used to assess a venture's solvency and determine whether or not a company is using its leverage appropriately.

Additionally, it is employed to assess the cash flow stability of an enterprise. A venture's financial capacity to satisfy long-term obligations can be ascertained by comparing its total non-current liabilities to its cash flow. For example, if the cash flow is consistently high, this indicates that the business endeavor can effectively manage its debt load with a reduced risk of default. A prospective investor can also benefit from having a good understanding of a company's cash flow stability and leverage usage. It immediately assists them in determining whether or not doing business with a company would be profitable for them. For example, creditors might decide it is not worthwhile to work with a company that frequently uses its primary resources to pay off debt. Nevertheless, a company that uses a lot of leverage in conjunction with stagnant cash flow might scare off potential investors. Nevertheless, to understand how non-current liabilities help to gauge such vital aspects, investors and business entities must assess specific ratios as well.

7.3.4. Different Financial Ratios Involving Non-Current Liabilities

Particular financial ratios can be used to assess a venture's potential as an investment vehicle in addition to determining its ability to pay off debt.

Here's a list of a few of such financial ratios which involve non-current liabilities.

1. **Debt Ratio:** The aforementioned ratio provides a reasonable indication of how frequently a company uses liability leveraging by comparing its total liabilities to its total assets. A lower percentage suggests that the business is lowering its level of leverage and has a solid foundation for stocks. In a similar vein, a higher ratio suggests a higher likelihood of financial risk exposure.

   Formula: Debt ratio = Total Liabilities/ Total Assets

2. **Debt to Equity Ratio:** The ratio is calculated by dividing a venture's total debt by its total equity. An excessively high ratio suggests that insufficient equity is being used to fund the business endeavor. Owners of businesses can learn from these results and address their shortcomings appropriately.

   Formula: Debt-to-equity-ratio = Total Liabilities/Total shareholders' Equity

3. **Cash Flow to Debt Ratio:** This ratio helps gauge how readily a business venture can pay off its existing debt by utilizing its cash flow.

   Formula: Cash flow to debt ratio = Cash flow/Total liabilities

A higher ratio shows that a company is stable financially and has the ability to accelerate debt payments when needed. Conversely, a lower ratio indicates a less solid financial position.

7.3.5. Difference Between Various Liabilities

The primary difference between non-current liabilities and other types of financial obligations of a business can be highlighted as Table 7.1:

Thus, it can be concluded that non-current liabilities are essential to understanding the present and potential financial status of a business endeavor. Investors find it useful to emphasize a company's potential for investment. In a similar vein, company owners would be able to make the required financial decisions that are in line with better management by regularly balancing their liabilities.

Table 7.1. Difference Between Various Liabilities

Type	Current Liabilities	Non-Current Liabilities	Contingent Liabilities
Definition	It comprises those liabilities which must be written-off within a financial year or business cycle. They are also known as short-term liabilities.	These liabilities are usually written-off in more than one year or business cycle. They are also known as long-term liabilities.	They mostly comprise obligations which may or may not be realized in a given financial year.
Treatment in books of accounts	It is posted on the right side of the Balance Sheet above the 'Non-Current Liabilities.'	They are recorded on the right side of the balance sheet below 'Current Liabilities.'	It is recorded twice in a Balance Sheet. The first treatment is recorded as an expense under the Income Statement, and the second is recorded on the right side of the Balance Sheet as well.
Examples	Some of the examples of current liabilities include accounts payables, short-term loan, trade payables and outstanding dues.	Debentures, mortgage loans and bonds are some of the non-current liabilities examples.	Guarantee for loans, lawsuits and claim against product warranty are some of the examples of contingent liabilities.

Source: https://groww.in/p/non-current-liabilities.

Did you get it?

1. Learn about debt to equity ratio
2. Describe the cash flow to debt ratio

CASE STUDY

MANAGING LIABILITIES IN A SMALL BUSINESS

John owns a small retail business specializing in handmade jewelry. Over the past few years, his business has experienced steady growth, but he's now facing challenges with managing liabilities as he plans to expand his operations.

1. **Situation:** John's business primarily operates on a cash basis, but he occasionally uses trade credit to purchase raw materials and supplies for his jewelry-making. Additionally, he has taken out a small business loan to finance equipment purchases and inventory expansion.

Source: https://images.businessnewsdaily.com/app/uploads/2022/04/04072500/accounting_Jirapong_Manustrong_Getty.jpg.

2. **Challenges:**
   - **Cash Flow Management:** John finds it challenging to balance his business's cash flow while meeting various financial obligations, including rent, utilities, payroll, and loan repayments.
   - **Supplier Liabilities:** With increasing demand for his products, John's supplier liabilities have grown, and he's concerned about maintaining good relationships with suppliers while managing his cash flow effectively.
   - **Loan Repayment:** John's small business loan carries monthly repayments, which add to his financial commitments. He worries about the impact of loan repayments on his business's profitability and growth prospects.
   - **Expansion Plans:** John wants to expand his product line and possibly

open a second retail location. However, he's unsure about the feasibility of these plans given his current liabilities and financial constraints.

3. **Strategies**
   - **Cash Flow Forecasting:** John implements a robust cash flow forecasting system to track incoming and outgoing cash flows. This helps him anticipate periods of cash crunch and plan accordingly.
   - **Negotiating Terms with Suppliers:** John negotiates favorable payment terms with his suppliers, such as extended payment periods or discounts for early payments, to ease the burden of supplier liabilities on his cash flow.
   - **Loan Restructuring:** John explores options for restructuring his existing business loan, such as extending the loan term or refinancing at a lower interest rate, to reduce monthly repayments and improve liquidity.
   - **Cost Control Measures:** John implements cost control measures, such as optimizing inventory levels, reducing non-essential expenses, and negotiating better terms with service providers, to free up cash for business expansion.
   - **Alternative Financing:** John considers alternative financing options, such as invoice financing or crowdfunding, to raise capital for his expansion plans without adding to his existing liabilities.
4. Outcome: By implementing these strategies, John successfully navigates the challenges associated with managing liabilities in his small business. He improves cash flow management, strengthens supplier relationships, and positions his business for sustainable growth and expansion.

SUMMARY

- Liability refers to an organization's legal obligation or responsibility to settle debts, fulfill contractual agreements, or address claims resulting from past actions or events.
- It encompasses various types, including financial liabilities such as loans, accounts payable, and bonds payable, as well as legal liabilities arising from lawsuits, accidents, or breaches of contract.
- Liabilities are typically classified as current liabilities, which are due within one year, and long-term liabilities, which are payable over a longer period.
- Managing liabilities involves ensuring adequate liquidity to meet short-term obligations while balancing long-term financial stability and solvency.
- Organizations often use leverage, or debt financing, to fund operations and investments, leveraging the potential returns of borrowed funds against the costs and risks associated with debt.
- Effective liability management involves assessing and mitigating risks associated with debt, including interest rate risk, credit risk, and liquidity risk, through strategies such as hedging, diversification, and debt restructuring.
- Accurate measurement and disclosure of liabilities are essential for financial reporting and compliance with accounting standards, providing stakeholders with transparency and clarity regarding the organization's financial position and obligations.
- Liability management decisions must consider various factors, including interest rates, market conditions, creditworthiness, and regulatory requirements, to optimize the organization's capital structure and financial performance.
- Failure to manage liabilities effectively can lead to financial distress, credit downgrades, increased borrowing costs, and even bankruptcy, highlighting the importance of prudent debt management practices.
- Proactive liability management requires ongoing monitoring, analysis, and adjustment of debt levels and repayment schedules to adapt to changing business conditions, minimize risks, and support sustainable growth and profitability.

REVIEW QUESTIONS

1. Define liabilities in accounting and finance. Discuss their significance in financial reporting and analysis within organizations.
2. Differentiate between current liabilities and long-term liabilities. Provide examples of each and explain how they impact a company's financial position.
3. Discuss the importance of understanding a company's debt structure. How does the composition of liabilities affect a company's risk profile and financial health?
4. Analyze the relationship between liabilities and liquidity management.
5. Explain the concept of leverage and its relationship to liabilities.

MULTIPLE CHOICE QUESTIONS

1. **Which of the following best defines a liability?**
   a. Assets owned by a company
   b. Obligations or debts owed by a company
   c. Investments made by a company
   d. Revenue generated by a company
2. **Which of the following is an example of a current liability?**
   a. Long-term loan
   b. Accounts payable
   c. Machinery
   d. Common stock
3. **Which financial statement primarily reflects a company's liabilities?**
   a. Income statement
   b. Statement of cash flows
   c. Balance sheet
   d. Statement of retained earnings
4. **What is the formula for calculating the debt-to-equity ratio?**
   a. Total liabilities / Total assets
   b. Total liabilities / Shareholder's equity
   c. Total assets / Total liabilities
   d. Shareholder's equity / Total assets
5. **Which of the following is considered a long-term liability?**
   a. Accounts payable
   b. Salaries payable
   c. Mortgage payable
   d. Accrued expenses
6. **What does the term "accrued liabilities" refer to?**
   a. Debts that have been paid off
   b. Debts that are not yet due
   c. Debts that have been forgiven
   d. Debts that have accumulated interest
7. **Which type of liability represents money received in advance for goods or services?**
   a. Accounts payable
   b. Accrued liabilities

c. Deferred revenue

d. Mortgage payable

8. What happens to a liability when it is paid off?

a. It remains unchanged

b. It increases

c. It decreases

d. It becomes an asset

9. How do creditors' claims on a company's assets differ from shareholders' claims?

a. Creditors have priority over shareholders in asset claims

b. Shareholders have priority over creditors in asset claims

c. Creditors and shareholders have equal claims on assets

d. Creditors have no claims on a company's assets

10. Which financial ratio measures a company's ability to meet short-term obligations using its most liquid assets?

a. Debt-to-equity ratio

b. Current ratio

c. Return on assets

d. Asset turnover ratio

Answer to Multiple Choice Questions

1. (b); 2. (b); 3. (c); 4. (b); 5. (c); 6. (b); 7. (c); 8. (c); 9. (a); 10. (b)

REFERENCES

1. Anderson, S. E., Jones, L. C., & Reed, T. N., (2012). *Insurance Fraud: Losses, Liabilities, and September 11; Issues in Accounting Education*, 1119–1130. Instructional case.
2. Barth, M. E., Hodder, L. D., & Stubben, S. R., (2013). Financial reporting for employee stock options: Liabilities or equity? *Review of Accounting Studies, 18*(3), 642–682.
3. Chasteen, L. G., & Ransom, C. R., (2007). Including credit standing in measuring the fair value of liabilities – let's pass this one to the shareholders. *Accounting Horizons*, 119–135.
4. Fried, A., Holtzman, M. P., & Rotenstein, A., (2015). Lost and found: Revenue recognition standard offers advice on booking liabilities and breakage income for unredeemed gift cards. *Journal of Accountancy*, 32–36.
5. Graham, A., & Maher, J. J., (2006). Environmental liabilities, bond ratings, and bond yields. Environmental accounting: Commitment or propaganda. *Advances in Environmental Accounting & Management*, (3), 111–142.

6. Harrison, W. T., Horngren, C. T., & Thomas, C. W., (2019). *Financial Accounting*. Chapters 11 and 12. Pearson.
7. Horngren, C. T., Sundem, G. L., Stratton, W. O., Burgstahler, D., & Schatzberg, J. W., (2017). *Introduction to Management Accounting*. Chapters 10 and 11. Pearson.
9. Libby, R., Libby, P. A., & Short, D. G., (2017). *Financial Accounting* (Chapters 11 and 12). McGraw-Hill Education.
10. Spiceland, J. D., Thomas, W. A., Herrmann, D. T., & Shaw, J. J., (2020). *Financial Accounting* (Chapters 11 and 12). McGraw-Hill Education.
11. Stickney, C. P., Weil, R. L., Schipper, K., & Francis, J., (2009). *Financial Accounting: An Introduction to Concepts, Methods, and Uses*. Chapters 9 and 10. Cengage Learning.
12. Warren, C. S., Reeve, J. M., & Duchac, J., (2018). *Financial and Managerial Accounting* (Chapters 11 and 12). Cengage Learning.
13. Weygandt, J. J., Kimmel, P. D., & Kieso, D. E., (2019). *Financial Accounting* (Chapters 9 and 10). Wiley.
14. Wild, J. J., Shaw, K. W., & Chiappetta, B., (2018). *Financial Accounting: Information for Decisions* (Chapters 10 and 11). McGraw-Hill Education.

CHAPTER 8

DuPoint Analysis

LEARNING OBJECTIVES

After studying this chapter, you will be able to:

- Understand the overview of DuPont analysis
- Discuss on DuPont analysis ratios with economic adjustments
- Know the asset and liability ratios by adjusted ROE performance group

INTRODUCTORY EXAMPLE

DuPont Corporation

Founded in 1802, DuPont Corporation, an American conglomerate, has significantly contributed to industrial innovation and chemical advancements worldwide. DuPont's operations span diverse sectors, including agriculture, electronics, materials science, and safety solutions. Utilizing the DuPont Analysis, the corporation enhances its financial management and performance evaluation. By dissecting Return on Equity (ROE) into its constituent parts—profit margin, asset turnover, and financial leverage—DuPont Corporation gains deeper insights into its operational efficiency and financial health. The company's profit margin, indicative of its ability to convert revenues into profits, reflects its effective cost management and pricing strategies across its product portfolio. Meanwhile, asset turnover measures the efficiency with which DuPont utilizes its assets to generate sales, highlighting its operational effectiveness and market penetration. Moreover, DuPont carefully manages its financial leverage, balancing debt usage to amplify returns while mitigating risk. Through DuPont Analysis, DuPont Corporation assesses its competitive positioning, identifies areas for improvement, and aligns strategic initiatives with its financial objectives. By leveraging this analytical framework, DuPont sustains its legacy of innovation, fosters shareholder value, and maintains its reputation as a global leader in science-driven solutions.

UNIT INTRODUCTION

DuPont analysis, named after the DuPont Corporation, is a financial performance measurement method that analyzes the return on equity (ROE) by breaking it down into three components: profitability, efficiency, and leverage. This analysis provides deeper insights into the factors driving a company's ROE and helps identify areas for improvement.

DuPont analysis breaks down ROE into its components: net profit margin, asset turnover, and financial leverage. Net profit margin measures the company's profitability by examining the percentage of revenue that translates into profit after deducting expenses. Asset turnover evaluates the company's efficiency in generating revenue from its assets by comparing sales to total assets. Financial leverage assesses the impact of debt on ROE by analyzing the proportion of debt financing compared to equity financing.

By dissecting ROE into these components, DuPont analysis enables stakeholders to understand the sources of a company's profitability and efficiency and how leverage influences overall returns. For instance, a company may have a high ROE due to strong profitability but could be heavily leveraged, posing risks related to debt repayment. Alternatively, a company may have a moderate ROE with a balanced mix of profitability, efficiency, and leverage, indicating stable and sustainable performance.

DuPont analysis helps management pinpoint areas for improvement. For instance, if ROE is low, management may focus on enhancing profitability through cost reduction initiatives, increasing asset turnover by optimizing asset utilization, or adjusting leverage levels to achieve an optimal capital structure. By understanding the interplay of these components, companies can make informed strategic decisions to enhance financial performance and create long-term shareholder value (Figure 8.1).

The decomposition of ROE allows investors to focus on the key metrics of financial performance individually to identify strengths and weaknesses.

- The DuPont analysis is a framework for analyzing fundamental performance originally popularized by the DuPont Corporation.
- DuPont analysis is a useful technique used to decompose the different drivers of return on equity (ROE).
- An investor can use analysis like this to compare the operational efficiency of two similar firms. Managers can use DuPont analysis to identify strengths or weaknesses that should be addressed.

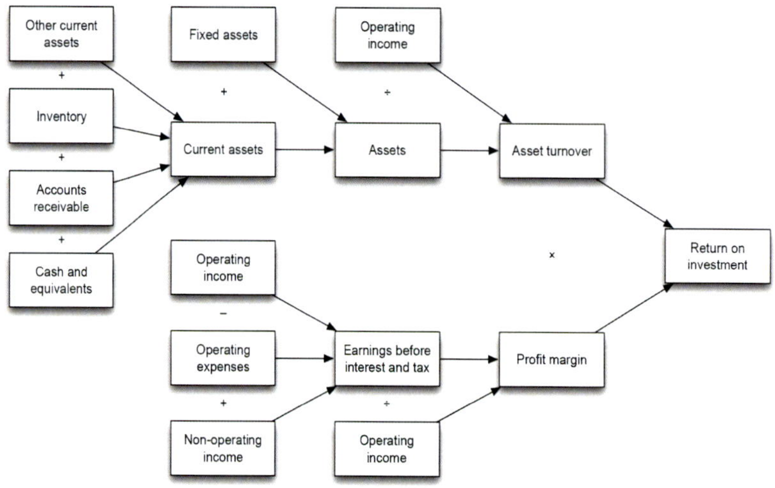

Figure 8.1. *DuPont model.*

Source: https://upload.wikimedia.org/wikipedia/commons/thumb/e/ec/DuPontModelEng.svg/1200px-DuPontModelEng.svg.png.

8.1. OVERVIEW OF DUPONT ANALYSIS

→Learning Objectives

- Discuss the role of DuPont analysis in financial planning
- Define the importance of DuPont analysis
- Describe the benefits of DuPont analysis
- Explain the advantages and disadvantages of DuPont analysis
- Write the decoding DuPont analysis

A multi-step financial equation called DuPont analysis can reveal information about the underlying performance of a company. A detailed examination of the main indicators influencing a business's return on equity (ROE) is offered by the DuPont model. The DuPont analysis is also known as "the DuPont model." These names come from the DuPont Corporation, which developed the model back in 1920.

An extension of the basic ROE formula is the DuPont analysis formula. The three distinct components that determine return on equity are taken into account by this extended formula: equity multiplier, total asset turnover, and net profit margin. The DuPont model deduces that a business can raise its return on equity by leveraging its assets more wisely, maintaining a high profit margin, and increasing asset turnover based on these factors. The DuPont analysis equation is:

DuPont analysis = net profit margin x asset turnover x equity multiplier

Each of these factors represents the result of a separate formula. When you replace the factors in the DuPont analysis equation with the formulas that make up each component, the DuPont analysis equation looks like this:

DuPont analysis = (net income / revenue) x (sales / average total assets) x (average total assets / average shareholders' equity)

1. **Net Profit Margin**: The ratio known as the net profit margin shows how much profit a company makes on each dollar of revenue after subtracting its costs. By dividing a company's net profits by its total revenues, you can find the net profit margin. When written as an equation, the formula for calculating net profit margin is:

   Net profit margin = net income / revenue

   An often used metric to assess profitability is net profit margin. Return on equity rises in tandem with a company's net profit margin. Net profit margin's main idea is that a company can raise its profit margins by raising prices, cutting expenses, or doing both at once.

2. **Total Asset Turnover**: Total asset turnover is a ratio that shows how well a company uses its resources to produce income and close deals. Divide the company's revenue by the average asset value to get the total asset turnover. The equation used to represent the total asset turnover formula is:

   Total asset turnover = revenue / average assets

   The return on equity of a company rises in tandem with its total asset turnover ratio. The total asset turnover ratio and net profit margin of a business typically have an inverse relationship. Accordingly, a company's asset turnover rate will decrease as its net profit margin increases and vice versa. This enables precise comparisons between a business that employs a low-profit, high-volume business model and a company that uses a high-profit, low-volume business model by investors and financial decision-makers. Next, based on their comparison, they can decide which business does a better job of maximizing return on equity for its owners.

3. **Equity Multiplier**: The equity multiplier indicates the percentage of a company's return on equity ratio that comes from debt and gauges its level of financial leverage. By dividing a company's average total assets by its average shareholders' equity, you can calculate its equity multiplier. The formula for calculating the equity multiplier is:

   Equity multiplier = average assets / average equity

   A company's return on equity ratio rises in tandem with its equity multiplier. A company should ideally use just enough debt to fund operations and expansion while avoiding excessive debt, which lowers the equity multiplier. Occasionally, a company will attempt to increase its return on equity ratio by taking on more debt. The DuPont analysis model provides investors with a precise gauge of the company's financial leverage to utilize in their investment decisions by incorporating the equity multiplier into its formula.

Keyword

Financial leverage is the strategic endeavor of borrowing money to invest in assets. The goal is to have the return on those assets exceed the cost of borrowing funds that paid for those assets.

8.1.1. The Role of DuPont Analysis in Financial Planning

A company's strategic planning process must include financial planning in order to ensure that it has the resources necessary to meet its objectives within the allotted time. DuPont Analysis is useful when financial planning is being done. The DuPont Analysis has a direct bearing on financial planning because it can pinpoint a company's strong points and areas in need of development. For example, it may be necessary to evaluate a company's asset investment strategy if its asset turnover is low. The financial plan can provide specific details and an outline of how changes in company policy can be brought about by identifying areas of concern. Additionally, a company's capital structure decisions may be impacted by its understanding of financial leverage through the use of DuPont Analysis. A company may be unduly dependent on debt to finance its assets if its equity multiplier is high. This realization may spark a discussion about the company's debt management approach and ultimately result in a deleveraging strategy. Lastly, DuPont Analysis can clarify whether there are any particular areas the company should aim to meet or surpass by offering a thorough breakdown of its ROE.

Keyword

Financial plan is a document that details a person's current financial circumstances and their short- and long-term monetary goals.

8.1.2. Importance of DuPont Analysis

DuPont analysis holds significant importance in financial analysis and decision-making processes for various stakeholders, including investors, creditors, analysts, and company management.

1. **Comprehensive Evaluation**: DuPont analysis provides a holistic view of a company's financial performance by breaking down ROE into its constituent elements. This enables stakeholders to understand the specific drivers behind changes in ROE over time and identify areas of strength or weakness within the business.
2. Identification of Performance Drivers: By analyzing profitability, efficiency, and leverage separately, DuPont analysis helps pinpoint the primary factors influencing a company's ROE. Stakeholders can assess whether improvements in ROE are driven by enhanced profitability, better asset utilization, or changes in the capital structure, allowing for targeted strategic interventions.
3. **Comparative Analysis**: DuPont analysis facilitates meaningful comparisons of financial performance across companies, industries, and time periods. Investors and analysts can benchmark a company's ROE components against industry peers to assess relative strengths and weaknesses, identify industry trends, and make informed investment decisions.
4. **Risk Assessment**: DuPont analysis assists in evaluating a company's financial risk profile by examining its leverage

component. A high proportion of debt financing relative to equity may increase financial risk and impact the company's ability to generate sustainable returns. Understanding the balance between leverage and profitability is crucial for assessing risk-adjusted returns and making prudent investment choices.

5. **Strategic Decision Making**: DuPont analysis informs strategic decision-making processes by highlighting areas for operational improvement and capital allocation. Management can use insights from DuPont analysis to optimize profitability, enhance operational efficiency, adjust the capital structure, and allocate resources effectively to maximize shareholder value.
6. **Financial Planning and Forecasting**: DuPont analysis aids in financial planning and forecasting by identifying historical trends in ROE components. By analyzing past performance, management can develop more accurate forecasts, set realistic financial targets, and monitor progress towards strategic objectives over time.
7. **Investor Communication**: DuPont analysis enhances investor communication and transparency by providing a clear and structured framework for discussing financial performance. Companies can use DuPont analysis to articulate the key drivers of their ROE, explain changes in performance metrics, and address investor concerns regarding profitability, efficiency, and leverage.

8.1.3. Benefits of DuPont Analysis

DuPont analysis offers several benefits for investors, financial analysts, and company management:

1. **Deeper Insight into ROE Components**: DuPont analysis dissects return on equity (ROE) into its component parts, including profitability, efficiency, and leverage. This breakdown provides a more comprehensive understanding of the factors driving ROE and allows stakeholders to identify specific areas of strength or weakness within a company's financial performance.
2. **Identification of Performance Drivers**: By analyzing the individual components of ROE, DuPont analysis helps investors and analysts identify the key drivers of a company's profitability and efficiency. For example, a low ROE may be attributed to weak profitability, inefficient asset utilization, or excessive leverage. Understanding these drivers enables stakeholders to focus on areas for improvement and make informed investment decisions.
3. **Comparison Across Companies and Industries**: DuPont analysis allows for meaningful comparisons of financial performance across companies and industries. By evaluating the relative contributions of profitability, efficiency, and leverage to ROE, stakeholders can benchmark companies against industry peers and identify outliers or industry trends.
4. **Assessment of Financial Health**

and Risk: DuPont analysis provides insights into a company's financial health and risk profile. For instance, a high ROE driven by strong profitability and efficient asset utilization may indicate a healthy and sustainable business model. On the other hand, a high ROE driven primarily by leverage may signal increased financial risk and vulnerability to economic downturns.

5. **Strategic Decision Making**: DuPont analysis informs strategic decision-making by highlighting areas for operational improvement and capital allocation. For example, management may use DuPont analysis to identify opportunities to enhance profitability, optimize asset utilization, or adjust the capital structure to improve overall returns for shareholders.
6. **Forecasting and Planning**: By analyzing historical trends in the components of ROE, DuPont analysis helps stakeholders forecast future financial performance and develop strategic plans. For instance, management can use DuPont analysis to project future profitability, assess the impact of changes in operating efficiency, or evaluate the potential implications of altering the company's capital structure.
7. **Investor Communication and Transparency**: DuPont analysis enhances investor communication and transparency by providing a clear and comprehensive explanation of a company's financial performance. By breaking down ROE into its constituent parts, companies can effectively communicate their financial results and strategies to investors, analysts, and other stakeholders.

Did you know?

The DuPont analysis, named after the DuPont Corporation, has its roots in the early 20th century when the DuPont Corporation sought to better understand and manage its return on equity (ROE). While the analysis itself wasn't officially developed until the 1920s, the principles it encompasses have been integral to the corporation's financial management since its inception.

8.1.4. Advantages of DuPont Analysis

DuPont Analysis has many more benefits than just figuring out a company's return on equity. Through the computation of the three ratios found in the DuPont formula—the equity multiplier, asset turnover, and net profit margin—it provides a comprehensive understanding of the financial and operational procedures that support a business's profitability. In particular, by analyzing net profit margin, it provides insight into a company's capacity for both cost containment and profit generation. Analyzing asset turnover sheds light on how effectively a business uses its assets to produce income. Additionally, by evaluating the equity multiplier, it provides information about the degree of risk a business assumes when using debt to finance its operations.

1. **Profitability Insights**: The DuPont Analysis's net profit margin section reveals how well a business turns a profit from its sales. Businesses can enhance their cost-control and profit-centric strategies by concentrating on this ratio.
2. **Assets Utilization**: The asset turnover ratio aids in a company's understanding of how effectively its

assets are being used to produce revenue. A lower ratio suggests that an organization might be overspending on assets that aren't being utilized effectively, indicating the need for strategic adjustments to asset management.

3. **Financial Leverage Assessment**: By using the equity multiplier, a company can determine how much of its funding comes from debt. With this information, a business can decide on its capital structure with knowledge.

8.1.5. Disadvantages of DuPont Analysis

While DuPont analysis offers valuable insights into a company's financial performance, it also comes with certain limitations and disadvantages:

1. **Simplification of Complex Factors**: DuPont analysis simplifies return on equity (ROE) into three main components: profitability, efficiency, and leverage. However, financial performance is influenced by numerous other factors, such as industry dynamics, competitive pressures, economic conditions, and strategic decisions. Ignoring these complex factors may lead to an oversimplified assessment of a company's financial health.
2. **Reliance on Historical Data**: DuPont analysis relies heavily on historical financial data to calculate and interpret financial ratios. While historical trends can provide valuable insights into a company's performance, they may not necessarily reflect future outcomes. Changes in market conditions, regulatory environments, technological advancements, and other external factors can impact future financial performance, rendering historical analysis less relevant.
3. **Interpretation Challenges**: Interpreting the results of DuPont analysis can be challenging, especially when individual components of ROE move in opposite directions. For example, a company may experience an increase in ROE due to higher leverage, but this may also result in increased financial risk. Distinguishing between sustainable improvements in profitability, operational efficiency, and prudent use of leverage requires careful analysis and consideration.
4. **Limited Predictive Ability**: While DuPont analysis provides insights into past financial performance and trends, its predictive ability for future outcomes is limited. Changes in market conditions, industry dynamics, competitive landscape, and macroeconomic factors can significantly impact a company's financial performance, making it difficult to forecast future ROE based solely on historical trends.
5. **Data Availability and Quality**: DuPont analysis relies on accurate and reliable financial data to produce meaningful results. However, data availability and quality can vary across companies and industries, making it challenging to conduct consistent and reliable analyzes. Inaccurate or incomplete financial information can distort the results of DuPont analysis and undermine its effectiveness as a decision-making tool.

6. **Does Not Account for Non-financial Factors**: DuPont analysis primarily focuses on financial metrics and does not account for non-financial factors that may influence a company's performance, such as corporate governance practices, management expertise, brand reputation, customer loyalty, and innovation capabilities. Ignoring these qualitative factors may result in an incomplete assessment of a company's overall competitiveness and long-term sustainability.
7. **Lack of Contextual Understanding**: DuPont analysis provides numerical insights into a company's financial performance but may lack contextual understanding of industry-specific dynamics, business models, and competitive strategies. Without considering these contextual factors, stakeholders may misinterpret the results of DuPont analysis and make suboptimal decisions regarding investment, risk management, and strategic planning.

Keyword

DuPont analysis is a useful technique used to decompose the different drivers of return on equity. An investor can use analysis tools like this to compare the operational efficiency of two similar firms.

8.1.6. Decoding DuPont Analysis

Acquired investors pay close attention to return on equity (ROE). It is a reliable indicator of how successfully management generates value for a company's owners. However, given its susceptibility to actions that both raise and decrease the stock's value, the figure may be deceptive. Investors may be misled into thinking a company is a good investment when it isn't if ROE components can't be broken down (Figure 8.2).

Figure 8.2. *Decoding DuPont analysis: A tool for enhanced financial insight.*

Source: https://media.licdn.com/dms/image/D5612AQFafsdwtHsxdA/article-cover_image-shrink_720_1280/0/1704515373409?e=2147483647&v=beta&t=GzMZZuVe6n8EzBt3gN27l8xjjdq5xLQt9ZoFl5y_M9U.

8.1.6.1. Return on Equity (ROE)

The beauty of ROE is that it is an important measure that only requires two numbers to compute: net income and shareholders' equity.

$$ROE = \frac{\text{Net Income}}{\text{Shareholder Equity}}$$

In general, an increase in this figure indicates that the rate of return on shareholders' equity is growing, which is positive for the business. The issue is that this figure can also go up if the business takes on additional debt, which would reduce shareholder equity. This would raise the leverage of the company, which may be advantageous, but it will also raise the risk of the stock.

Keyword

Shareholder equity (SE) is a company's net worth and it is equal to the total dollar amount that would be returned to the shareholders if the company must be liquidated and all its debts are paid off.

1. **Three-Step DuPont:** A deeper understanding of ROE is required to prevent false presumptions. This need was met in the 1920s by the DuPont Corporation, which developed an analysis technique that breaks down ROE into a more intricate equation. DuPont analysis reveals the reasons behind changes in the quantity.

There are two variants of DuPont analysis: the original three-step equation, and an extended five-step equation. The three-step equation breaks up ROE into three very important components:

ROE=NPM × Asset Turnover × Equity Multiplier

Where;

NPM=Net profit margin, the measure of operating efficiency

Asset Turnover=Measure of asset use efficiency

Equity Multiplier=Measure of financial leverage

- **The Three-Step DuPont Calculation:** Taking the ROE equation: ROE = net income / shareholder's equity and multiplying the equation by (sales / sales), we get:

$$ROE = \frac{\text{Net Income}}{\text{Sales}} \times \frac{\text{Sales}}{\text{Shareholders' Equity}}$$

We now have ROE broken into two components: the first is net profit margin and the second is the equity turnover ratio. Now by multiplying in (assets / assets), we end up with the three-step DuPont identity:

$$ROE = \frac{\text{Net Income}}{\text{Sales}} \times \frac{\text{Sales}}{\text{Assets}} \times \frac{\text{Assets}}{\text{Shareholders' Equity}}$$

This equation for ROE breaks it into three widely used and studied components:

ROE=NPM × Asset Turnover × Equity Multiplier

We have ROE broken down into net profit margin (how much profit the company gets out of its revenues), asset turnover (how effectively the company makes use of its assets) and equity multiplier (a measure of how much the company is leveraged). The usefulness should now be clearer (Figure 8.3).

An increase in a company's net profit margin or asset turnover will increase its return on equity (ROE), which is highly positive for the business. But if the company was already suitably leveraged and the rise is due to the equity multiplier, then this just makes matters more hazardous. Despite the increase in ROE, the stock may still be worth more of a discount if the company is becoming overly leveraged. There's a chance the business is underleveraged. It might be indicative of improved self-management on the part of the business in this instance.

Analyzing a company in this manner can be very beneficial even if its ROE has not changed. Assume a business releases data and its return on equity remains constant. A DuPont analysis examination could reveal that the company's net profit margin and asset turnover both declined, which are bad indicators. The only explanation for the ROE's stability was a significant increase in leverage. This would be a bad sign regardless of the company's initial state.

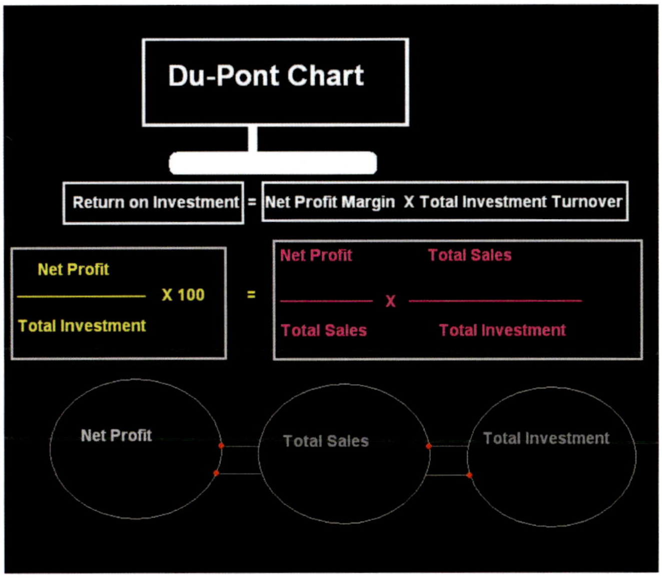

Figure 8.3. *DuPoint chart.*

Source: http://1.bp.blogspot.com/-TZ7yDzq3xIw/TvKuHVkjSaI/AAAAAAAAHMc/iq-mhyRruJI/s640/du+pont.PNG.

2. **Five-Step DuPont:** The DuPont equation, also known as the extended version, dissects net profit margin into five steps. The three-step formula showed us that increases in leverage, asset turnover, and net profit margin will generally result in higher ROE. The five-step formula demonstrates that higher leverage does not always translate into higher ROE.

- *The Five-Step Calculation:* Since the numerator of the net profit margin is net income, this can be made into earnings before taxes (EBT) by multiplying the three-step equation by 1 minus the company's tax rate:

$$ROE = \frac{EBT}{S} \times \frac{S}{A} \times \frac{A}{E} \times (1 - TR)$$

Where;

EBT=Earnings before tax

S=Sales

A=Assets

E=Equity

TR=Tax rate

Since earnings before taxes (EBIT) is just the earnings before interest and taxes (EBIT) less the interest expense incurred by the company, we can break this down one more time. So, if there is a substitution for the interest expense, we get:

$$ROE = \left(\frac{EBIT}{S} \times \frac{S}{A} - \frac{IE}{A}\right) \times \frac{A}{E} \times (1 - TR)$$

where:

IE = Interest expense

The practicality of this breakdown is not as clear as the three-step, but this identity provides us with:

ROE= (OPM × AT–IER) × EM × TRR

Where;

OPM=Operating profit margin

AT=Asset turnover

IER=Interest expense rate

EM=Equity multiplier

TRR=Tax retention rate

If the company has a high borrowing cost, its interest expenses on more debt could mute the positive effects of the leverage (Figure 8.4).

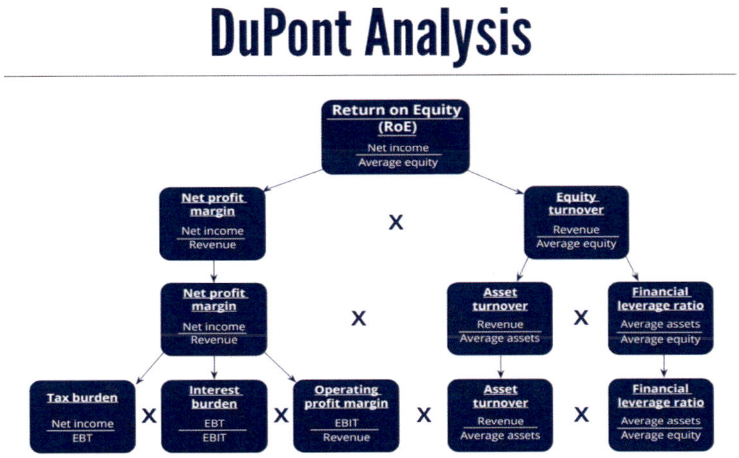

Figure 8.4. *DuPont-analysis.*

Source: https://365financialanalyst.com/wp-content/uploads/2020/10/DuPont-Analysis-%E2%80%93-A-Pyramid-of-Ratios-image.png.

Did you get it?

1. How does DuPont Analysis break down return on equity (ROE) into its constituent parts?
2. What do you mean by shareholder equity (SE)?

8.2. DUPONT ANALYSIS RATIOS WITH ECONOMIC ADJUSTMENTS

→Learning Objectives

- Learn about adjusted operating profit margin
- Know the adjusted asset turnover ratio
- Describe the adjusted leverage multiplier
- Define the adjusted return on equity

DuPont analysis ratios with economic adjustments enhance traditional DuPont analysis by incorporating economic factors that affect a company's financial performance. These adjustments allow for a more accurate assessment of a company's return on equity (ROE) by considering economic conditions and trends that may impact profitability, efficiency, and leverage.

Incorporating economic adjustments into DuPont analysis involves several steps. Firstly, it involves analyzing economic indicators such as inflation rates, interest rates, exchange rates, and industry-specific factors to identify their impact on a company's financial metrics. For example, high inflation rates may erode purchasing power and affect profitability margins, while fluctuating interest rates may influence financing costs and leverage ratios.

Secondly, economic adjustments are applied to financial ratios within the DuPont analysis framework. For instance, adjustments may be made to net profit margin to account for changes in input costs due to inflation or currency fluctuations. Similarly, asset turnover ratios may be adjusted to reflect changes in consumer spending patterns or shifts in market demand.

Moreover, economic adjustments can help assess the impact of regulatory changes, technological advancements, or geopolitical risks on a company's financial performance. For instance, changes in government policies or trade agreements may affect revenue streams, operating costs, and market dynamics, thereby influencing key DuPont analysis ratios.

By integrating economic adjustments into DuPont analysis, stakeholders gain a more comprehensive understanding of the drivers behind a company's ROE and can make more informed decisions regarding investment, risk management, and strategic planning. It allows management to identify emerging trends, anticipate potential challenges, and adapt their financial strategies accordingly to maintain competitiveness and enhance shareholder value amidst changing economic conditions.

8.2.1. Adjusted Operating Profit Margin

Adjusted operating profit margin refers to a modified calculation of the operating profit margin that incorporates certain adjustments to provide a clearer picture of a company's operational efficiency and profitability. These adjustments are typically made to exclude one-time or non-recurring items, extraordinary expenses, or other factors that may distort the true operating performance of the business.

To calculate the adjusted operating profit margin, the operating profit (also known as earnings before interest and taxes, EBIT) is adjusted to remove specific items that do not reflect the ongoing operational performance of the company. These adjustments could include:

1. **Non-recurring expenses**: Expenses incurred as a result of one-time events, such as restructuring costs, litigation settlements, or asset write-offs, are excluded from the calculation to isolate the core operating performance.
2. **Extraordinary items**: Certain events or transactions that are unusual in nature and infrequent in occurrence, such as gains or losses from the sale of assets, are adjusted to provide a more accurate representation of the company's ongoing operations.
3. **Accounting changes:** Adjustments may be made to account for changes in accounting policies or principles that impact the reported operating profit, ensuring consistency in the measurement of profitability over time.

By making these adjustments, the adjusted operating profit margin provides investors, analysts, and stakeholders with a clearer understanding of the company's underlying operating performance and its ability to generate profits from core business activities. It helps in evaluating the sustainability and quality of earnings, as well as comparing the operational efficiency of the company with industry peers.

Adjusted operating profit margin is a valuable metric for assessing management effectiveness, identifying areas for improvement, and making informed investment decisions based on a more accurate representation of a company's financial health and performance.

Keyword

Operational efficiency is the ability of an organization to reduce waste in time, effort, and materials as much as possible, while still producing a high-quality service or product.

8.2.2. Adjusted Asset Turnover Ratio

Adjusted asset turnover ratio is a financial metric that assesses a company's efficiency in generating revenue from its assets, with adjustments made to account for specific factors that may affect the accuracy of the traditional asset turnover ratio. The traditional asset turnover ratio is calculated by dividing net sales by average total assets.

Adjustments to the asset turnover ratio may be necessary to provide a more accurate reflection of a company's operational efficiency and asset utilization. These adjustments could include:

1. **Non-Operating Assets**: Non-operating assets, such as investments in marketable securities or excess cash holdings, may distort the asset turnover ratio. Adjusting for these assets ensures that the ratio focuses solely on assets used in the company's core operations.
2. **Depreciation and Amortization**: Since the asset turnover ratio is based on total assets, which include both tangible and intangible assets, adjustments may be made to account for depreciation and amortization expenses. Excluding these non-cash expenses provides a clearer picture of the company's ability to generate revenue from its productive assets.
3. **Seasonality and Cyclicality**: Companies operating in industries with seasonal or cyclical demand patterns may experience fluctuations in asset turnover throughout the year. Adjustments may be made to smooth out these fluctuations and provide a more meaningful measure of asset utilization over time.
4. **Asset Impairments**: Write-downs or impairments of assets can distort the asset turnover ratio by artificially inflating or deflating total asset values. Adjusting for these impairments helps in assessing the true efficiency of asset utilization.

By adjusting the asset turnover ratio, investors, analysts, and management can gain deeper insights into the company's operational efficiency and capital productivity. It enables better comparisons across time periods and with industry peers, leading to more informed decision-making regarding investment, strategic planning, and resource allocation.

Ultimately, the adjusted asset turnover ratio provides a more accurate assessment of how effectively a company is utilizing its assets to generate revenue, which is crucial for evaluating overall business performance and identifying areas for improvement.

8.2.3. Adjusted Leverage Multiplier

The adjusted leverage multiplier is a financial metric that evaluates a company's capital structure by measuring the proportion of debt financing relative to equity financing, with adjustments made to account for specific factors that may impact the accuracy of the traditional leverage multiplier. The traditional leverage multiplier is calculated by dividing total assets by shareholders' equity.

Adjustments to the leverage multiplier are typically made to provide a more accurate representation of the company's financial risk and leverage position. These adjustments may include:

- **Non-operating Liabilities**: Non-operating liabilities, such as short-term borrowings used for financing purposes or liabilities related to discontinued operations, can distort the leverage ratio. Adjusting for these liabilities ensures that the ratio reflects the company's core operational leverage.
- **Off-balance Sheet Liabilities**: Certain obligations or contingent liabilities that are not recorded on the balance sheet may impact the company's financial risk profile. Adjusting for these off-balance sheet liabilities provides a more comprehensive view of the company's leverage position.
- **Capitalized Leases**: Lease obligations that are capitalized and recorded as debt on the balance sheet may inflate the leverage ratio. Adjusting for capitalized leases helps in evaluating the true extent of the company's debt burden.
- **Non-recurring Financial Items**: One-time or non-recurring financial items, such as restructuring charges or asset write-downs, can distort the leverage ratio. Adjusting for these items ensures that the ratio reflects the company's ongoing financial position.

Remember

A lender will set a limit on how much risk it is prepared to take and will set a limit on how much leverage it will permit, and would require the acquired asset to be provided as collateral security for the loan.

By making these adjustments, the adjusted leverage multiplier provides a more accurate assessment of the company's capital structure and financial risk. It helps investors, analysts, and stakeholders evaluate the company's ability to meet its financial obligations, assess its solvency and liquidity, and make informed decisions regarding investment and risk management strategies.

Overall, the adjusted leverage multiplier serves as a valuable tool for understanding the financial health and risk profile of a company, allowing stakeholders to gain deeper insights into its leverage position and make more informed decisions about its future prospects and stability.

8.2.4. Adjusted Return on Equity

In the DuPont Analysis, return on equity serves as the main indicator of how shareholder value is created. It can be understood as the return on each dollar invested by shareholders, or in this case, equity. It is the outcome of the Equity Multiplier, ATO, and OPM. Depreciation and building value adjustments have been made to the ATO in order to calculate this ratio. Depreciation, the current liability for rental expense, and intangible assets are taken into account when adjusting the equity multiplier. On average, the group with the lowest performance has negative returns to equity. There are two causes for this. The practice's reported balance sheet either shows intangible assets or the practice makes a negative cash profit. Negative equity is the outcome of purchasing intangible assets. ROE will be negative until the loan is paid off or the intangible assets are fully amortized. Low-performing practices typically have higher debt levels than assets and are heavily leveraged. The ROE in the Low-Mid group is almost zero.

Due to owner withdrawal, profits are likewise nearly nonexistent, and little is invested back into the business. Due to high owner withdrawal and consequently low investment, the Low-Mid group has the lowest ATO and OPM, despite their comparatively higher leverage multiplier expected to boost returns. Profit and ATO in the Mid-High group are comparable to those in the best-performing group. The highest performing group can be identified by the leverage multiplier, ATO, and high profits. To attain this caliber of performance, the Mid-High group ought to concentrate on judicious and well-funded investments. The highest group's ROE is significantly higher than that of their peers because of a compounding effect in which they perform better across the board in all business processes, resulting in a significantly higher total return. The High group serves as proof that a company's overall performance can be enhanced through effective management of the entire business system.

Investment and the use of financing increase returns both now and when the practice is sold in the future, surpassing the short-term profitability goal of raising returns. The analysis also revealed that the middle-performing groups have the highest levels of in-group stability. They include ROE in almost all ratios where their standard deviation is the lowest. Conversely, the practices with the lowest performance typically have the highest standard deviation, while the practices with the highest performance typically fall in the middle. The variations in performance volatility among groups provide insight into practice age, style, and aptitude for management. Performance practices, in particular the Low-Mid group, seem to be mature practices where owners are happy with their current position and therefore have low levels of investment, even though practice age is unknown in our sample and this hypothesis cannot be confirmed. It is assumed that the practices at the top and bottom are relatively new endeavors with varying degrees of success.

Did you get it?

1. **Evaluate the non-operating liabilities**
2. **Discuss about capitalized leases**

8.3. ASSET AND LIABILITY RATIOS BY ADJUSTED ROE PERFORMANCE GROUP

→Learning **Objectives**

- Discuss on current ratio
- Define the debt coverage ratio
- Describe the debt to assets
- Explain the debt to equity

Asset and liability ratios by adjusted return on equity (ROE) performance groups provide valuable insights into how efficiently a company utilizes its assets and manages its liabilities to generate returns for shareholders. By categorizing companies based on their adjusted ROE performance, stakeholders can analyze how different levels of profitability and efficiency impact various financial ratios.

Asset turnover ratios, such as inventory turnover, receivables turnover, and fixed asset turnover, can be compared across different adjusted ROE performance groups to assess how effectively companies are generating revenue from their assets. A higher asset turnover ratio indicates better efficiency in asset utilization and revenue generation, whereas a lower ratio may suggest inefficiencies in asset management.

Likewise, liability ratios, including the debt-to-equity ratio, debt ratio, and interest coverage ratio, can be analyzed across adjusted ROE performance groups to evaluate how companies finance their operations and manage their debt obligations. A lower debt-to-equity ratio and debt ratio generally indicate lower financial risk and better capital structure management, while a higher interest coverage ratio reflects the company's ability to meet its interest obligations.

By comparing asset and liability ratios across different adjusted ROE performance groups, stakeholders can identify trends, outliers, and areas for improvement within each group. Companies with high adjusted ROE and favorable asset and liability ratios may be considered well-managed and financially sound, while those with low adjusted ROE and unfavorable ratios may require closer scrutiny and potential remedial action.

Overall, analyzing asset and liability ratios by adjusted ROE performance groups provides a comprehensive view of a company's financial health, operational efficiency, and risk profile. It helps investors, analysts, and stakeholders make informed decisions regarding investment, risk management, and strategic planning based on a deeper understanding of the relationship between profitability, asset utilization, and capital structure.

8.3.1. Current Ratio

The current ratio is a financial ratio that measures a company's ability to meet its short-term obligations with its short-term assets. It is calculated by dividing the company's current assets by its current liabilities.

The formula for the current ratio is:

$$\text{Current Ratio} = \frac{\text{Current Assets}}{\text{Current Liabilities}}$$

Current assets are assets that are expected to be converted into cash or used up within one year, such as cash, accounts receivable, inventory, and short-term investments. Current liabilities are obligations that are due within one year, including accounts payable, short-term debt, and accrued expenses.

The current ratio provides insight into a company's liquidity and its ability to cover its short-term liabilities. A ratio greater than 1 indicates that the company has more current assets than current liabilities, suggesting that it is capable of meeting its short-term obligations. A ratio less than 1 indicates that the company may have difficulty covering its short-term liabilities with its current assets.

While a high current ratio may indicate strong liquidity, excessively high ratios may suggest that the company is not efficiently utilizing its assets. Conversely, a low current ratio may signal liquidity issues or difficulty in meeting short-term obligations, which could pose risks to the company's financial health.

Overall, the current ratio is an important financial metric used by investors, creditors, and analysts to assess a company's short-term financial strength and liquidity position. It provides valuable insights into the company's ability to manage its working capital and meet its immediate financial obligations.

8.3.2. Debt Coverage Ratio

The Debt Coverage Ratio (DCR) is a financial ratio that measures a company's ability to cover its debt obligations with its operating income. It is commonly used by lenders and investors to assess the company's ability to generate enough cash flow to meet its debt service requirements.

The Debt Coverage Ratio is calculated by dividing the company's net operating income (NOI) by its total debt service (TDS). The formula for the Debt Coverage Ratio is:

$$\text{Debt Coverage Ratio (DCR)} = \frac{\text{Net Operating Income}}{\text{Total Debt Service}}$$

Net Operating Income (NOI) typically represents the company's income from operations before interest, taxes, depreciation, and amortization (EBITDA) or other non-operating items. It is a measure of the company's ability to generate income from its core business activities. Total Debt Service (TDS) includes all the payments made by the company to service its debt obligations during a specific period. It usually includes interest payments, principal repayments, and other financing-related expenses. A Debt Coverage Ratio of 1 or higher indicates that the company's operating income is sufficient to cover its debt obligations. A ratio below 1 suggests that the company may have difficulty meeting its debt service requirements with its current level of operating income. Lenders and investors typically have their own minimum acceptable Debt Coverage Ratio thresholds, depending on factors such as industry standards, risk tolerance, and the terms of the loan agreement. A higher Debt Coverage Ratio is generally considered more favorable, as it indicates a stronger ability to service debt obligations and withstand economic downturns or unexpected challenges.

Overall, the Debt Coverage Ratio provides valuable insights into a company's financial health, solvency, and ability to manage its debt effectively. It is an essential tool for assessing creditworthiness, evaluating investment opportunities, and making informed financial decisions.

Remember

The debt-service coverage ratio (DSCR) is used to assess a company's or individual's overall financial health. DSCR compares available cash flow to debt and measures whether an entity has the ability to pay its debt in cash.

8.3.3. Debt to Assets

The Debt to Assets ratio is a financial metric used to evaluate the proportion of a company's assets that are financed through debt. It indicates the extent to which a company relies on debt financing to fund its operations and investments. The Debt to Assets ratio is calculated by dividing the company's total debt by its total assets.

The formula for the Debt to Assets ratio is:

$$\text{Debt to Assets Ratio} = \frac{\text{Total Debt}}{\text{Total Assets}}$$

Total debt includes all of the company's outstanding debt obligations, including short-term and long-term debt, bonds payable, and other liabilities. Total assets represent all of the company's resources and investments, including current and non-current assets such as cash, accounts receivable, inventory, property, plant, and equipment. The Debt to Assets ratio provides insight into the company's financial risk and leverage. A higher ratio indicates that a larger portion of the company's assets is financed through debt, which can increase financial risk and vulnerability to economic downturns or changes in interest rates. Conversely, a lower ratio suggests that the company relies less on debt financing and may have a stronger financial position.

The optimal level of debt to assets varies by industry, business model, and financial objectives. Industries with stable cash flows and low-risk profiles may be comfortable with higher levels of debt, while others may prefer a more conservative approach with lower debt levels to minimize financial risk.

Investors, creditors, and analysts use the Debt to Assets ratio to assess a company's capital structure, financial stability, and ability to manage its debt obligations. It is an important tool for evaluating creditworthiness, comparing companies within the same industry, and making informed investment decisions.

8.3.4. Debt to Equity

The Debt to Equity ratio is a financial metric used to evaluate the proportion of a company's financing that comes from debt relative to equity. It provides insight into the company's capital structure and financial leverage. The Debt to Equity ratio is calculated by dividing the company's total debt by its total equity.

The formula for the Debt to Equity ratio is:

$$\text{Debt to Equity Ratio} = \frac{\text{Total Debt}}{\text{Total Equity}}$$

Total debt includes all of the company's outstanding debt obligations, such as loans, bonds, and other liabilities. Total equity represents the residual interest in the company's assets after deducting its liabilities, including common stock, preferred stock, retained earnings, and other equity accounts.

The Debt to Equity ratio helps investors, creditors, and analysts assess the company's financial risk and leverage. A higher ratio indicates that a larger portion of the company's financing comes from debt, which can increase financial risk and the company's vulnerability to economic downturns or changes in interest rates. Conversely, a lower ratio suggests that the company relies more on equity financing and may have a stronger financial position.

The optimal level of debt to equity varies by industry, business model, and financial objectives. Some industries may tolerate higher levels of debt to finance growth opportunities or take advantage of tax benefits associated with debt financing, while others may prefer a more conservative approach with lower debt levels to minimize financial risk.

Investors and creditors use the Debt to Equity ratio to assess a company's capital structure, financial stability, and ability to manage its debt obligations. It is an important tool for evaluating creditworthiness, comparing companies within the same industry, and making informed investment decisions. Additionally, changes in the Debt to Equity ratio over time can provide insights into the company's financial strategy and performance trends.

Did you get it?

1. Can you explain how adjusted ROE performance groups are formed and utilized in financial analysis?
2. How do analysts interpret variations in asset and liability ratios within different adjusted ROE performance groups?

ROLE MODEL

FRANK DONALDSON BROWN

Frank Donaldson Brown (1885–1965) was born in Baltimore on February 1, 1885, the son of J. Willcox Brown and Ellen Turner Macfarland. Brown entered Virginia Polytechnic Institute (VPI) in 1898 at the age of 13, graduating four years later with a degree in electrical engineering. Today, the student union at VPI is named for him.

He became the chief financial officer at DuPont Corporation in 1912 and later General Motors Corporation (GM) in 1921. At both companies, Donaldson Brown developed accounting innovations that led to the success of both organizations. These innovations included the DuPont Return-on-Investment (ROI) formula in 1914. However, ROI was not Brown's only contribution to financial management. His dealer ten-day reporting system at GM was widely and rapidly adopted throughout the auto industry. His ideas to support a variety of forecasting and planning techniques supported decentralized corporate management, and his pricing processes were cutting-edge developments that others emulated. Flexible budgeting at General Motors also was implemented during his administration in the early 1920s.

Brown began his career in 1903 with the Baltimore & Ohio Railroad, but soon moved to the Sprague Electric Company, a subsidiary of General Electric. He stayed with that company until 1907 when he went into business for himself in a coal-moving company and then went to work in 1909 as a salesman of explosives for the DuPont Company. In 1912, DuPont general manager, Hamilton Barksdale, a first cousin who was married to a duPont*, recognized Brown's abilities and asked him to join the staff. In June 1916, Brown married Barksdale's daughter, Greta duPont Barksdale, which gave him a kinship that some considered necessary for advancement at DuPont. He was elected to the DuPont board of directors in 1918 and remained thereon until his death 47 years later. He served on the DuPont board's Finance Committee for 45 years. He died on October 2, 1965, at the age of 80.

ROI was Brown's most prominent contribution and the technique achieved status as a dominant approach to financial management by the 1950s. As a national standard-of-performance measure, it was supported by varying sources including the American Management Association as well as in the teaching materials of academics, especially Robert N. Anthony of the Harvard Business School. The impact of these forms of dissemination led to ROI being adopted eventually at the Ford Motor Company when its previously autocratic centralized style of Ford family management was replaced by a team known as the Whiz Kids, led by Harvard Business School alumnus Robert McNamara and a former GM vice president, Ernest R. Breech. This is indicative that the innovations developed by Brown are among the most important of those initiated in 20th century corporate America, and thus among the most important in the development of 20th-century accounting and financial management thought.

Although it was at DuPont that Brown developed many of his concepts, it was at GM where he was able to put them to work. Brown's title was officially that of chief financial officer, but he was also essentially what is known today as the chief information officer at both companies—a role that effectively supported GM's decentralization. The practices initiated by Donaldson Brown enabled DuPont and General Motors to cope with the challenges of large companies seeking to balance centralized vs. decentralized decision-making. Brown's ideas were made known through his writings, publications, and speeches, and ultimately by incorporation in textbooks, classrooms, and academic literature. Trade organizations and financial publications, for decades up to the present, have disseminated ROI materials. Furthermore, his disciples helped in spreading his influence far beyond GM and DuPont.

SUMMARY

- DuPont analysis is a financial performance measurement tool that decomposes return on equity (ROE) into its component parts to provide insights into the drivers of profitability and efficiency.
- The DuPont analysis breaks down ROE into three key components: profitability (net profit margin), asset utilization (total asset turnover), and financial leverage (equity multiplier).
- Total asset turnover measures how efficiently a company utilizes its assets to generate sales revenue, reflecting its operational efficiency and asset management practices.
- DuPont analysis can be used for benchmarking against industry peers, identifying best practices, setting performance targets, and formulating strategic initiatives to enhance financial performance and shareholder value.
- DuPont analysis has limitations, including its reliance on accounting data, sensitivity to accounting policies, and potential masking of underlying issues by aggregating multiple factors into a single metric, necessitating careful interpretation and consideration of contextual factors.
- It enables management and investors to assess the impact of various factors, such as pricing strategies, cost control measures, asset utilization initiatives, and capital structure decisions, on overall profitability and return on equity.

REVIEW QUESTIONS

1. Define DuPont analysis and explain its significance in financial analysis.
2. How does DuPont analysis break down a company's return on equity (ROE) into its component parts?
3. What does the profit margin component of DuPont analysis measure, and how is it calculated?
4. Discuss the advantages of using DuPont analysis compared to analyzing ROE alone.
5. Provide examples of strategies that a company could implement to improve its return on equity based on insights gained from DuPont analysis.

MULTIPLE CHOICE QUESTIONS

1. DuPont analysis is a financial technique used to:

a. Evaluate the performance of competitors

b. Assess a company's return on equity (ROE)

c. Determine the market capitalization of a company

d. Calculate the net present value (NPV) of a project

2. **The DuPont analysis breaks down return on equity (ROE) into which components?**
   a. Profit margin, asset turnover, and financial leverage
   b. Revenue, expenses, and taxes
   c. Assets, liabilities, and equity
   d. Inventory, accounts receivable, and accounts payable
3. **Profit margin, in the DuPont analysis, is calculated as:**
   a. Net income divided by total assets
   b. Net income divided by sales revenue
   c. Total assets divided by equity
   d. Sales revenue divided by net income
4. **Asset turnover, in the DuPont analysis, is calculated as:**
   a. Net income divided by total assets
   b. Net income divided by sales revenue
   c. Sales revenue divided by total assets
   d. Total assets divided by equity
5. **Financial leverage, in the DuPont analysis, is calculated as:**
   a. Net income divided by total assets
   b. Net income divided by sales revenue
   c. Sales revenue divided by total assets
   d. Total assets divided by equity
6. **In DuPont analysis, an increase in profit margin can result from:**
   a. Increased sales revenue
   b. Decreased sales revenue
   c. Decreased expenses relative to revenue
   d. Increased financial leverage
7. **An increase in asset turnover, in DuPont analysis, indicates:**
   a. Improved efficiency in utilizing assets to generate sales
   b. Decreased efficiency in utilizing assets to generate sales
   c. Increased expenses relative to revenue
   d. Decreased financial leverage
8. **The DuPont analysis helps investors and analysts:**
   a. Assess a company's liquidity position
   b. Evaluate a company's profitability, efficiency, and leverage
   c. Determine a company's market share
   d. Calculate a company's cost of equity

9. A high return on equity (ROE) calculated using DuPont analysis indicates:

a. Poor financial performance

b. Efficient use of assets to generate profit

c. Excessive financial leverage

d. Declining profit margins

10. DuPont analysis is particularly useful for comparing:

a. A company's financial performance over time

b. A company's financial performance with its competitors

c. A company's financial performance with industry benchmarks

d. All of the above

Answer to Multiple Choice Questions

1. (b); 2. (a); 3. (b); 4. (c); 5. (d); 6. (c); 7. (a); 8. (b); 9. (b); 10. (d)

REFERENCES

1. CFA Institute, (2013). *Financial Statement Analysis: A Practitioner's Guide*. John Wiley & Sons.
2. Choi, K. W., Park, H. J., Shin, S. Y., & Yang, I. S., (2007). Analysis of profitability and its affecting factors in restaurant franschise firms. *Korean J. Food Cookery Sci., 23*(2), 270–279.
3. Gibson, C. H., (2017). *Financial Reporting and Analysis: Using Financial Accounting Information*. Cengage Learning.
4. Groppelli, A. A., & Ehsan, N., (2000). *Finance* (4th edn., pp. 444, 445). Barron's Educational Series, Inc.
5. Ittelson, T. R., (2009). *Financial Statements: A Step-by-Step Guide to Understanding and Creating Financial Reports*. Career Press.
6. Jordan, B. D., Miller, T. W., & Dolvin, S. D., (2017). *Fundamentals of Investments: Valuation and Management*. McGraw-Hill Education.
7. Kang, S. W., (2008). Research on the evaluation of the differences in financial variables of chain restaurants using multivariate analysis of variance. *Korean J. Cul. Res., 14*(1), 21–38.
8. Koller, T., Goedhart, M., & Wessels, D., (2015). *Valuation: Measuring and Managing the Value of Companies*. John Wiley & Sons.
9. Magee, R. P., & Pankin, M. J., (2011). *The Magic of Financial Analysis: Understanding Financial Statements in Your Business*. AMACOM Div. American Mgmt. Assn.
10. Marshall, H., (2022). *DuPont Analysis*. Investopedia.
11. Mulford, C. W., & Comiskey, E. E., (2002). *Creative Cash Flow Reporting: Uncovering Sustainable Financial Performance*. John Wiley & Sons.

12. Mulford, C. W., & Comiskey, E. E., (2002). *The Financial Numbers Game: Detecting Creative Accounting Practices*. John Wiley & Sons.
13. Phillips, M., (2015). *The DuPont Invention That Changed How Things Work in the Corporate World*. Quartz Publication.
14. Stickney, C. P., Brown, P. R., & Wahlen, J. M., (2019). *Financial Reporting, Financial Statement Analysis, and Valuation*. Cengage Learning.
15. Subramanyam, K. R., & Wild, J. J., (2014). *Financial Statement Analysis*. McGraw-Hill Education.

Index

FSC
www.fsc.org
MIX
Papier | Fördert gute Waldnutzung
FSC® C083411

Kolibri 360 GmbH
Ferdinand-Jühlke-Straße 7
99095 Erfurt, Deutschland
produktsicherheit@kolibri360.de